For Tim

STARS
✧ AND ✧
SKELETONS

STARS
✧ AND ✧
SKELETONS

Tales of Life with
My Schizophrenic Brother

DAVID ROBINSON

THREE UNCLES
PUBLISHING

**THREE UNCLES
PUBLISHING**

Copyright ©2024 David Robinson
All rights reserved.
Published by Three Uncles Publishing
P.O. Box 150419, San Rafael CA 94915
ISBN 978-1-952785-00-9
Library of Congress Control Number: 2023951517
www.threeunclespublishing.com

TABLE OF CONTENTS

Acknowledgments

Karen and Tim,
my harshest critics and my biggest fans,
thank you for being both.

Patty – what beautiful work.

Joanie, Trevor, Annemarie, Luanne, Daniel, Mary, Hugh,
Stacey, Marty, Colette, Jeff, Jean, John, Dan –
Your feedback was always wise.

Rachel - what a pleasure.

And a huge thanks to folks in the
Storyline writers' workshops:
Kevin, David, Bekah, Alan, Craig, and Eleanor.

FOREWORD

For over a decade, Dave Robinson and I worked together as he shaped Creative Interfaces, the non-profit in which he serves as Executive Director. I marveled at the many talents he possessed, both artistic and administrative, and the vision he held of supporting others in their personal growth, be it spiritual, creative, or both. When he approached me and said he had written a book and could I possibly read the manuscript, I marveled again at his dedication of dreaming a dream and then nurturing that dream into a reality.

Not everyone can comprehend the loss of a loved one to schizophrenia, the feeling that the person you knew in childhood, bright, inquisitive and clever, filled with promise and potential, has plunged headlong into an abyss of uncertain depth and darkness. Hands outstretched and almost falling in after them, you wave frantically into the void, desperate to bring them back again, to see them whole and free.

STARS AND SKELETONS thrust me back into my own childhood, a time when siblings and friends navigated the landscape of discovery and the challenges of growing up. As I read the manuscript, I saw instantly the parallels between the journey Dave describes and my own. I felt invested in the characters because we shared the experiences of growing up in the '60s, coming of age in the '70s, and then both encountering a sudden, horrific interruption in that otherwise common narrative, as though a rock was hurled through a window, the shattered glass scattered into hundreds of indistinguishable shards. We stand in the middle wondering what on earth just happened, and how we pick up the pieces and put them back together again. That rock that disrupts and redefines lives is schizophrenia.

If you have a loved one or know someone who suffers from mental illness, you will empathize with the characters and relate to their journey as I did in my personal experiences with an older brother struggling with schizophrenia. If you have not, this book will knit you to the characters in their childhood so that you are comfortably strapped in with them on the wild and unpredictable ride, with its joys and its sorrows, its examination and its understanding of the illness, and the wholly unanticipated outcome.

~ Mary Bihr
VICE PRESIDENT, GLOBAL PUBLISHING, LUCASARTS,
A DIVISION OF LUCASFILM (RETIRED)

INTRODUCTION

This book is made up of a series of short stories lifted from the life experienced by my brother Tim and me. Each story falls within a larger story arc that follows us through the decades of our lives from Tim's birth to nearly the present day. They are written in chronological order except for the three scenes in the cemetery found at the beginning of each of the book's three parts.

My brother Tim's life, as well as my own, transpired among a host of family members and friends, and while I mention many of them, I focus mainly on my relationship with Tim. I've used the real names of some people and changed the names of others—to honor their privacy, or simply because I am no longer in touch with them and it seemed respectful.

As is often the case with human beings, we don't always recall events in the same way. The family members and friends whose stories overlap with mine have their own memories and perhaps would tell our stories with various differences. This is a good thing. As we humbly compare notes and share our stories with each other, those differences reveal the unique perspective of unique individuals, providing opportunities to know each other more deeply. In the end, I have done my very best to represent all the events and circumstances as they occurred.

Tim's mental illness surfaces in Part Two. His choices and behavior during that time resulted in consequences that some readers will find disturbing. I have included scenes that I believe to be essential to understanding his journey. My examination of his illness is not clinical, but familial and relational. I want to simply tell the stories from my perspective as a brother close to him throughout the whole experience.

Each of us is born from above
and from below.
We are in essence as celestial as the stars
and as grounded
as old bones.

✧ ✧ ✧

PART ONE

TALES OF BOYHOOD

Graves are strange. The presence of the deceased mixes with their absence, both in the same space.

The starry night over the Kansas prairie slowly yielded to the coming dawn as I walked among the graves, reading the names of those whose stories were finished. Some may yet be told; others are forgotten. I noticed their ages, especially if they were young. One man was twenty-three when they put him in the ground. "I wonder if anyone remembers his story," I thought to myself, followed immediately by the next thought: "That could have been my brother." I stopped and sat down on the stone, remembering what my brother Tim was like at that age, casually oblivious to the doom right in front of him. Silence ruled the moment, interrupted only by a few birds beginning to stir themselves awake. The sun hadn't appeared yet, but the eastern sky glowed with a promise of warmth.

My brother's story needs to be told. I know Tim's story like I know my own. The words of a thousand conversations from every stage of life, full of commingled heartache and shared humor—propelled us into a connected experience. Our stories overlap and mix like two rivers that flow together in some parts. It's difficult to distinguish whether the water is from this one or that one. Telling his story by itself is impossible. To tell his, I must tell parts of my own.

Life brought troubled times soon enough, and I tend to remember those first. But there in that quiet place, I wanted to recall the younger years—the times of innocence, when being a kid seemed like the whole of reality and the future was measured only by how big a kid you'd become. In that world of childhood, my brother Tim was purely himself, not yet tainted by worry, fear, anxiety, or self-doubt. For much of Tim's adulthood, he looked back at his childhood with longing, sometimes tortured by the irretrievability of that existence.

I watched in my mind as images from childhood played like a silent movie. Each scene took the images further back in time, as far back as I could remember, forming the backstory that brought me to where I sat among the graves. I recalled one of my earliest memories: it was nighttime and I could see the stars through a window. They seemed close. They felt like friends. I felt a presence with me that I can't quite name, except to call it a simple childlike sense of God. It was a warm, enveloping feeling of peace—and more than that, something personal, as if an invisible hand was pointing upward, showing me the stars.

Many times throughout my life I have felt that presence, and in every case two things have been the same: First, I have always had the feeling of marking a moment—a bookmark in the story of life. The other is the same feeling of peace and connection, exactly like that first time.

"Thank you," I uttered under my breath, grateful for a peaceful place from which to stop and remember.

Most of the memories brought to mind a life outdoors. I suppose the indoor memories just couldn't compete. They happened in a string of various houses, each one different from the next. As we moved from one place to another, I became aware that what we called "home" would, at some point, change again. Life outdoors was more constant. The weather might change, but the outdoors, no matter where we were, was always connected to everywhere else outdoors— one huge world where all our different homes could be found under the same sky. Thinking of it that way seemed to help whenever we were uprooted, leaving friends and favorite places behind—following Dad to the next thing.

I watched in my imagination as memories of my family showed themselves like movies in my mind: mysteries, comedies, adventures, romances, and sometimes horrors. The memories grouped in my imagination like a hundred short stories arcing into a chronicle of shared experiences—tales of my brother and me. ✧

Chapter One
1962 – 1968

Parents are like shuttles on a loom.
They join the threads of the past with
threads of the future
and leave their own bright patterns as they go.

~ Fred Rogers
Mister Rogers' Neighborhood

HEY TIMMY

I enjoyed the feel of the warm sidewalk against my four-year-old legs as I sat down. I looked down the street where I saw my older brother Doug and several other boys casually riding their bikes in my direction. I crouched down low behind the hedge, waiting.

It was a sunny Southern California day. Our lives at that time revolved around a simple house in a suburban neighborhood while Dad was stationed at Point Mugu Naval Air Station. Unlike the other dads in the neighborhood, he wore a Navy officer's uniform, which made him seem important.

"That's my man. You look great, Honey," commented my mom, her eyes beaming with admiration. I watched him put his officer's hat over his short, dark wavy hair. Dad was tall, strong, and wore it well. That uniform made me feel important too.

Sometimes Dad would put me in the car with him and we'd travel to another Navy base in San Diego. I tend to remember warm days—the sun shining into the car as I rode with my dad, or one of my favorite sensations, the feel of the warm sun on the sidewalk. This, of course, caused a problem if bicycles were cruising down the same sidewalk.

There it is—that clear memory among the vague images of life at that time—sticking my head out from behind the hedge to surprise my brother and his friends, then feeling the black bicycle tire mushing its rubbery tread into my skin as it rolled over the side of my head, squashing the top of my ear against my skull. Then it was over, or so I thought for one split second until the back tire provided a second helping.

Running into the house, I found Mom brushing her dark brown hair in front of a mirror. She met me with a smile, followed by a look of concern. "What happened to your head?"

"It got run over." The delayed tears felt free to flow now that Mom was with me. I figured I would cry as long as she offered comfort, and I could certainly generate tears when necessary. "I was just trying to surprise them," I explained. My head was scraped up a bit, but in truth it didn't hurt that much.

Doug ran into the house with a concerned look. "Is David okay?"

Mom nodded, then looked up to the sudden sound of someone else who was also crying. "Oh, we woke the baby," said Mom, as she left me to attend to him.

I watched Mom holding Timmy, the new recipient of her doting affection.

For as long as I could remember, I had been the youngest brother. Not anymore. My role would now change forever.

"Hey, Timmy." I spoke quietly, not wanting to startle him. When I startled him, he would cry for a while which is not what I wanted.

"How you doin' today?" He was staring at the wall, or the slats on his crib, or maybe at nothing. A fine tuft of blond baby hair stuck straight up above his forehead.

"You're going to look like me," I declared. My big brother Doug had darker skin than mine and very dark, full, wavy hair. I was blond—usually sporting a crew cut.

"I wonder when you'll be big enough to play outside."

Suddenly, as if he had just become aware of my presence, he turned his head and looked at me.

"You wanna play outside?"

A huge grin landed on his face and stayed there.

"Mom, Timmy wants to play outside," I hollered to the other room.

"You leave him be," was the response.

"But he wants to play," I shouted back. "Don't worry Timmy," I said softly. There will be lots of time to go out and play."

Impossibly, his grin got even bigger.

TWINKLE TWINKLE BOOM

Several months after Tim was born, the Navy transferred Dad to the Naval Training Center in San Diego. We moved to another house where Tim had his first birthday. Soon after, Dad all but disappeared when they stationed him aboard a ship in the Pacific Fleet. He was gone for months—a long time for young kids.

One evening, Mom told Doug and me to go get in the car and wait for her. The December sunset brought the night's darkness early and a few stars came into view. Timmy stood in the front yard looking up. He seemed to think the night sky was something alive, that it was not far away but close, offering something and expecting a response. He and I shared that perspective.

He stood in silence, pointing upward, transfixed. He wanted to touch the heavens, but he was too short.

Mom's voice responded as she picked him up and sang Twinkle Twinkle Little Star. He'd been restless, and the sight of the stars and moon quieted him.

The babysitter showed up and Mom left her with Tim, still looking into the sky as we drove off to our big rendez-vous at the Navy base.

Bright lights flooded the pier as The USS Hopewell approached, churning up the dark seawater, slowly brought to berth where we stood waiting.

Dad was returning from West Pac—six months aboard a

Navy ship in the Western Pacific.

"Your dad brought home some presents for you boys." Mom's big smile had been stuck on her face from the moment the ship came into view.

Doug was intrigued. "Presents?"

He and I looked at each other with excitement.

We toured the ship with Dad that night. I felt excited to be aboard with all the sailors, some of whom were unloading wooden crates onto the dock.

Two of those crates were delivered to our house later that evening. We all stood in the front yard watching Navy personnel unload the gifts from Dad.

Doug and I took to guessing what was in the crates. Tim took to staring at the sky. Even when Mom pointed to the crates being carried into our house, Tim seemed far more interested in the stars.

The next morning, Doug and I were up early, Tim following us around. "Dad, when can we open the boxes?" Doug yelled.

Dad was in his room with Mom, his muffled voice calling from the bed. "Pretty soon."

"No, now!" I shouted.

"Soon," yelled Dad.

"You boys be patient," came Mom's voice through the door.

My parents realized they wouldn't get any privacy anyway, so they came out, and the unpacking began. It was a noisy business, requiring tools, but the loot slowly emerged: Two bicycles.

"English racers," Dad announced with a smile.

"Wow. English racers," Doug and I repeated. We didn't know what that meant, but they were bikes, and we couldn't have been happier.

Tim suddenly paused his otherwise perpetual motion and stared at Dad as if he had just recognized him. "Daddy!" he squealed, trying to catapult himself across the floor in a fast hobble—falling forward and barely catching himself with each step. He slammed into Dad's knee, and Dad picked him up. "Timmy—how you doin' buddy?" Tim's excitement at seeing Dad modeled outwardly what my brother Doug and I were feeling.

That night we all went back to the base where the Navy was hosting an event involving fireworks. We spread a blanket on a huge lawn, ready to watch the fireworks with a crowd of celebrating people.

Tim watched the stars come out, one by one.

The crowd cheered as the first sudden burst of light scattershot itself in all directions.

Tim opened his mouth in shock, startled by the sight and sound. We thought he would like it, but he cried uncontrollably, trying to say something no one understood.

All of us tried to console him, without success. Finally Mom put together what he was trying to say. He thought the moon was exploding.

MOM, HILLBILLIES, AND COAL TRAINS

Our mother came off as a very put-together woman. She wore dresses, curled her hair, and kept herself always looking and smelling good. However, she wore no jewelry, not even a wedding ring. She also carried a big secret. Or, maybe surprise is a better word, as she had no shame about it. People would often lean in, interested, when they learned about her past.

"Fleta, you came from where?" they would ask with obvious incredulity.

Yes, our mom's name was Fleta.

She enjoyed telling stories from her childhood, and we enjoyed hearing them. "Boys, if you ever hear people talking about hillbillies, that's me. I'm a hillbilly."

The world of her childhood was comprised of mountainous terrain, ravines, two or three creeks, an abundance of trees, a valley, and, at one time, a small wooden house put together so poorly that she could feel the wind on the inside, even when all the windows and doors were closed. There was a railroad track on which trains, usually coal trains, would rumble past any time of the day or night. She was the oldest of three kids, unless I count Uncle Harry, who died before Mom was born. It was a family of five—the Rhodes family.

She could visit neighbors if she walked around a hillside or across the valley. She made the acquaintance of a few cows, goats, and hound dogs. The dogs would often be hanging out in their usual habitat—an old wood porch that may have been painted once, long ago, complete with a shotgun or two leaning against the wall, a couple old chairs, and the sounds of human voices wafting through the window.

Other sounds—aside from the trains, the hound-dogs, and the voices, might include various domestic animals, such as guinea hens, chickens, roosters, and maybe the whinny of an overworked mule, anxious to finish out his day.

You might also hear animals being killed and prepared for dinner. Everyone living in Mom's valley became proficient at preparing animals, both domestic and wild, for the table. Some families grew crops, but only one row at a time—like stair steps on the side of the hill, as most households had no flat land.

What you would not hear in our mom's valley, were cars, or the sound of a tractor, or any vehicle at all, except the ever-present coal train. You would not hear the sounds of a store, or a post office, or a police station, as those things were far away.

On a bad day, you might hear the wailing of a woman who had lost a son to another family locked in a vicious blood feud still smoldering from the days of the civil war. When this happened, there was no one to call, and no phone on which to call them. The residents of our mom's valley were governed by whatever cooperation could be arranged. Some of the feuds cast a darkness over families who carried the scars from lost sons who had been murdered, and another kind of scar from sons who had themselves murdered in vengeance. This was Breathitt County, Kentucky, in the 1930's and 1940's. "Bloody Breathitt" they called it then. It was the land of hillbillies, lawless feuding, and moonshine. It was also the land of strong, capable, self-governed people who made a rich and sustainable community that still remains.

Mom's childhood home did not include things like electricity or plumbing. Her family depended on coal stoves in the winter, used both for cooking and for warmth. They traded goods with neighbors, some of whom lived just a ten-minute walk away, while a trip to see others would take most of the day. It was a do-it-yourself world. They were experts at acquiring, preparing, and storing whatever food the land provided. When someone died, there was no professional to call, and Mom's mother often played the role of undertaker.

But, after considering all the aspects of Mom's backwoods home, one thing surfaces as unique. It wasn't the lack of modern conveniences. That would have been experienced by many at the time. I measure the remoteness of her world by something else: Roads.

Whether it's rough country dirt roads, or paved highways, roads are a basic ingredient of civilization. Hers was a community that had none. I had to sit with that idea for a long time to begin to understand the world Mom came from.

If someone wanted to leave that valley, they packed a mule or hiked for days. If one of Mom's family members or neighbors wanted to travel very far, they had a system that involved putting up a marker in a particular place near the railroad, then hiking a ways down the tracks where they would wait. When the engineer on the train saw the marker, he would stop the train, and the hiker would become a passenger. Some of my mom's neighbors lived out their entire lives without ever leaving that valley.

Mom's father introduced the first motor vehicle late one summer by driving it on a small, mostly dry riverbed from another community. It was a rough trek, and he eventually emerged from a creek at one end of the valley. I don't know what kind of vehicle it was, but most locals had never seen a car, so they just called it a car. Leave it to a man named Rhodes to show up with the first one.

There was a school in the valley, but only because a small group of people, including Mom's dad, built one. He was a visionary, a spiritual leader who was determined to make the valley into something civilized.

Mom attended that school. She left on Monday mornings, stayed at the school all week, and returned on Fridays. It was a long valley, and sometimes the trek involved riding the train. She continued until she finished high school, and then became the first person from that valley to go away to college.

She said it was at college that she saw her first commercially manufactured bar of soap. That small fact always helped me see her life in perspective. She also encountered roads— many of them. In a way, the rest of her life was a never-ending discovery of new ones.

THE ALL-SEEING EYE OF MOM

We three boys each had two birthdays at the house where we got our bicycles, then moved to another house about ten blocks away. Tim turned three at the new place. I turned seven.

One day, Tim was entertaining himself in our room at the end of the hall. He pulled the bottom dresser drawer most of the way out. Then he pulled out the next one, but not as far, then the next one part way, until he had the drawers set up like steps. He climbed the drawers, intending to stand on top of the dresser.

"You be careful climbing like that!" Mom yelled from the living room.

Tim had no idea that she could see his reflection in the glossy lacquered surface of the cabinet door on her Hi-Fi console in the hall. At that moment, he believed two things: Mom knew everything, and Mom saw everything. He was sure he could never misbehave without getting caught.

Mom enjoyed her Hi-Fi console, often playing music from her classical record collection. We three boys drifted to sleep to the sound of Mom's collection. Grieg's Hall of the Mountain King, Tchaikovsky's Nutcracker, and music by Dvorak, Brahms, and others. Mom often situated herself so she could see into our room by looking at the reflection in the glossy cabinet. Doug and I eventually figured this out, but Tim thought she could see through walls. Of course we affirmed that belief whenever he questioned it.

When Mom wasn't listening to her classical records, she kept the radio tuned to a Christian radio station. The station she preferred played a combination of very traditional church music, interspersed with Christian teaching and preaching. We had no TV, and that station was the only outside influence she allowed into our home. So we experienced many of our formative years with almost no exposure to popular music or other cultural influences. Knowledge of the larger culture was limited to school and whatever we encountered in someone else's home. Much of this was by Mom's design. When I was a young boy, I didn't realize it was intentional, I just thought it was a matter of Mom's taste.

But like the reflection in the glossy Hi-Fi cabinet, she positioned herself in our lives so as to monitor the influences we encountered. She was a good mom and that's what good moms do. As we grew we spent more and more time outside the house. She monitored us closely with people and cultural influences, but gave us enormous freedom outdoors. One might say she allowed us freedom with the earth, but not much with the world.

Our house in Spring Valley came with a huge bonus: open land, one corner of which started right across the street. Rolling, grassy hills stretched on for miles, providing room for endless adventure. We just called it "The Field."

We found many trails winding through the tall golden grass, and where there were none, we blazed our own, leaving footpaths in the wild oats behind us. The summer scent of tarweed from the field left its indelible brand on our souls. We hiked among lizards basking on sun-baked rocks, and among snakes, tarantulas, scorpions, ground squirrels, and other more elusive creatures. One favorite place in the field was the cactus fort—a large clump of cacti about the size of a house. It took a while to find a way inside between the maze of needles, but we did, and in the middle was the perfect hideout.

We brought Mom some branches of the perforated hollow wood-like remnant of dead cactus. "Oh, cactus skeleton," she said, delighted. Mom always liked natural things like that.

Exploring the field gave me a feeling of freedom. That feeling followed me into other places as well: other neighborhoods, other wild areas, and the homes of other people my family didn't know. In those explorations, I encountered new things of which Mom would not have approved—"worldly things" as she called them. I developed secrets I wouldn't share with her, such as watching TV at someone else' house—shows she would not have allowed, or reading magazines or comic books. The only magazines I ever saw at home were either church-related or Mom-approved children's publications, or perhaps Readers Digest. As for comic books, they were not allowed, nor were playing cards. Movie theaters were questionable as well. Sneaking off to the movies wasn't difficult. The challenge was the ticket price. I seldom had money.

Perhaps Mom disapproved of too much. Or perhaps I was too sneaky. Either way, our bond was compromised and I never felt I could be fully open with her. Tim's experience was different. Mom's sheltering restrictions made him feel safe and protected. He valued his bond with Mom more than he valued his freedom.

DAD, RELIGION, AND THE MILITARY

Dad was an interesting individual. He was fun-loving, deadly serious, and unpredictable.

"I'm not much for raising kids," Dad told Mom when they were engaged to be married. "That'll pretty much be your job."

She probably figured he would catch on once kids came into existence.

Dad's home was Lawrence, Kansas, where he and his friends enjoyed hunting, fishing, and other outdoor sports. He lived there until attending college in Illinois, where he met

Mom. She was the storyteller, whereas Dad would only occasionally mention his childhood. His upbringing was something of a mystery.

Our dad was a doer. His nature might be summed up in the question, "Why watch when you can participate?" He used to tell us about how he played football when he was young—a lot of football. He was definitely a fan of the game. But unlike many fans, he had no interest in watching football on TV. He didn't follow any particular team and sometimes even confused the names of football teams with baseball teams. He simply had no interest unless he was a player on the field.

He demonstrated that get-involved attitude everywhere—except perhaps in the lives of his children. Getting his attention was somewhere between difficult and impossible for us. His mind was usually elsewhere. Mom was the exception. She could get his undivided attention and hold it for as long as she wished. I suppose he was a great husband; Mom always spoke of him with deep respect and affection. As for being a father, we three boys loved him, but we often wished for more than he offered.

Dad spoke almost endlessly about ideas he would come up with on the spur of the moment. If we were in a restaurant, he would likely talk about his unique ideas for opening a restaurant of his own. If we were in a store, he might launch into a monologue about how to make a better store.

Dad's work was sometimes difficult to describe. An extreme do-it-yourselfer, he could build just about anything. He was also a public speaker, an activist, and a mentor. He was both a soldier and a preacher. Proudly patriotic, he served with three branches of the military: the Army in Germany, the Navy around the Pacific Rim, and the Marines in Vietnam. His military service was something of an enigma in that he loved the military but he often had trouble with authority.

In high school, he was guilt-ridden about something—I never found out what it was. Amid those feelings, he attended a church where he experienced a spiritual breakthrough. He described it as "swapping the guilt for joy." Whenever he mentioned that experience, he always wore a big smile. His religious convictions became central to every aspect of his life from then on.

He found a perfect niche for himself when he became a Navy chaplain. That role provided the military context he enjoyed, respect for his religious life, and significant personal freedom.

Tim was transfixed as the military parade finished its final maneuver, gave a unified salute, and marched away. It wasn't a real parade—more of a drill or a rehearsal, but it left an impression on us kids. Tim was fully attentive.

"I like the swords," he stated.

"Yeah, I wish we could have swords," I returned.

That was a Saturday.

Monday morning, Dad was dressed in his Navy uniform, headed for the door when Tim intercepted him.

"Daddy, where's your sword?"

"My sword? What do you mean, buddy?"

"At the parade they had swords."

"Oh, yeah, the dress uniforms. That was great, wasn't it?"

"Do you have a sword?"

"I'm a chaplain. Chaplains don't wear swords."

Tim seemed disappointed. "I think chaplains should wear swords," he stated with strong childlike conviction.

A patriot, Dad spoke passionately about his military duty,

but he chose the one role that would intentionally put him in war zones armed with little more than a Bible and a flashlight.

THE GUMBALL HEIST

The water in the gutter backed up about thirty feet as I finished the dam I'd been making out of dirt and other debris. The water dutifully rerouted itself through the channel I designed at the end of the dam, then found its way to the storm drain about ten feet away.

As I washed my arms off with the water hose, I discovered I'd lost my big plastic Batman ring. "Oh, man!" I said to myself. I looked everywhere. No luck. I liked that ring. I got it the previous week from a twenty-five-cent gumball machine. I gave up the search and went to look for something else to do.

I played with our dog, Inky, for a while. Dad had surprised us when he brought the black dachshund home a few weeks earlier. Easily distracted, I noticed my stilts lying on the ground and picked them up.

Hanging onto the redwood poles at my side, I got my feet in place and walked across the grass in front of our house, then out onto the sidewalk, enjoying the large strides one can only experience on stilts. Dad had made them recently, and I enjoyed them immensely. I imagined what it might be like to actually be this tall as I roamed the sidewalk from my artificial height.

Johnnie and Petey from down the street walked by admiring my stilts. "I've got a pair of those," stated Johnnie.

"I had a pair too, but they fell apart," Petey chimed in.

Thoughtlessly, Johnnie gestured toward Petey and started the sing-song classic: "Nana nana naaa na, you don't have any."

"Shut up," responded Petey, laughing and shoving Johnnie.

The little girl with the hound dog was sitting on the curb laughing at Tim and Pauly, who had climbed down into the storm drain on the edge of the street. None of us knew her name and she never talked much. She smiled often enough, but I always felt sadness from her. She roamed the neighborhood with her dirty brown hair and that big hound, her personal canine angel that faithfully watched over her. The big dog sniffed around our fence. Inky was on the other side of the fence whining and barking in response.

Kyle came speeding down the street on his blue stingray bike. "Hey Dave, wanna go kype some candy at the store?" Kyle was tall with blond spiky hair—not because it was stylish, but because he never combed it. He was strangely fond of shoplifting—candy in particular. One of the older boys called him "Kyle the kyper." Even when he had money, he preferred the challenge of getting it out of the store without paying, and without getting caught.

"I don't know…"

"Come on! We don't have to steal anything. Just go to the store with me."

"Wait for me!" I heard my friend Greg, also on his bike, approaching from the other direction. Greg's curly black hair fell over part of his face as he rode his red adult-looking bike. I thought of Greg as my best friend at the time.

"Yeah, let's all go," said Kyle.

I dropped my stilts and grabbed my bike.

Pauly stuck his head out of an opening in the curb, climbing back out of the storm drain, much to the entertainment of the little girl with the hound dog.

Greg hollered to Pauly: "Hey Pollywog! Tell Mom I went to the store with Kyle and Dave." Pauly was Greg's little brother.

In the parking lot next to the store, we came across some small disks about the size of nickels. They were made of hard cardboard-like material and scattered on the blacktop next to one of the parking spaces.

"You can use these in the gumball machines as nickels." I commented, fabricating some made up nonsense.

"Wow," responded Greg, as he grabbed a handful of them and ran into the store. To my complete surprise, Greg inserted one into a five-cent gumball machine, turned the handle, and out came two gumballs. He proceeded to try again with the same result.

Scrambling over each other, we ran back out to the parking lot to gather a supply of the fake nickels. Ten minutes later, we had pockets full of gum and candy.

Somehow, using the fake coins didn't feel like stealing. It felt like outsmarting the machines, which was different.

Back out in the parking lot, we found Johnnie, who had missed out on the fake nickels. "Hey, give me some," he begged.

"Nana nana naaa na, you can't have any!" I sang, enjoying the poetic justice.

We examined our take. "It's like Halloween!" exclaimed Greg.

"Check it out." said Kyle surprising us when he reached into his pockets and pulled out, not only gumballs, but also several large candy bars and a box of Junior Mints. Kyle had been busy. Now we felt like thieves. The candy was great, but it came with guilt, which was its own expense; using real nickels would have been cheaper. Despite those guilty feelings, I kept a handful of those little nickel slugs to use again later.

We all grabbed our bikes and headed back. As we approached my house, we passed the little girl with the hound dog. She gave her usual wave but didn't say anything. Tim was getting a talking-to from my mom about staying out of the storm drain. Dad had come home while we were out, and about twelve Navy sailors were hanging out in the yard and the house. The presence of all the sailors meant a barbecue.

"How come there's so many people here?" asked Kyle.

"Dave's dad likes to have these big meals with lots of people," responded Greg.

Tim ran up to me with something in his hand. "David, I found your Batman ring in the sewer." Sure enough, there it was. It must have fallen off my finger when I was making the dam in the gutter. Tim stood there beaming, waiting for my approval.

"Ooh, Thanks," I said. "That's great!"

"It's not a sewer," commented Mom. "It's a storm drain. We've got a lot of company. Get yourself cleaned up."

Kyle went home with his loot, Greg hung out with the sailors, and Inky enjoyed heaps of attention from all the young men. It was a good Saturday.

The balmy southern California days were full of wondrous opportunities. We were like wind chimes. We thought we were making our own music, not realizing we had simply been placed in the perfect breeze.

CREEPY FLASHER

Treks through The Field were not always fun.

On one occasion, I was with a few friends about a mile from home, when we found a place where someone had dumped a bunch of construction debris. In our world, this was a treasure trove. We found broken pieces of marble slabs, asphalt roofing shingles, and a whole pile of safety glass bits. To an adult, this was useless junk. To us, it was the raw materials for creative expression.

We loaded up as much as we could carry, hiked back to our homes, and went to work. My friend Greg and I worked together. We took the pieces of marble, made interesting shapes out of the roofing material, and then glued it all together with bits of broken safety glass on top. Of course, we called the glass bits "diamonds." We sculpted all sorts of shapes until we ran out of material.

Tim came into the garage to watch us. "Can I make one?"

"Too late. We already ran out of stuff," replied Greg, much to Tim's disappointment.

I always had mixed feelings about Tim. When I was with friends my age, I left him out of whatever we were doing because he was too young. But when it was just the two of us, I liked his company. Even as a kid, I was aware that approval from me or from Doug meant the world to him.

The next day, Greg and I packed a sackful of food and prepared to go gather more treasure. Tim followed us around, hoping to tag along.

"I wanna go too!" he cried, as we headed out.

"You're too young," yelled Mom from another room. Tim looked at the floor. "I wish I was four," he mumbled. Then the shameless begging started. "Mom, I wanna go! David will be there."

After some fairly intense complaining from Tim, and me promising to watch him, Mom relented, and we headed out. He managed to keep up—an impressive feat for someone that small. We were joined by several other kids, and made our way back to the same place, looking for more loot.

As we rummaged through the piles, we noticed a man watching us. Normally we wouldn't have cared, but there was something about this guy that seemed different from other adults. He came a little closer and just stood there, staring at us. We pretended to ignore him.

After a good haul, we decided it was time to eat. We broke out our bags of food and sat down in a circle, some on rocks, and some in flattened-out dry grass.

Immediately, the man was with us, joining our circle. He was standing, sort of towering over us. His face was round with a dark, full head of hair. "You boys wanna see something?"

I wasn't sure what he meant. Aside from Tim, the average age in our group that day was about seven. Stephen was the oldest. He was nine. Most of us weren't quite old enough to identify the vibe this guy was giving off. Our friend Ricky, looking a little confused, but wanting someone to say something, said, "Yeah, okay." Ricky was the smallest of us except for Tim.

The man was holding his hands together in front of him, looking somewhat normal. Then, dropping his hands to his side, he stood there, proudly exposing himself. We all stared, silently. I'd seen adults naked before, mostly my dad. But this was different. He wasn't really doing anything, but he scared me.

"Oh, man," said Ricky, awkwardly. No one else said anything, but Ricky was always talkative.

Tim didn't even seem to notice.

Two or three of us looked at our food and continued eating, wishing the man would go away. After a long minute or two, he left—jogging away up the trail, still exposing himself to the world.

"That guy was an idiot," said Greg, with disdain in his voice. Stephen was probably afraid, but he sounded angry. "We're lucky he didn't take out a knife and kill us."

Those words startled Tim, who then looked up, completely oblivious to what had just occurred.

Stephen was the oldest. I figured he knew something I didn't. I felt disturbed, but wasn't sure why. That disturbed feeling stayed with me, but I never talked about it. I didn't know what to say.

We lost interest in our treasure. The day was now filled with a disquieting quiet.

Weeks earlier, at school, Ricky had told me about something that happened to him—something a man had done to him, but I hadn't understood.

"Oh, man," Ricky said again. His eyes teared up and the usual sound of his talkative voice was conspicuously silent for the rest of the day.

RATTLES, ROCKS, AND RHYTHM

The Anza-Borrego desert heat radiated from the rocky outcrops, cacti, and pale orange sand as we hiked with Dad. Mom said she would enjoy some alone time so she stayed at our campsite. We took in the desert, listening as Dad pointed out various land formations and the occasional lizard, tarantula, or other small creature.

Dad was taking us on a road trip to Kansas through the American Southwest. This was something we'd done before and always loved.

Doug, who walked a short distance ahead, suddenly jerked his legs up in wild, rapid contortions like he was trying to get off the ground. At first I laughed at his youthful spindly limbs, flailing in all directions, then I saw the full-size diamondback rattlesnake that had been sunning itself right where he was about to step. He jumped and twisted awkwardly as the viper coiled into position, ready to strike. It froze, waiting, motionless but for the energetic announcement from its tail.

Dad responded with protective aggression. "Boys, get back behind me." He then killed the snake with several blows from a large rock.

Jamming a stick through the snake's body, he held it up by the stick.

"There," said Dad. "It's dead now. It can't hurt you."

I felt the long, scaled body, looking closely at the diamond patterns on its back.

Tim stared, wide-eyed, not understanding. He couldn't figure out why it was dangerous, and then it wasn't. This was his first exposure to death.

We returned to our mom, snake in hand.

She tried to make out what we were carrying. "Oh, my goodness. Is that a rattlesnake?"

"Yup," answered Doug. "I almost stepped on it."

"Oh my." She looked at Tim. "Were you afraid?"

"Daddy was there," replied Tim, incredulous, fully believing that Dad's presence meant there was nothing to fear.

I looked at the rattle at the end of the snake's tail. "Dad, can we keep its rattle?"

Dad got out a pocket knife and took hold of the snake's tail. He removed the rattle and got rid of the body of the snake. The rattle had about ten segments. When we shook it, it sounded like...well, a rattlesnake. We saved it to add it to our drawer of treasures when we got home. I suppose that was gross and unsanitary, but it was also typical, given the kind of boys we were.

My brothers and I were always collecting treasures, especially those acquired on road trips across the vast North American landscapes. We would gaze out the car window at the warm deserts with rugged mesas glowing in the evening sun. Those images burned deep into our souls. When we stopped along the way, we often experienced something that would become a significant memory later. We explored old adobe ruins, small remnants of ghost towns, and many natural land formations.

Looking out the car window, we noticed a row of teepees on a raised area a mile or more from the road. We were just close enough to see their shapes, lined up in front of a hillside. We had constructed small teepees on occasion in our yard, and on some of our outdoor adventures, but these were the real thing. We watched as they slowly faded out of sight.

Within minutes, we saw a sign that read "Indian Trading Post" and a large arrow pointing to a small collection of buildings a little ways off the road. The three of us erupted into shameless begging.

"Dad, can we stop?"

"Come on, Dad, it's an Indian trading post! We have to stop!"

Mom looked at Dad. "It's a long drive, Honey, let's give them a break."

As I got out of the car, I was struck by how quiet everything seemed. I could hear a couple of kids in the distance, and an old wood frame screen door closing as someone disappeared into a small building. The sound of our car doors seemed loud. I felt out of place, like a tourist—welcome, but an outsider.

The inside of the small trading post store was mesmerizing. Everything they sold was stuff we wanted. Some knives with decorative leather sheaths caught my attention but I knew I couldn't afford them. I only had pocket change, and while Mom and Dad might buy something for us occasionally, a sheath knife would be unlikely. I came across another favorite, a small bin full of polished stones. A man wearing an old straw-colored cowboy hat sat in a wooden chair watching me. Somewhat shyly, I asked him how much the stones cost. I don't recall what he said, but I remember the feeling of elation when I realized I could afford some. I carefully chose three: obsidian, tiger-eye, and a turquoise mix. All of them were tumbled and polished. The obsidian piece was also called an Apache tear.

Those three stones felt like treasure. At home, I loved gathering colorful stones and using them to make artistic creations.

"Dave, look!" said Tim, pointing to several toy drums. "I want a drum!"

To our surprise, Dad asked Tim which drum he liked best. Tim made a choice, and Dad took it down and handed it to him. Tim carried it around with that huge smile he'd sometimes wear. Doug picked out a wooden pop gun that shot corks and Dad paid for all the items. I got to keep the polished stones and my money too.

Hitting the road again, we stopped at the famous meteor crater in Arizona. Tim loved anything connected to space, which included meteors once he found out what they were. We also visited Carlsbad Caverns and many other fun sites on our way to Kansas.

Between the snake rattle, Doug's pop gun and Tim's drum, the backseat soundtrack for that trip was memorable. My treasure was silent, and much longer lasting.

At home, I had a small wooden box with a secret lock that made it difficult to open if you didn't know how. When we got home, I put my three stones in the box.

EEW!

"No!" cried Tim as he fled the room, leaving Mom standing there holding out a teaspoon filled with the nasty medication. It was sort of the color of tomato soup, but the similarity ended there.

"Young man, you come back this minute!" she hollered after him.

"No!" he yelled back, determined to win this battle of wills. He had tasted the stuff before and had no intention of repeating the experience.

She spoke sternly. "Timothy, you have to take this."

"Dave," he yelled, "Save me!"

"I had to take it, now it's your turn," I responded.

It was horrible stuff, but it was better than having pinworms.

Pinworms.

Worms.

What could be worse?

The medication, apparently.

"I'll just keep the pinworms." Tim suddenly reasoned, but Mom didn't see it his way, and, catching up with him, held out the spoon once more.

"It's disgusting—It tastes like evil!" The whining continued. He looked up at Mom, his face pleading for mercy. She looked down at him. Hers was always a face of mercy.

All at once, he opened his four-year-old mouth and took it. His body squirmed oddly, as if he were becoming a worm himself, followed by some heavy breathing and an indescribable guttural sound.

"Very good, son."

Twenty minutes later, Tim approached Mom again. "Mom, will the pinworms taste the medicine?"

"Hmm, I imagine so."

"Good," he said boldly, as he headed outside. "That makes me feel better."

POOR INKY

We all looked up when we heard knocking. The sun shone through the nine square panes of glass in the front door. A tall, serious-looking man stood on the porch, waiting.

Dad answered the door.

"Is this your dog?" he asked, holding her lifeless body. "I'm so sorry. She was in the road—I didn't mean to hit her."

Dad answered quietly, gently reaching for the dog. "Oh, yes. This is Inky."

With tears in his eyes, Dad laid Inky in the grass and sat beside her. We all gathered around.

Dad loved animals. We seldom saw him cry, but when he did, an animal was often involved. Mom was less attached to the dog, but she sat down in the grass as well, putting an arm around Dad.

It was a quiet afternoon, and we mourned Inky's early departure. Her sleek black body lay on the grass. Tim squatted beside her, petting her smooth black fur from head to toe, "Poor Inky. Poor Inky." He continued to repeat the petting and the same words over her body, unaware of his effect on everyone else. Our grief had changed; now we were all feeling for Tim as well. After the rattlesnake, this was his second taste of death. This time, he didn't like it at all.

THE MOON

"Hey Dave, we should buy this telescope," said Doug, showing me the ad in the catalog. "I can't pay for it myself, but if we team up, we can afford it for sure."

He was right.

A few weeks later, after much dreaming over the picture in the catalog, I heard Doug yelling something from the front door.

"What's going on?" I responded, running out of the bedroom.

"It came! We got a notice. It's at the store. Mom, we have to go to the store to pick up our telescope!"

A couple of hours later, we were in the middle of our living room, excitedly tearing into the box.

We spent the afternoon looking at just about everything through the telescope. Doug pointed it toward the top of a telephone pole about half a block away, aiming for a small orange rectangle up near the wires. "High voltage," he mumbled.

"Lemme see!" Sure enough, there in the eyepiece, that little sign looked huge.

We were hooked. Doug and I spent much of the afternoon looking at distant houses across the field, power lines, people's windows, traffic—even distant plants in some random person's yard. Suddenly, every little thing was exciting.

"I can't wait for it to be night, so we can see the moon," Doug said.

Tim joined us. "I wanna see the moon!" he exclaimed, clearly fascinated by the telescope.

Finally, night fell, and even Mom and Dad joined us.

"Will we see the man in the moon?" asked Tim.

"Probably," I responded, messing with Tim's head. "If he's out. Sometimes he goes inside the moon and you can't see him."

"No honey," answered Mom, "There's no man. That's just an expression because sometimes the moon looks like it has a face."

Tim appeared deflated. "No man in the moon?"

Dad spoke up. "I hate to disappoint you, but I'm not sure we have a moon at all tonight, boys."

We hadn't thought of that. And Dad was right; there was no moon. We turned our attention to the stars.

"It's good to look up," said Mom. "It reminds us of how small we are."

"My teacher says there is no 'up' in space. She says we feel like we're looking up into the sky, but you could also say we're looking down into it or out across it. Out in space it's all the same."

"Your teacher's pretty smart," said Mom.

"Wow!" said Doug, as he looked through the scope. "This is great!"

"Lemme see!" I shouted.

We all spent the next part of the evening looking at stars through the telescope.

"They're beautiful," said Mom. "They look like jewels in the sky."

"How 'bout that," said Dad as he took a turn.

Tim was next. He looked, but he was silent—transfixed. He resisted when it was someone else's turn. He was really taken by the telescope and the magical experience it offered.

When we got a good view of the moon about a week later, we were all pretty excited. The moon, covered as it was in craters and shadows, was amazing for each of us, especially Tim. Once again, he was silent, riveted by what he saw.

For weeks at school during art, I drew pictures of the moon. I even sculpted a little moon, complete with tiny mountains and craters.

On a road trip not long after, Dad took us to the Palomar Observatory. It was, at the time, the largest telescope in the world. Tim loved it. Not much could hold his attention more than the mystery of the night sky.

THREE THOUSAND MILES

Dad sat reading the paper as Mom called us all into the room. "The Navy transferred your dad to a different base, so we're going to drive our new car to San Francisco and live there," announced Mom. "We're going to live under a bridge in a place called Treasure Island."

I wasn't sure what she meant. "Under a bridge?"

Doug looked excited. "Treasure Island?" Doug was a reader. In all likelihood, he had already encountered the classic Robert Louis Stevenson novel of the same name.

"It's a place called Treasure Island," said Mom. "And it's under a big bridge."

She had seen pictures of the island. It was situated near the middle of the Bay Bridge, although not actually underneath it.

Dad had recently flown to Kalamazoo, Michigan to buy a white Checker Marathon sedan direct from the factory. Tim was somewhat interested in the car, but he was more excited about the word "Kalamazoo."

"Dad went to Kal-a-ma-zooooo," he repeated, enjoying the sound. "Hey Dad, is Kalamazoo a zoo in Kalama?"

Dad didn't notice the question. Mom just laughed.

"San Fran-siskee-o," muttered Tim, more intrigued with the word than the news. By this time he was five.

Dad drove us from San Diego to San Francisco, but being Dad, he first took us on an elaborate three-thousand-mile road trip, zigzagging across the country. We camped in the desert and in the mountains. We visited the Meteor Crater in Arizona again, much to Tim's delight. We stopped at Aunt Elwyn's house in Kansas where Dad grew up, then went on to The Garden of the Gods, Dinosaur National Monument, The Great Salt Flats, and many other places.

We stayed at our aunt's house for several days—a place we loved for a lot of reasons, one of which was her classic porch swing. Tim loved to sit on the swing with Mom or Dad, taking in the summer evenings.

One highlight for Tim on that road trip occurred at a mountain town somewhere along the way. We stopped at a pet shop after Tim and I begged to go in. A large cage, taking up a sizable space in the store, housed a young lion for sale. Tim and I stared at the lion, keeping a few feet of space between us and the cage bars. Tim was nervous.

"He's just a big kitty cat." The pet shop owner approached the cage and stuck his hands through the bars. The lion stood up with his front paws on the bars above the man's head as the man proceeded to energetically scratch the big cat on its ribs. The lion seemed to enjoy the attention.

In those days, pet shops could pretty much sell whatever they could acquire. This was terrible if you were an animal, but if you were a kid intrigued with animals, venturing into pet shops was a great experience. We encountered many animals that would never be allowed nowadays, including monkeys, baby alligators, and, well, lions.

Tim loved the lion, but what really caught his interest were some Keeshond puppies. He desperately wanted to take one home. That didn't happen, although it was a sign of things to come.

Back in California, we settled in the city of Concord,

twenty-five miles east of the San Francisco Bay. Dad commuted to work as one of four chaplains on Treasure Island. On Sundays, we all went with him. The base chapel became our church.

Doug, Tim and I loved our new neighborhood. It came with a whole lot of kids. If you hate kids, you'd say it was infested. For perspective, on Halloween night, Mom passed out candy to over two hundred little superheroes, monsters, clowns, faeries, ghosts, witches, and skeletons.

CHAPTER TWO
1969 – 1971

---

*"It is easier to build strong children
than to repair broken men."*

*~ often attributed to
Frederick Douglass*

Treasure Island

Sitting in the chapel on Treasure Island, I looked out the window, bored with the sermon. It was my own dad preaching, but that didn't make it interesting. All I could think about was the table of cookies waiting in the other room. I noticed a monarch butterfly on the edge of the window outside. Then I noticed two more flying by the same window, then a couple more. I watched as Monarchs kept flying by—dozens of them.

I leaned over toward Tim. "Look at all those butterflies!" I whispered energetically.

"I wish church would end, so we could get some cookies and go outside," he responded.

Eventually, it was time for everyone to stand and sing "Eternal Father Strong to Save". That was our cue. The chapel services always ended with the same hymn—a very military hymn. At last, everyone somberly sang the final words: "O hear us as we cry to thee, for those in peril on the sea."

Trying to look relaxed and respectful, we made for the doors and freedom. We had to see what the deal was with all the butterflies.

We were not disappointed. We looked around for a few moments, lost in pure wonder. Within minutes, even most of the adults came out to see. Thousands of butterflies swarmed the area around the chapel. Moving like an orange fluttery cloud, they kept coming from over the bay across the island.

"'How is this possible?" someone asked. "We're in the middle of the bay."

I didn't know about their annual migration. I just knew this was amazing. I took off with Tim following behind, through a cloud of golden butterflies. We ran, laughing like we'd never seen anything like it—which we hadn't.

Suddenly I remembered the refreshment table inside

with cookies waiting to be eaten.

The butterflies had distracted everyone, and I made it to the table unseen. Tim showed up soon after, and there we stood, alone in front of a long table of cookies. Feigning nonchalance, I subtly picked up as many cookies as I could hold, added a few to my pockets, and walked away scarfing my loot.

"Does it get any better than this?" I asked myself. "A swarm of butterflies, all the cookies I can eat, on a warm day in a place called Treasure Island." Having consumed many cookies from my personal stash, I went back to the table, now crowded with adults. "Why are they taking all the cookies?" asked Tim. "They're grown-ups. Aren't cookies for kids?"

Worming between adults, I was loading up a second stash when Mom stopped me with a look of disapproval.

"Young man, you go straight to the car and wait there."

My punishment was perfect. I had two pockets full of cookies that she didn't know about. There I was, sitting in the back seat on a beautiful day with a good supply of cookies. Nice.

Dad's new Checker Marathon offered a lot of space between the front and back seats, sort of like a limousine. Tim came out and joined me, moving across the car floor from the left window to the right, and back again, watching whatever was happening outside.

I thought it might be fun to introduce him to the car's cigarette lighter.

"Tim, look at this. You can make it hot by pressing it in and waiting a little while. When it pops back out, it'll be red hot!"

"Wow," exclaimed Tim, when he saw the hot lighter activated. "What's it for?"

"It's for lighting cigarettes. Too bad we don't smoke."

I may or may not have suggested that Tim could brand the vinyl seat with lighter-shaped circles, but whether I own that or not, it's what he proceeded to do.

When the family was back in the car, my dad didn't make his usual motions to start driving. He just sat there looking at my mom. "Mom tells me you made quite the impression on the table of refreshments."

"Yeah. I had a few cookies. Isn't that what it's there for?"

Mom looked at me seriously. "How many cookies did you eat?"

"I don't know, a few, maybe eight." I knew I had to pick a relatively high number to make it believable.

"Son, I want the real truth. How many cookies did you eat?" Mom knew me well enough to know I would have kept count.

I got the distinct feeling that we wouldn't be moving until I confessed.

"What's the big deal? They're just cookies."

Mom continued with the pressure. "Several people mentioned that they couldn't have any because one of the chaplain's kids took so many. How many did you eat?"

I hadn't realized I'd caused disappointment for someone else. I felt bad about that. "Twenty-two," I mumbled.

Both parental faces turned toward me, wide-eyed. They got out of the car, talked softly with each other for several minutes, and then got back in. Dad started up the engine, and off we went to Concord. I wondered what they had said to each other. I soon found out when Mom spoke up.

"David, you are not to have any cookies of any kind for a month."

Then, just as I was about to protest the oppression, Dad's voice suddenly interrupted me.

"What in the world?" he exclaimed.

He happened to look down and saw the circular rings of melted seat vinyl. "How did those get there?"

I put on my best dumb face. "I don't know."

Tim looked desperate. He was only following my counsel when he'd done it, but he'd done it, and he hated conflict with our parents.

They later punished us, but seeing the pained look of disappointment on Dad's face was also punishment. He loved that car, and we hated disappointing him.

MAN IN THE MOON

The summer of 1969 brought a few changes to our world. Doug was now twelve, I was nine, and Tim was six.

Tim gently rubbed his hand along the contours of Mom's big pregnant tummy.

"Mommy, was Davy jealous of me when I was born?"

"Why do you ask that, Honey?"

"Because I think I'll be jealous when the new baby is born."

As it turned out, Tim wasn't jealous at all. His happiness was obvious when our sister Beth arrived. He was delighted to have a baby sister, although he would have to wait about five weeks before meeting her. She had seizures soon after birth and had to stay in the hospital. It was a while before Mom could bring her home.

The doctors told Mom and Dad that Beth would not develop mentally—that she wouldn't be able to do much of anything. They said Beth might remain "like a vegetable."

"I don't like it when they call Beth a vegetable," muttered Tim. Even at six years old, he felt the term was disrespectful. He talked about her every day, often asking when she would come home. He also missed Mom, who was at the hospital more than she was home.

Finally, the day arrived. "Boys, your mother is bringing the baby home tonight. I want each of you to make yourselves available for whatever your mom needs." When they came in, Tim hung back at first, but soon wanted to get close.

"Can she play?" inquired Tim.

"Not yet," answered Mom. "You need to be very gentle."

Tim gently ran his finger across her forehead. The doctors had shaved the front half of her head as part of monitoring her brain activity, so there was a lot of forehead to touch. He leaned in, staring. "Hi Beth," he said, as she stared back.

He had trouble being excited and gentle at the same time, so he redirected his energy and ran out to the backyard to play with Keesha, the new puppy.

He spent part of every day with the little Keeshond. It was the same breed he had seen in that pet shop that had the lion. His delight was unquenchable when Dad had brought the puppy home the previous week.

"A puppy and a baby sister at the same time!" he proclaimed.

I was thrilled beyond words to have a little sister. We'd always been only boys. That was different now. I tried to conceal my excitement, acting nonchalant about the whole thing, but I couldn't stop thinking about her.

I went out to the yard where Tim and Keesha were playing. He had also gained the attention of several kittens, who were themselves just a few weeks old.

Tim looked thoughtful. "David, if Inky had lived, would we still have Keesha?"

"Wow, maybe. I don't know. I guess maybe not."

Tim stared at Keesha, then grabbed her, rolling on the

grass in a playful blur of striped T-shirt and fluffy gray dog fur.

We heard Dad inside saying something about a TV. We ran in, and to our surprise, he was fiddling with a medium-sized television he had just brought in from the car.

Aside from a few months in San Diego, we'd never had one. Friends at school thought it was strange, and would often ask, "What do you do at night?" I never understood the question.

"Hey boys, I thought we could all watch the moon landing together." Dad was pretty excited and started hooking up the set. "I rented this TV for a month."

We all sat around the dinner table that night. A lot was happening at once. Dad talked about the Apollo Eleven astronauts, and how they were inspiring people. Mom talked about how well Beth was doing. Tim talked about Keesha. Doug joined with Dad, talking about the astronauts and where they were at that moment in their lunar journey. "They named the lunar lander 'The Eagle' and it's gonna land on Sunday," he announced. I talked about wanting to keep the TV.

That Sunday evening, Beth slept peacefully next to Mom on the couch.

Tim sat next to them.

The world stopped.

The Eagle landed.

Tim sat up with a satisfied smile. "Now there really is a man in the moon."

MISCHIEF AND DECEPTION

I was bored and looking for something to do, so I wandered into the kitchen to see what Mom was up to. She was occupied, preparing dinner—or maybe not dinner, but some sort of recipe. She had just finished organizing several ingredients and had them out on the counter, waiting and ready, while she disappeared into another part of the house for a while. I perused the various items like a curious shopper, not knowing what I was looking for. Off to the left, sitting by itself, was a tall glass, about two-thirds full of what appeared to be apple juice. I picked it up and gave it a sniff. Vegetable oil.

I don't know how the mind of a nine-year-old works, but I must have operated mine something like my mother operated her kitchen. It seemed I had various thoughts prepared and ready, like ingredients laid out and organized, waiting for the appropriate opportunity to present itself.

I set the glass of oil back down on the counter, but my mind was already spiraling into that place where mischief was made. I heard Tim playing outside. I stuck my head out the back door. Tim was playing with several kittens while their mother watched curiously from a patio chair. He looked up at me, his face innocent and unsuspecting.

"Hey Tim," I spoke straightforwardly, putting on a generous tone, so as to make my foul plan more likely to succeed. "Wanna taste something super delicious?" He looked just slightly suspicious—only for a moment, then got up. "Yeah, what is it?"

"It's a special kind of extra good apple juice that Mom got for us." Invoking Mom's name added credibility, which I needed. "Apple juice?" He seemed uninterested. "No, I don't want any."

"You never tasted this kind before."

"Why, what's it like?"

"It's really good. It's the best you can imagine."

Tim walked toward the door in his short pants and bare feet, more curious than thirsty, and stepped into the kitchen. I held the glass of oil, smelling it, pretending to be entranced by the aroma. "I already had a full glass, this one's for you. But you have to drink it fast to get the flavor." I handed him the glass.

Cautiously, Tim held the glass to his lips. He stopped. He looked suspicious again, but then, choosing to trust me, he began to gulp the oil.

I didn't know it was possible to chug down a drink and throw up at the same time. Tim produced a noisy gulping, gagging, spewing spectacle, like a sporadic fountain, just as Mom walked into the room.

At first, she seemed mystified. "Why would you drink vegetable oil?" she asked Tim, who was beginning to recover. Then she looked at me. I could see her mind working, connecting the dots as she read my face. I expected to be punished, but she seemed at a loss. "What possessed you to do such a thing?" she asked me. What indeed—that was the real question. Tim looked at me, completely lost.

Mom told me to tell Tim I was sorry for lying to him. I complied, but I was merely placating her.

My mischievous trickery worked. I succeeded, but I didn't like how I felt. Something about my mom's question got to me.

A while later, I was in the backyard playing with the kittens. Tim came out and joined me. I couldn't shake the dark feeling inside. "Tim, I'm sorry I lied to you," I said, this time on my own without parental oversight. "I just thought it would be funny."

Tim pressed his forehead against the forehead of one of his furry friends. "Hey kitty, wanna taste something super delicious?" We both laughed.

I still felt something wrong inside, but I also felt forgiven.

✧ ✧ ✧

ONE WHEEL IS BETTER THAN TWO

I paused, calming myself and focusing on my balance as I held on to the stop sign pole for stability. I was determined to ride my one-wheeled Christmas present at least ten or fifteen feet. I let go of the pole and moved forward a few feet, pedaling slowly, arms waving, trying to balance. I suddenly lost all control. Falling forward, my arm shot quickly behind me, catching the blue vinyl seat before it hit the sidewalk. Finally, I caught the unicycle before it hit the ground. "Yes!" I shouted. Tim heard me and came outside.

I was nowhere near able to ride it yet. My goal at the moment was simply to keep from destroying the seat, which had already taken heavy damage by crashing repeatedly into the concrete.

I walked my one-wheeler back toward the stop sign, distracted for a moment by Jimmy, out on his driveway across the street: Ka-joink, ka-joink, ka-joink... His light brown hair flopped up and down rhythmically as he went for a new record on his pogo stick. His personal best was two thousand jumps without stopping.

Suddenly my afternoon was interrupted by Eddy, an older kid I barely knew and wanted to keep it that way. He stood in the street—white t-shirt, freckled face, and blond hair sticking up in what was once a flat-top. "You can't ride that thing!" he taunted.

"Yes, he can!" yelled Tim, confidently.

I knew Tim was scared of Eddy, but he felt courageous because I was there. Tim didn't realize that I was afraid of Eddy too.

Eddy chuckled as he sneered. "Prove it!"

Now I was in a difficult position. I had already told Tim that I could ride this thing. And I believed I could; I was in the process of proving it to myself. It would just take another week or two.

"So, ride it," Eddy continued, his voice loaded with ridicule.

I got on the seat, my feet on the pedals and my hand firmly grasping the stop sign pole. Tim watched with a confident smile. Eddy watched with a sneer, shaking his head.

My lack of skill was about to be exposed to a local bully and my little brother at the same time. I didn't like where this was going. It seemed that bluffing was my only option.

I put my feet on the pedals, let go of the pole, gave two or three turns of that unicycle wheel, deliberate and assured, then let it fly forward right out from under me, caught it by the seat, standing tall and proud as if I'd done it.

I needed to maintain Tim's impression of me, which outweighed my fear.

"No Eddy, you prove it. You can't ride one of these can you?" I held the unicycle out for him to try. I knew this could cost me more damage to the seat, but my brother was watching.

Eddy gave a loud laugh—a single squawk, and for a moment, he was at a loss. Whatever might come next, I owned that moment.

"What a dork," mumbled Eddy as he walked away, leaving me to my practice, and Tim to his illusion that I could do what I couldn't do.

Every day that followed, the damage to the seat continued. Foam rubber escaped from each of the four corners. I put tape over it, but the tape couldn't handle the concrete any better than the vinyl seat cover.

Then it happened.

I let go of the stop sign, kept my eyes straight ahead, and pedaled, carefully keeping the wheel underneath me. My arms flailed in ways that made dignity impossible, but I rode that thing and kept riding it all the way down the block. I fell only when I tried to turn around.

A few days later, I made a point of whizzing past Eddy's house on my one humble wheel. I saw him working on something in his garage. His dad was watching him. "Come on stupid, do it right. Don't you know anything?" yelled his dad, slapping him on the side of his head.

For one long second, Eddy's eyes met mine. And in that second, he looked different. He could have been my brother. I saw past the bully to the boy.

I rode past Eddy's house, then past the school where several small kids pointed and cheered. I rode past Jimmy, still out on his driveway, going for height this time. Jimmy's pogo stick was great, but not as good as touring the neighborhood on a unicycle. I rode over the bridge that crossed the creek where I would sometimes catch frogs. I rode past the older couple's house whose names I could never remember. They waved from their porch. As I approached our house, Tim was watching me from the window, once again wearing that confident smile.

QUARTERS 212-A

"Quarters 212-A," said Tim proudly. "That's our new house."

After a few moments, he spoke up again. "Dad, will we still go to Treasure Island sometimes?"

Dad had been transferred to the Naval Weapons Station, where he would now be the base chaplain. It was just on the other side of town, so this move was only a few miles.

"Probably not," said Dad.

"I like Treasure Island," said Tim.

"I do too," I commented.

"Well, we're here now. I think you'll like this place, too."

The moving truck backed up to our side of the beige-colored military duplex. One of the movers flung open the back door and everyone began carrying our stuff into the new house.

When the couch was in place, Mom sat down holding Beth. She now focused her attention on the little face in her lap. Beth, as it turned out, was doing quite well. Despite the seizures she'd had after she was born, she developed well, gaining energy and personality. She thrived and we all enjoyed her immensely.

Doug came running around the side of the house looking excited about something. "Dave, you gotta see all the land behind this place! Have you been out there yet?" We both ran around the house and up a small embankment. "Check it out!"

I could see why he was excited. "Wow, this is great! We've got the whole countryside in our backyard."

A week or so later, Dad came home earlier than expected.

"Doug, David, go get in the car, we've got an errand to run and your presence is required." When Dad used that expression, it often meant something fun was about to happen.

"I wanna go too!" hollered Tim.

"But your presence isn't required," said Dad, with a smirk.

Tim looked like he was about to come unglued, so Dad preempted.

"Ok, buddy, you can come along."

We parked at one of the Navy offices and went inside. A sailor in uniform took Doug's picture, then mine. He disappeared into another room for a while as we waited in gray metal chairs that had black leather padding that wasn't soft.

"Are we gonna take my picture?" asked Tim.

"No buddy, you don't need one."

The sailor finally emerged with two laminated cards in his hand. He handed one to Doug and the other to me.

"Navy ID cards!" Doug and I exclaimed almost simultaneously.

"Thanks!" said Dad to the guy who made the cards, and we headed back to the car.

"I wanna be in the Navy too!" cried Tim, as he threw himself into the wide space between the front and back seats. There was ample room for Doug and I to stretch out our legs and admire our new ID cards while Tim threw a fairly wild tantrum.

Living on the base made these cards necessary. ID was required to get into just about anywhere. Of course, Tim, being too young to do much on his own, didn't get one yet—a fact about which he was clearly disturbed.

With those cards, we enjoyed access to the little four lane bowling alley, as well as the gym. The best part about the gym was the trampoline, where we would annoy the military personnel by occupying it way longer than was fair. Our favorite was the "Country Store," a gift shop on base with a good supply of candy. It was there that I fulfilled a long-term desire when I finally acquired my first sheath knife.

I stared at that card until I convinced myself that I was in the Navy. When I flashed the card, I could even board the Navy ships, or so I told myself. In truth, I was following behind my dad each time.

ID cards aside, the best part of living on that base was the open land, where we would disappear, spending long summer days building forts, chasing jackrabbits, and playing army with other kids.

Sometimes Mom had to run errands outside the base,

and we would scramble into the car to go with her. "Mom, where are we going?" asked Tim, as she drove us out the main gate and turned left on Port Chicago Highway. The three of us watched the world go by from the back seat.

"I've got some errands downtown," said Mom.

Tim looked concerned. "Not on base?"

"No, there's a lot of things we need to do off the base."

Tim looked thoughtful.

We looked out the window at the houses, the stores, and the people on the sidewalk. But we didn't just look, we looked from the loft of our new Navy selves, down our noses, onto the general population.

"Civilians," said Doug.

"Yeah," responded Tim with disdain. "Civilians."

DIRT BOMBS AND OLD BONES

One day my brothers and I managed to get ourselves on the front page of the Contra Costa Times.

We were at the top of a small hill, along with my friend Skipper, in the process of digging foxholes—a necessary element if one is to effectively play army. The idea was to form two enemy holes about fifty feet apart, each large enough for at least one boy to hide in. Then we would gather and prepare our "bombs."

To acquire a bomb, we would grab as much tall grass as we could with one hand and pull it out of the ground. If the ground was right, the roots would come out of the ground along with a large dirt clod. We would then pick up the whole thing by the grassy end opposite the dirt clod, swing it around to create good momentum, and then release it. The effect was a beautiful comet-like projectile—the clod followed by its grassy tail—hurtling toward the enemy. When it landed, we would experience a satisfying explosion of roots and dirt. We also had an ample supply of toy guns, including Tim's giant plastic bazooka, but our favorite weapon was always the grass bomb.

Unfortunately, the area had recently been plowed, so we had to bring in a supply of grass bombs from down the hill. Of course, we used Tim for this, loading him up with grass bombs and making him carry them. With a good supply, we continued the work with our shovels.

That's how I found myself digging a hole in the ground that day. It was a hole none of us would ever forget. My energetic digging was suddenly blocked by the presence of something made of wood. I continued to dig, pounding at the wood until it broke away all at once, and I found myself down on the ground looking into the decayed, long-since-dead face of a real human skeleton.

There was a quiet pause as our revelry was overwhelmed by the unexpected reality in front of us. I experienced a feeling that I can only describe as being startled in slow motion. I don't recall who ran first, but a kind of herd mentality took over and the four of us found ourselves running down the hill in various states of fear as if the old bones were chasing us. Tim's six-year-old legs had trouble keeping up with the rest of us, especially with his giant plastic bazooka.

Running wildly into the house, producing a cacophony of shouting, the message was clear: "Dad, Dad, we found a skeleton!" We found Dad, otherwise occupied, who gave his usual nod: "Uh huh."

"What should we do?" Dad was used to the boyish adventures we got ourselves into and was not really listening. "I don't know, bring it home I guess."

Outside again, the woman who lived next door heard us. She took me by the arm, her brown braids coming undone, causing a wild look as her partially loose hair moved in the afternoon breeze. "Show me what you found."

Hesitantly, I led her back up the hill to the hole where the jawbone and teeth were conspicuously exposed less than two feet below the surface. Immediately, she knelt and began to dig away the dirt and old rotten wood. As she removed the dirt, the shape of the coffin came into view. It was narrow at the head and foot, and wider at the shoulders, like coffins I'd seen in pictures of the Old West. Square nails and wood pegs stuck out of the old boards as she pulled them up.

The bones gradually revealed more of themselves, and the coffin's occupant began to look like what it was: a dead person's skeleton. My legs shook, my kneecaps rapidly vibrating up and down as I watched her clear away the dirt. I tried to calm myself, but I couldn't make my legs stop shaking.

The woman stood up, made some comment under her breath, and went back to her house for something. Skipper and my brothers showed up again, and there we all stood, looking down on the dead.

I was still afraid, as were they, but less now that we were all together. Our boyhood spirit of adventure began to return. Overcoming our fear, we circled up around the discovery. I don't know who made the first move, but soon we were picking up bones and examining our find. Instead of being soldiers, we were now archaeologists. Before long we found ourselves carrying a large paper grocery sack, filled with human remains, into the house to show Dad.

This time, Dad's response was a little more animated, as was Mom's, and that day became a family legend, involving the police, the coroner, all four boys' pictures in the paper, and most of all, fame among the other kids at school.

Soon after that, Tim and I were back on the knoll where we made the find. We lay on the ground, thoughtfully looking up into the afternoon sky.

"Who was the skeleton?" asked Tim.

"I don't know."

"It was a real man, right?"

"Yes. Or maybe a woman."

Something had changed. Finding a real person's bones was more than merely a boyhood adventure.

"What's it like to be dead?" asked Tim.

I didn't know what to say. We looked at the sky for a while, lost in his question.

Men came and excavated the hill, but they found no other graves. Against all odds, we had managed to dig directly into a lone grave in a wide-open area of rolling hills. They told our parents that it was likely the grave of someone who died in the late 1800s, possibly while traveling, as there was no evidence of any settlement.

Much to my disappointment, the coroner's office took the skeleton away. Tim, however, was relieved. He said he had trouble sleeping the night after our find. Before going to bed, he went out to where he could see the paper sack on the floor near the back door. He just stared, disturbed by the lifeless bag of bones.

Perhaps I shouldn't admit this, but the coroner didn't get everything. We managed to squirrel away a rib, a kneecap, a few teeth, and a piece of wood with an old square peg sticking out of it. These were added to our drawer of random boyhood treasures.

JOLLY ROGER

I loved kites. I once won a blue ribbon in a kite flying contest put on by my school. The ribbon confused me a bit, as I had always heard that a blue ribbon signified first place. My blue ribbon was clearly marked "2nd."

The kites in the store were each rolled up in a long package, usually quite colorful. The color would reveal a little bit about the kite. Upon unrolling it, we'd find the two sticks inside, along with the paper kite. At that point, we would find out what sort of image was on the kite. They came in all sorts of styles and colors, but one could never know for sure what their kite would look like until it was unrolled after it was purchased.

"I want a Jolly Roger Kite," I told Tim, as we rummaged through the bin.

"What's a Jolly Roger?" he asked.

"You know the skull and crossbones you see on a bottle of poison?"

"Yeah."

"That's Jolly Roger. It's what you see on pirate ships—the black flag with the skull."

I don't suppose either one of us had seen actual bottles of poison, but we got the idea from cartoons and comics.

"I want a Jolly Roger kite too," he said, excited.

"Well, we only have enough money for one kite." Just then, I noticed one of the packages had no colors—just black and white. "Ooh, this has to be it," I said, "The one I'm looking for is black with a white skull on it, and this kite looks like it's mostly black."

We got home and opened it up.

"Yes!" I exclaimed. "It's the one I wanted!"

Tim seemed intrigued with the image. "Yeah," he said,

"That's what they put on bottles of poison."

"Or pirate flags!" I exclaimed. "Or kites!" I put the kite together, attached a tail made of old rags, and began tying it to my supply of string.

Tim had run off and returned with a piece of paper and a pencil. "Dave, can you draw a Jolly Roger on this?"

Ever the artist, I was accustomed to drawing at someone's request. "Yeah, sure." I drew the image on his piece of paper.

"Now write the word 'poison' under the bones."

I wrote the word "POISON" under the bones, and Tim ran off with it.

I took my new kite out, but there wasn't much wind, so the experience mostly involved a lot of running back and forth with the smiling skull behind me, not able to gain much loft.

When I came back into the house, Tim was standing on a stool in front of the stove, boiling a small pot of odd-smelling liquid. Mom came into the kitchen. "What's that smell?" she asked.

"I'm making poison," answered Tim.

"Oh, goodness," said Mom, humoring him as she walked by. She had trained us to use the stove from an early age and didn't think much about it.

He had a bottle on the counter with my drawing attached as a label. Using a funnel he'd found, he carefully poured some of the liquid into the bottle and put the pot back on the stove.

Mom suddenly returned, this time with a curious look on her face. "Tim, what is that?"

"Poison."

"What's in it?" she asked, looking into the pot which contained a tea-like substance with a bunch of leaves in it.

"It's oleander tea."

"That's oleander? Oleander is poisonous!"

"Mom, I just told you, I'm making poison."

"And what were you planning on doing with it?"

"Nothing. I just wanted a bottle of poison."

"Oh, goodness, Tim, if you want to play like that, you can just put some colored water in the bottle and call it 'poison'."

"No, Mom, it has to be poison!"

They argued like that for a while, then she supervised Tim as he poured out the toxic tea under the oleander bushes, and thoroughly washed the pot.

It was probably an oversight, but Mom failed to make Tim pour out the liquid that was already in the bottle. With a look of victory, he carried his appropriately labeled bottle to his room, where he put it on the shelf with other treasures. And yes, it was full of poison.

THE PURPLE BUS

Suddenly our life in the Navy came to an abrupt halt. Dad decided to move us off the Naval Weapons Station, about ten miles down the road to a house in Pleasant Hill. An idea had been simmering in his mind and he wanted to see it through.

As a chaplain, Dad had a lot of success gathering young sailors together in study groups that resulted in meaningful personal growth. His influence helped them gain a foothold on a healthier life. He enjoyed such work and found significant personal fulfillment himself.

His vision now was to leave the Navy and start gathering young people of all sorts for something similar: study groups, spiritual retreats, and recreational outings associated with personal and spiritual development.

Culturally, this was part of what was later known as "The Jesus Movement," and we found ourselves in the middle of it. People still called my dad "Chaplain" but instead of sailors, he was surrounded by teenagers, students, and hippies.

"Dad, you can just let me off here," I said, as the two of us cruised down Viking Way toward my school. I was in the seventh grade, and my dad was driving me to school in a purple bus. This was not a van, a camper, or a large family vehicle that might be called a bus. It was an actual bus, like the school buses I watched ahead of us as they filed into the front driveway of my school.

"Dad, you can just let me off here," I said again, slightly louder.

"What's that buddy?"

"You can just stop here. We're close enough to the school."

"Oh, that's alright, I don't mind taking you all the way."

I tried again. "It's pretty crowded in there, why don't you just stop here."

Getting Dad's attention was never easy. He was always on a mission, and today his mission was to gain exposure for his new ministry work. He figured a big purple bus with his new logo on the side would get people talking and asking questions. He wanted to get the bus out into the community to be seen.

Being seen was the one thing I was trying to avoid.

Too late. Dad pulled into the large circular driveway with all the normal school buses, waiting as they emptied their cargo of kids, so he could capitalize on the most visibility.

"Okay buddy, I'll see you later," he said as he scanned the crowd. I stepped off the bus with everyone watching and tried to discreetly walk into the school.

"What's 'This Way'?" inquired two of my classmates. They had misread my dad's logo.

"It's not 'This Way,' it's 'His Way'," I corrected.

"Whose way?" asked one.

"What's 'His Way'?" asked the other.

This was the exact sort of moment I was afraid of. I barely understood what Dad was doing, but if anyone asked me about it, I felt obligated to try and manifest Dad's confidence and proudly explain. I generally failed.

"It's something my dad's doing," I said, and kept walking.

"Oh, so it's your dad's way."

"I guess."

In my third-period class that day, I overheard someone say I was in the Partridge Family; a TV show about a family that drove around in a multicolored bus.

The upside of having a bus often came when it was parked. It provided a great hangout space for my friends and me, as well as a place for solitary refuge.

I suppose Dad's plan worked. Before long, he had won the trust of many parents, frequently filling that bus with high schoolers and taking them on weekend retreats, canoe trips, and other similar outings.

His promotional methods were unorthodox. When he wanted to gather young people for an event, he tended toward reverse psychology.

"You probably wouldn't like what we're doing," he'd say to some local teenager. "There won't be much time for fun. It'll be intense. It's not for everyone."

They loved the bus, and they loved my dad.

Walking up to the house one evening, I could see about fifteen energetic teenagers filling the porch and part of our yard near the front door. I knew my dad was inviting young people to our house, and I figured he'd drawn this crowd. Then I discovered this was just the overflow. No less than seventy teenagers filled our house and spilled out into the yard.

Our family was changing.

THE CRAZY GUY IN SAN FRANCISCO

Sometimes my brother Doug and I would lay the newspaper out on the living room floor. We would look for anything interesting, which often led to comics. When we finished reading those, our eyes would meander through the paper, looking at whatever caught our attention.

"Wow," said Doug, pointing to the page. I looked at what he was reading, and joined him, a paragraph behind. It was about a guy in San Francisco who had gone crazy and mutilated himself. According to the story, the young man had injured himself so badly, that he ended up blinding both his eyes and completely severing one of his hands. We talked about it for a while as boys sometimes do, with a dramatic sort of intrigue. We even speculated how someone might physically do those things. Tim was with us, focused on the comics, but hearing everything we said.

That night on my bed, I thought about that guy and felt the horror of it disturbing me and keeping me awake. I couldn't stop my imagination. I kept thinking about what it would be like to experience those things and why he would do it to himself. If he had hurt himself accidentally, it would still be horrible, but it would be easier to think about. The thought of him doing it to himself, on purpose, got to me. The more I thought about it, the more it disturbed me. The more it disturbed me, the more I kept thinking about it.

Horrified by my thoughts, I curled up under my blankets in the dark.

I know Tim was listening to Doug and me that day because he mentioned that story more than once in the years that followed. His imagination had hijacked his thoughts like mine did. In his young imagination, he said he pictured the guy running down the street with his eyes pulled out, screaming and waving his bleeding arms with his hands cut off. We knew that picture was imaginary, but there was no getting rid of the image. "What would it really look like?" we asked each other, and then we'd speculate. These were the kinds of conversations we could only have when Mom wasn't around. It was the stuff of nightmares. It didn't seem real.

Tim Meets Jesus

"I hate slacks," complained Tim as the five of us walked up the hill on a Sunday morning with Mom. We were all there except Dad. "I feel like I'm wearing pajamas. And what's with these polished shoes? You can't do anything in these."

As active boys accustomed to outdoor adventures, Tim and I always hated dressing up for church. Doug was an adventurer as well, but he didn't seem to mind so much. It was different for Beth. We thought of her like a little flower, made to be pretty.

Beth wore a yellow dress as she held Mom's hand—everyone walking at her pace. "It's important to give God your best." said Mom in response to Tim's complaint.

I thought about that, but it didn't make sense, so I questioned Mom. "If God is everywhere, and knows everything, then he was at home with us before we dressed up, right? So, what difference does it make?" Mom gave me a familiar look—a patient smile that somehow conveyed annoyance as well. I had pestered Mom with many similar questions over the years. Occasionally, she had a decent answer, but not today. Today she just seemed frustrated with us.

"You boys look nice. All I ask is that one day a week you dress up and act civilized."

Several neighborhood boys were out playing in tee shirts and cut-offs like we wore every other day of the week. "I hope they don't see me," said Tim.

"Hey, Tim!" shouted one of the boys. "Where ya goin'?"

Tim tried to turtle into his sport coat, pretending not to hear.

"Hi boys, we're on our way to church," responded Mom. "Would you like to come with us?"

They just stared, not knowing what to say. "F★ck that," muttered an older brother standing nearby.

Tim looked up at Mom. "Mom, did you hear that?"

"Yes, and I don't ever want to hear you boys talk that way."

Swear words got a big reaction from Mom, and Tim noticed. Later that afternoon, when she was on the phone, he stood just out of her reach and boldly shouted the "F" word a few times so the person on the phone could hear him. As the chaplain's wife, Mom found this frustrating.

She got off the phone. "Tim, come here, I want to talk with you about those words." She thought that perhaps if she told him the meaning of the words, it might help inspire a little more propriety. She explained that the "F" word was a nasty way of saying how a mom and a dad would mate and produce children (yes, our mom used the word "mate").

Since Tim could see there were four kids in our family, he immediately went out and told his friends that our parents had f★cked four times.

At school the next day, Tim chose liberation from the rules we'd been taught. He ran out of class for recess to the field, gleefully shouting "F★ck, F★ck, F★ck-a-Roooo…!"

He was exhilarated—like a captive animal finally making an escape and running free. Looking around with a big rebellious smile on his face, he expected someone to look horrified and maybe send him to the principal's office.

He waited a while.

No one noticed.

Nothing happened.

That evening, I overheard Mom talking with Tim. "You know, Jesus watches over us from Heaven. But he's also here with us in spirit too. When we talk with him, he helps us." She looked at Tim and smiled sweetly. "I think the time is right for you to meet Jesus."

Stifling laughter, I wanted to shout, "Meet Jesus? What are you gonna do, kill him and send him to Heaven?" But I kept quiet, knowing I'd get in trouble if I made light of it.

Tim looked delighted to hear what she said. The two of them sat in his bedroom, praying, as I stood around the corner listening. Tim told Mom that for a long time, he'd wanted to experience faith. He said he had tried to connect with God on his own but was unable to until now. He felt lighthearted and free. For several days, he seemed downright happy.

I was aware that something real was happening in him, but I was also aware of something else that I couldn't name. I could not yet articulate the distinction between real faith and its imitation sometimes found in religious trappings. I knew both were present in our family, but I couldn't explain it, not even to myself.

Within a couple of weeks, Tim changed again.

"Dave, do I have to tell my friends about God? I think I

have to tell them about God so I can go to Heaven when I die."

We sat on the little retaining wall in our backyard. Keesha ran back and forth with Tim throwing a toy to her. She brought it back to him, pushing it against his knee to get his attention.

I thought about what he asked, and I wasn't sure what to say. I sometimes felt the same obligation. I was taught that we were supposed to tell people about God so they could believe in him and be saved from Hell. But I was also taught that God was the one who would send them to Hell if they didn't believe in him. It always confused me.

"I don't know why God would send people to Hell and try to save them from Hell at the same time," I commented. "It's hard to know what to tell people."

Tim looked thoughtful. "At church, they said I'm supposed to tell people about God, but I hate it. I wish I didn't have to." He had somehow gotten the idea that in order to keep a connection to God, he had an obligation to tell his friends about it and to convince them to come to church— sort of like a multi-level marketing plan for God's love. It was a lot of pressure for a nine-year-old.

Tim remained unsettled about his faith, but he took to reading the Bible. He always read the Bible after that.

He was with his friend Ben the next day after school. Ben seemed preoccupied. "My grandpa died," he said, confiding in Tim.

Tim was quiet for a few moments, then replied. "You should be happy."

Ben looked disturbed. "What do you mean I should be happy?!"

Tim had read about Heaven in the bible. He recalled a verse that even said, "To die is gain."[1] He figured Ben's grandpa was better off having died. But Tim hadn't lost a loved one yet. He didn't understand Ben's grief. Not only had he failed to comfort his friend, but he made it worse. Later Ben began ignoring Tim and even took to mocking him. When Tim tried to talk to him, Ben was unfriendly.

The rejection from Ben was the first time Tim felt he'd lost someone. As a result, he began to learn about grief himself.

[1]PHILIPPIANS 1:21 (NIV)

CHAPTER THREE
1972 – 1977

*"When we are children we seldom
think of the future.
This innocence leaves us free to enjoy
ourselves as few adults can.
The day we fret about the future is the
day we leave our childhood behind."*

~ *Patrick Rothfuss*
The Name of the Wind

DAD'S FAITH

Sitting in the purple bus on a Saturday morning, I nursed my thirteen-year-old angst while watching my dad work on the other side of the parking lot.

"Come on, buddy!" he yelled, "there's a lot of work to get done."

Somehow my dad had acquired a two-acre property in Concord a couple miles from our house in Pleasant Hill. The place included five buildings and a parking lot. It had been used for storing and repairing trucks for the telephone company but had stood vacant for a year or two. It wasn't much to look at—concrete, steel, and a lot of dust.

He was convinced we could turn this old truck yard into something special. He envisioned a community center where people from the surrounding area could experience life-enriching activities. In his mind, it was a kind of church, although not necessarily in the traditional sense. I looked around. All I envisioned was what was in front of me: a parking lot, a big tin roof that covered an area where trucks used to park, and a few dismal-looking buildings. The fact that my dad had acquired it was impressive. But why? It was one of the ugliest places I'd ever seen.

My brother Doug was hard at work somewhere on the property.

"I'm not helping!" I hollered back.

Dad walked over and stepped up into the bus. "Listen, I brought you with me to get some work done. We're going to be working on this place for a long time. I suggest we get to it."

"No way!" I shouted. I felt he was taking me away from activities with my friends for no reason. I wanted nothing to do with this place.

I could see the anger forming on his face, but I was ready to stand my ground. The next few moments were quiet. He stood there with his hand on the pole at the top of the steps, looking down at the bus floor. I sat in one of the seats looking out the window. Slowly, the look on his face changed.

"Suit yourself," he said quietly, stepping off the bus and walking back across the parking lot. I was ready for a yelling match, but instead, he just looked hurt.

As I continued to look out the window, my hard attitude turned into an emotional pain that seemed to be forming in my throat. Dad was changing our lives in ways we didn't understand or want—at least Tim and I didn't. I was trying to load up enough anger at my dad to cover my uncertainty and fear.

Since leaving the Navy, Dad had decided to live "by faith," as he called it. Money was so short that I recall taking a sack lunch to school with a couple of pancakes in it. My mom had a lot of flour, so we had pancakes for breakfast, lunch, and dinner for a while. Fortunately, I liked pancakes, but I also felt the change brought on by the lack of income. I couldn't figure out why we had no money, but he was able to acquire this two-acre piece of land with five buildings.

Earlier that week, I'd heard my parents talking about a large bill that came in the mail. "How are we going to pay for this?" Mom asked Dad.

"I don't know," he replied, "but God will take care of us."

They continued opening the mail. There in the same stack, they found a check—a donation that amounted to the exact amount of the bill, plus ten cents.

"Goodness," said Mom, "This person wouldn't know anything about the bill."

They paid it that day, and the extra ten cents covered

the postage stamp. Even as kids, occurrences like that did not escape our notice. I wondered where this path of my dad's would lead.

The warm sun wafting into the bus felt good. With the warmth, I also felt the presence, so familiar in times when I was quiet. The feeling of that presence always brought out honesty within me. In that space, I began to see that my dad was trying to do something good. Staring at the tin roof and dusty concrete buildings, I let myself imagine what it could be like with people coming and going like my dad envisioned. I began to feel an interest. Nearly an hour passed.

I found Dad and Doug in one of the buildings, patching up a damaged wall.

"Alright, I'll help," I said quietly.

Several other people came in not long after I did. "Hey Chap!" said Gary, the one face I recognized. Gary always brought a smile and a "can do" attitude. He was a large man— strong and ready to work. A couple of years before that, he had nearly lost his life to extreme drug use. He experienced a dramatic recovery and now carried a genuinely joyful demeanor. He was also one of Tim's favorite adults, someone he enjoyed immensely.

"Oh, hi Gary!" responded my dad. Many people called my dad "Chap" since his chaplain days in the Navy. The nickname stuck, and he was always called either "Jim" or "Chap."

I spent the afternoon working with this crew my dad had somehow formed. Then I spent much of the following week doing it again.

Months went by, and in the end, the tin roof had become a building with walls. One of the buildings became a well-equipped place where people could work on their own cars, another building became a bookstore, and another was turned into a restaurant.

We had a grand opening. People came, and my dad's vision was realized. He had done nearly all of it with volunteer labor and donated materials. Such was the magnetic personality of my dad.

The tin-roofed building became a church, but not like any I had seen before. People called it The Barn. The gatherings were highly interactive; it was a place where people shared openly about what was going on in their lives and received encouragement and support.

Everyone at The Barn knew Tim as "that kid who's always running around." It was true; he pretty much spent all his time there running around causing harmless mischief. He was a fixture in motion, generally liked, and even loved, by the grownups surrounding him.

The unspoken dress code at The Barn was casual. Tim finally got to wear comfortable everyday clothes, much to his delight. Many gatherings ended with the whole group folding up the chairs and setting up a volleyball net. Everyone was welcome to play. Tim often joined the game, but sometimes he annoyed the other players when he would bounce the volleyball off his head as if he were playing soccer.

Tim particularly liked it when people shared openly in the gatherings. He paid attention, knowing this was something exceptional. He listened as Denny, a young man about twenty-four years old, spoke to the group. "Will you all pray for me that I can find a good car I can afford? I've got a new job, but it's difficult to get there on time. I need a decent car."

Jerry spoke up: "I have two cars. You can have one."

That night, Jerry signed one of his cars over to Denny, so Denny could drive it to work the next morning.

On the way home, Tim was deep in thought. "Jerry really

gave Denny his car?" he asked Mom.

"Yes, isn't that wonderful?" responded Mom.

Tim thought for a moment. "I like Jerry."

Dad called the whole place a church, even the garage where neighborhood people came in to work on their cars. "God's in that too," he would say.

Faith took on an observable quality at The Barn. Many people recovered their lives after spiraling addictions. Thieves made restitution, resulting in their own joy and healing. Rejected and marginalized people found a home where they were genuinely enjoyed.

Dad's innovative ideas sometimes drew criticism from other church people, but the local community in Concord responded generously. He had left the Navy with no financial backing and no specific business plan—just a simple vision, which was somehow becoming reality. For a few years, it felt good to be in our family. We enjoyed seeing how people benefited from Dad's vision. And beyond that, I made a number of friends that meant the world to me.

OF FAITH AND PHEASANTS

"So, let's see," I said, responding to my visiting cousins when they asked me about my bird hobby. "I've got fourteen homing pigeons, five chickens, four doves, nine quail, two ring-necked pheasants, two golden pheasants, two parrots, four finches, plus the babies hatching in the incubator in my room."

I'm not sure why, but birds became my thing for a few years. I built several bird cages in our yard, two large enough to walk in. My hobby was loud, dirty, and required a lot of work. I hung bird posters in my room, read bird books, learned most of the local wild species, and taught my little sister the names of all the birds on my walls.

While I was away at a friend's house, Tim's friend Bryan Reiff was at our house with Tim. Unlike most of our childhood friends, Bryan's family stayed in our lives throughout many moves and became lifelong friends. At that age, he and Tim were often inseparable.

The two boys decided they wanted to get a close-up look at my pair of golden pheasants. The male was possibly my most prized bird, and certainly the most beautiful. He sported striking blue, green, and scarlet feathers on his body, a deep yellow crest on his head, and a tail almost two feet long.

They unlatched the door and went into the cage together. The female scurried into her nest box, but the male strutted about, seeming to enjoy the attention. They sat next to each other in the cage, watching the bird until they felt satisfied, and went off to do something else.

"Oh, wait!" yelled Tim, a few moments later. "I left the door open!"

The male golden pheasant continued his strutting right out the door into the yard. Then, suddenly realizing where he was, he gave a couple of wing flaps and one strong jump, alighting on top of the fence that encircled our back yard.

"We need to catch it!" yelled Tim, fearful of what might happen to him when I came home and found out. At that moment, the gorgeous bird took flight and disappeared over the rooftops.

The two boys watched the bird vanish. Tim's voice was frantic. "What's Dave going to do to me?" Running into the house, they did the only thing they could: they told Mom.

Mom could have scolded Tim for letting the bird escape, but she always showed respect when we confessed our faults rather than hiding. She sat down with Bryan and Tim, and true to her form, prayed with them that they would find the pheasant.

Tim felt slightly better. He still didn't know what would happen when I got home, but at least Mom had been merciful.

The two boys had already planned to go for a hike, so Mom got a burlap sack and told them to take it along, in case they found the missing bird. Bringing the sack seemed ridiculous; the pheasant could have gone in any direction, and it wasn't hand-tamed anyway. But Mom insisted, so they took the sack and set out on their hike.

Not far from home, near a place everyone called Hangman's Hill, a row of pine trees grew next to the road. Next to the row of trees ran a barbed-wire fence. Beyond the fence, the walnut orchard was in full bloom. As they walked there, Tim stopped abruptly, looking through the pine trees and the fence, into the orchard. Right there among the walnut trees stood the golden pheasant in all his glory.

Tim felt a solemn amazement. He thought about Mom's prayer, and how she insisted they bring the burlap sack. Fully expecting the bird to fly away, he slowly climbed through the barbed wire fence, cautiously approached it, and gently reached out with both hands. Perfectly relaxed, the bird allowed Tim to pick him up and put him into the sack. They ran straight back home.

"Mom! Mom! We found it!"

"I'm not surprised," said Mom, and she wasn't. This aspect of our mom's faith was always a wonder to see. She seemed to have two types of faith; one was overly religious— even slightly oppressive, and the other was a wondrous sense of God's presence in her day-to-day life. When she sent Tim and Bryan out with the burlap sack, she truly expected them to bring my pheasant back home. She was not ignorant; she was aware of how unlikely it would be for them to find the bird. Her expectation was rooted in her experience of God actually listening to her.

When I arrived home, I went around to my various bird cages to check on them and feed them. The pair of golden pheasants greeted me in their usual way. I had no idea the male had spent part of the day in the walnut orchard.

Mom later told me about the escape, and what had happened. She strongly encouraged me to be gracious with Tim.

I was initially furious that Tim had let my prized pheasant escape. But, as I thought about it, I was amazed that they were able to return it without injury or incident. And although I was still young, I was not oblivious to the faith element demonstrated by Mom. My anger subsided.

"Hey Tim, I heard you had an adventure today with the golden pheasant."

"Are you mad at me?" asked Tim.

"No, everything worked out fine. And the pheasant got to have an adventure too."

Years later, as a young man, Tim doubted his own standing with God many times. He was caught between the overly religious kind of faith and the simple kind that brings peace with it. Though our mom was sometimes a strange mix, her tangible faith was contagious, and helpful when he struggled with his own self-doubt.

SMILING DANGER

Dad pulled the car into the Davidson's driveway in Monterey. These were old friends of Mom and Dad. They had four kids, three of whom were near us in age, which meant fun.

The older son, Dwight, was at least eighteen—much older than the rest of us. He was tall, with dark hair and a pleasant smile. Sometimes the four adults would listen as Dwight sang hymns for them, something he often did at church.

We only saw them every couple of years—a long time for growing kids. After some small talk and awkward silences, we would get reacquainted, and head off toward the beach.

We always enjoyed their place. We liked Monterey with its fascinating shoreline, fisherman's wharf, and many historical sites. It was also the land of John Steinbeck, adding the bonus of his legendary tales to the place.

"Try to keep up!" yelled Dwight as he took off toward the ocean, winding his way through the ice-plant-covered dunes.

"I'm the fastest!" responded Tim, zipping along on the loose sand. Dwight let him pass and watched as Tim gained even more speed when he hit the moist sand—much firmer under his feet.

Dwight watched Tim closely. "Wow, you are fast!"

We explored tide pools, swam if we felt like it, and watched scuba divers disappear into their underwater world.

"I'm gonna do that someday," commented Tim to no one in particular.

"I'm sure you will," responded Dwight, eyeing Tim with a smile.

We spent that night in sleeping bags on the living room floor. Dwight massaged Tim's shoulders and back. "That feels great," said Tim, innocently oblivious to anything but good intent.

I was uncomfortable with the way Dwight treated Tim, but I didn't know what to do about it. Dwight was older and the adults admired him. Tim was ten or eleven at the time.

The next day we were out on another outdoor adventure, after which we once again found ourselves stretched out on the living room floor with the Davidson kids.

Dwight was ready with another massage for Tim, but this time he waited until the lights were out and most of us had drifted into a good sleep, happy to be staying in this home that, in Tim's words, "felt like being in a storybook."

I was unaware of what happened next. Tim told me much later what happened and how it affected him.

Dwight worked for a while on Tim's back, then moved to his thighs. He then began touching Tim's private parts, startling Tim, who suddenly became overwhelmed with a disorienting fear.

"I think you should stick to just massaging my back," his voice choking.

Dwight smirked in the dim light. "I can see your face turning red."

Something happened to Tim that night, something no one knew about but him. He didn't know what it was, but something had changed. The joy of life became tainted. Trust, which had come so easily, was now a point of confusion.

HOW TO FREAK TIM OUT

"Found it!" I hollered as my shovel of dirt revealed the bones and remains of Sam the rooster.

"How can you stand it?" commented Carl, a friend from school. "That's so gross."

"I've dug up worse." I stated, matter-of-factly. "Help me gather these bones into a pile."

Carl laughed. "I don't think so. You can do that yourself."

I barely noticed as Carl eventually wandered off, leaving

me to my work. I spent the next forty-five minutes sorting and arranging. Artistic expression had always been my thing. My medium of choice at that moment was rooster remains.

The afternoon sun exposed every flaw, and I tried to correct each one, as I worked to perfect my masterpiece. Tim would be home soon, and I needed to have it ready by the time he arrived. Carefully laying out the leg bones, I was nearly finished.

About a year earlier, my red rooster, Sam, had died of something called coccidiosis. At least that was the diagnosis from our neighbor, Mr. Bishop. He had two aviaries in his yard and an impressive collection of birds. I figured he knew what he was talking about. I knew nothing about the disease itself, but I remembered the name, which I would repeat from time to time when I wanted to sound knowledgeable. Sam caught the disease, but it didn't actually kill him. It was a hatchet that did him in—a hatchet in my young hand.

My father insisted that I "put the rooster out of his misery" and suggested that I wring its neck or take a hatchet to it. The thought of wringing Sam's neck was more than I could handle. I figured I would make some terrible mistake and end up torturing the poor guy. That left the hatchet, which sounded equally terrible, but I felt less likely to make a mistake. In the end, Sam, my pet rooster died under my hand, and I felt like a murderer for weeks afterward. My dad said that being willing to kill animals was simply part of having them. He told me that nature was not always nice to creatures, and we had to be willing to kill out of kindness. That made sense in my head, but I never got used to it in practice, and it didn't feel like kindness.

For some reason, being kind to my younger brother came less naturally. And here I was, spending a good part of the afternoon in our backyard, digging up Sam's bones, and creating my own little monster to scare Tim.

I sorted the bones, piling the curved ones together, lining up the straight ones, and discarding anything that didn't fit my plan. I carefully laid out the design, organizing the bones into the shape of a miniature human. I constructed a rib cage, arms and legs, even hands and feet—sort of. It was impressive enough to scare me a little as it took form. The skull, of course, needed some work. The shape of Sam's head bone was just too different—it didn't look human at all. This was remedied by the use of a file and some other tools I found in the garage. It was still somewhat bird-looking, but sitting at the head of the little skeleton, it worked. The whole thing together looked very much like the bones of a little human being about a foot tall. It lay there on its back in the sunlight on top of the redwood retaining wall in our yard. I stood back, like a young Dr. Frankenstein admiring his work.

Tim and I agreed that fear was the worst feeling in the world.

Oddly, we also looked for ways to cause it.

When I saw Tim coming down the street toward our house, I mustered up a sufficient volume of fake fear, and ran out of the house yelling and looking terrified. I pretended I was surprised to find Tim and told him I had found something in the backyard that had freaked me out. I may or may not have even said something about leprechauns being real.

It worked. Tim was stunned by the mini-skeleton—getting as close as he could, while still keeping his distance. The look on his face told me that he was genuinely afraid, which I found satisfying.

His voice was tentative and nervous. "Where did it come from?"

"I don't know, I just found it lying here."

Of course, he insisted we show Mom. I had already accomplished my mission, so I didn't bother to object. Besides, a willingness to show Mom might make me look all the more sincere.

"Those look like chicken bones," my mom said. "David, did you dig up a dead chicken?" Tim suddenly looked enlightened, and perhaps a little relieved. We were then treated to a lecture about germs and the importance of leaving buried dead things underground out of sight.

To me, the conversation was background noise, a soundtrack to my continued admiration of my handiwork.

SPOOKED

Blake was a young man known at church for his musical talent. For a sixteen-year-old, his abilities on a piano seemed like magic and he could sing like an angel.

"Blake's dad will bring you home tomorrow," said Mom, as Tim got out of the car at Blake's house and Blake came striding out to meet him.

"You boys be good!" she said, casting a confident smile as Blake and Tim waved and went into the house. Tim's time with Blake wouldn't have happened naturally—it was something our mom and Blake's mom decided would be a good idea. Tim was twelve or thirteen at the time.

Blake plopped himself onto the couch to watch the TV, which was already on.

Tim sat down for a while. "What do you wanna do?" he finally asked Blake.

"What do you mean?"

"Are we just going to watch TV?"

"What else is there?"

Tim had expected to do something more active, but Blake seemed uninterested.

"You wanna see where we're sleeping?" asked Blake.

"Uh… sure."

Blake showed Tim his room.

"We'll sleep here," said Blake, bright-eyed and half-smiling.

Tim didn't relish sharing a bed with Blake, but he didn't want to upset the plan.

They watched TV for a while, enjoyed a nice dinner with Blake's parents, then back to the TV.

That night, Tim woke to an odd sensation. At first, he thought it was just Blake turning over in his sleep. But then he felt something moving in his underwear on his private parts.

It was Blake's hand.

Tim spoke up, surprised and afraid, "Hey!"

Blake shot out of the bed and out of the room, leaving Tim alone, feeling violated and confused.

Several minutes later, Blake returned without Tim's knowledge. He crawled silently on the floor toward the foot of the bed. From there, he slowly pulled the blankets off the bed, causing a rush of fear in Tim as the blankets seemed to move on their own. A moment later, he realized it was Blake.

"Knock it off!" said Tim, raising his voice without yelling loud enough to wake the rest of Blake's family.

"Wow, Tim, did you feel that? I think the room is haunted." Blake's behavior left Tim feeling disoriented, afraid, and angry.

"Haunted by you," responded Tim, afraid but trying to sound aggressive. He sat up, feeling trapped, waiting for morning. His thoughts produced only frantic questions. "Why am I even here? I hate this. Why did Mom think this was a good idea? What am I supposed to do?"

Blake continued saying something, but Tim no longer listened.

The next day Blake's dad drove Tim back home. "Tim, thanks for spending some quality time with my son. He needs good friends."

"Okay, yeah, sure," said Tim. He was quiet most of the way home, wondering what the adults had expected from him. He told no one what had happened until years later.

HANGING BY THE ANKLES

Normally, car hoists would be installed by a professional crew using industrial equipment to drill into the ground. Gary and Dad weren't the sort to throw money at a professional crew. No, they decided they wanted to install one in a hole dug by hand about seven feet deep. And that was after jackhammering through a concrete floor where the hoist was to be installed. That's when Tim and I showed up.

"You guys here to help?" hollered Gary as we approached.

"Yeah!" responded Tim. He wasn't all that interested in helping, but he liked Gary and wanted to please him.

We looked into the hole they'd dug, and Tim, of course, immediately got down and stuck his head in, examining it for the possibility of getting inside. He'd always liked holes in the ground. He made a pastime of digging holes—sizable ones—big enough to hide himself in, including two in our yard, and one under our house. I'm not sure if our parents knew about the one under our house.

When Tim stuck his head in the hole, I noticed a familiar smirk take over Dad's face. He and Gary had been discussing an idea before we arrived. The hole was currently about five feet deep and they couldn't get any deeper with shovels and a post-hole digger. They needed a depth of two more feet.

Dad retrieved a metal coffee can and said, "Tim, lay down with your head over the hole." When Tim did so, Gary and Dad picked him up by the ankles and began lowering him, coffee can in hand, all-too-willing prey, into the gaping mouth of concrete and dirt. He then filled the can with dirt while hanging upside down in the hole.

When the coffee can was full, they hauled Tim out, emptied it, and then lowered him into the ground again. Very slowly, the hole got deeper and deeper, until only his feet could be seen, one held by Dad, the other by Gary.

At first, Tim thought the process would be fun, but after being lowered about fifteen times, he started to complain about the process. As they pulled him up, he seemed flustered.

"Dad, you couldn't hear me yelling?" Tim asked, dumbfounded.

"Yelling? No. When were you yelling?"

"Just a minute ago, before you pulled me up. I needed to get out."

"Oh, sorry Tim," responded Dad, still smirking.

I hadn't heard him either. The dirt in the hole absorbed the sound.

From Dad's perspective, the process was working, and he encouraged Tim to stick with it. Eventually, however, Tim refused to go down again. They looked at me. "Dave, it's your turn. Besides, you're taller. You'll be able to go deeper."

The hole surprised me. Down inside, it was difficult to see, and even more difficult to hear. I filled the can, which they had tied to a rope, and they raised and lowered it past my upside down body as I filled it. I yelled for them to pull me up. My ankles hurt, and I needed to breathe air that I hadn't already exhaled forty or fifty times. None of us had thought of that. They couldn't hear me. I continued yelling. Finally Dad's voice yelled back: "What?"

"Pull me up!"

"What?"

"Pull me up!"

There's a reason God put our nostrils on the bottom of our noses and not the top. If you're ever hanging upside down in a hole with dirt spilling over your face, you'll notice this. So, there I was, heavy-headed from hanging upside down, nostrils full of dirt, mouth-breathing recycled air, yelling into the nearly soundproof walls of the earth which seemed determined to swallow me whole. And this was happening with the help of my dad, no less. I thought about Tim complaining as they raised and lowered him repeatedly. Now I understood.

Working with our dad was unpredictable. Sometimes it was fun, sometimes difficult, and sometimes dangerous. But we never really felt the danger. We still believed that Dad's presence somehow meant we were safe.

DOUBLE CRUSH BLUSH

Tim was a smart kid, but not academically driven. He always did well on tests, but he was behind others his age in school.

"I like my new school," commented Tim one day near the beginning of the seventh grade. He was on the floor, engrossed in his coin collection. He picked up a specific coin. "I wish I could have lived in our grandparents' time," he said, putting down the coin and picking up another. He loved his old coins, as well as other antiques. He liked his school, not for the education it offered, but for the old buildings in which the students met for class.

He also loved "treasure hunting," as he called it, which usually involved arranging ropes and buckets on an embankment overlooking Taylor Boulevard near our house. He would dig for quartz crystals, which he would find in abundance. "Those crystals have been in there for a thousand years," he would declare.

One day his teacher, Mrs. Halverson, found a wheat-back penny in her change as Tim stood near her desk. Tim wasn't fond of her tightly curled gray hair or her choice of dress— dark blue with white polka dots. He thought she was super old, probably born in the 1800s. Apparently, his love for old things didn't apply to aging women.

He sometimes got wheat pennies from the 1950s in his change, but this one was from 1939 which seemed ancient to him as a twelve-year-old.

"Oh, I love those!" he exclaimed. "Can I exchange a regular penny for it?"

"Oh, well, I might like to keep it myself," responded Mrs. Halverson.

"Come on, please?"

"Well, look at you. You really want this don't you?"

"Yeah!"

"Alright, I suppose I can trade you for a newer penny."

They traded, and Tim went to one of the tables in the lunchroom to get a closer look at his new old penny.

In his pocket, he also had several other old coins from his collection. He laid them out on the table, entertaining himself. Enthralled and preoccupied, he was only half aware of several students bringing their lunches to the same table.

His thoughts were interrupted by a lovely voice. "Aren't you going to eat?"

"Hmm?" He looked up into the face of one of his crushes,

Cheryl Clyde. She sat across from him, putting her long straight brown hair and her lovely face in the middle of his field of view.

"Uh…"

"What have you got there?" asked another voice, taking a seat right next to him.

"A penny" was all he heard himself say. It was his other crush, Laura Martinez—black hair, perfect oval face, and a sweet fragrance.

"Must be a special penny," said Cheryl with a smile.

In Tim's world at that time, these two girls were the height of feminine beauty. He could never decide which one he was more attracted to, but he always kept those thoughts to himself. He never even spoke to them.

Enraptured by Cheryl's smile, while simultaneously feeling the closeness of Laura beside him, the self-consciousness was almost unbearable.

"It's old," he choked out in a barely audible voice.

"What was that? asked Laura, barely able to hear him.

Unable to speak, he suddenly felt the dreaded red face, starting at the chin and rapidly rising until it covered his face with its ghastly hue.

The two girls spoke mostly to each other after that, while Tim sat lost in self-conscious anxiety, consoling himself by continuing to admire his coins.

THE PERIL OF PUPPIES AND PIGEONS

The four of us stood motionless. The moment didn't feel real. Mom had just called a family conference, something she did now and then when she and Dad had something to say to all of us.

"We need to get rid of Keesha. We can't take her with us." The words echoed in our heads.

Tim was trying to control himself, but he was failing. His face was beginning to give into the emotional pressure he was feeling—grief, anxiety, and probably anger.

Dad was the one who had acquired Keesha. He's the one who had named her and raised her when we were too young to know how. She had given birth to two litters of five puppies. We still knew some of those puppies and visited them on occasion. She'd been in our family for eight years— as long as our sister.

Beth began to cry.

We'd spent the previous few months adjusting to the idea of moving to the city. Dad wanted to move his ministry work into San Francisco, leaving us with very mixed feelings.

Tim's grief was obvious, but there was something else, too. He turned away, looking out the back door which stood open. Then he looked back at Dad and Mom as if he didn't quite recognize his own family. The idea of moving to the city was strange enough. But the discovery that Dad was giving up our dog in order to make the move left Tim feeling lost, like our family wasn't quite what he thought it was.

I was feeling it too but held myself together.

Doug looked sobered.

"Sometimes we have to make sacrifices for the sake of ministry," said Dad. The words were exactly the sort of thing I expected from Dad, but I didn't know he would go this far.

"I thought people stopped sacrificing animals a long time ago," I said, beginning to feel the edge of a coming anger.

"Come on, buddy," was Dad's only response.

I understood that pets are not human beings. I knew that sometimes things happen that require letting go of them. A natural disaster, for example, or war, or maybe even a difficult move. Was this like that? Was our move to San Francisco that sort of thing? I was angry. I also felt for Tim, who was profoundly bonded with the dog.

Suddenly I thought of all my birds. The flock of pigeons was free to fly away and would survive without me. But what about the others, the ones that needed daily care?

"Why can't we take her with us?" asked Tim.

"Yeah," rejoined Beth. "Please? We hafta keep her!"

"We just can't have pets in the new ministry center. It's too much to manage. If we took Keesha, then we would have to let everyone else bring pets, and it's just not appropriate."

Dad's explanation may have been sensible, but it didn't make us feel any better. We just sort of sat around after that, caught in a vortex of sorrow and grumpiness.

That afternoon I watched Tim playing with Keesha, trying to have fun. He couldn't seem to generate his usual energy.

A few days later, we transported the more exotic of my birds to the backyard of one of my parents' friends. Using materials from my cages, we set up an aviary in her yard. She didn't know much about how to care for them but knew our situation and wanted to be helpful. I had finally grown up enough to build some nice aviaries, but that was over now. During the next week, I gradually stopped feeding my flock of pigeons, hoping they would fly off to a new home. They stayed. I felt cruel, but I didn't know what to do about it.

Responding to the doorbell, Mom opened the front door, greeting a young couple standing on the porch. "We're here for the dog," said the man.

"Oh, it's a sad moment," said Mom, inviting them in.

Tim must have hugged Keesha fifteen times between the backyard and the front door. Taking the end of her leash, they put her in their car. Tim waved, trying to be friendly, but he fell apart as soon as they were out of sight.

Tim planned to visit them to see her every chance he got. He called them for weeks, before, during, and after our move. "Hey, can I come over this weekend?"

"This isn't a good time—maybe later," was the usual reply. Then one day they leveled with him. "I'm really sorry to say this, but we just had Keesha for a few days. After that, she got out into the street and was killed by a car."

It was summer. Normally this was Tim's favorite time of year, but in San Francisco it was different. He looked out his new window at the fog covering the city and felt a cold fog covering his soul.

*The sun still hadn't come up
in the cemetery.*

✧ ✧ ✧

PART TWO

No One Prepared Us

Remembering the San Francisco fog seemed to add a chill to the air. I stood up from my gravestone seat and walked awhile, taking in the early morning and continuing to read the inscriptions on the graves. More than usual that morning, I felt both the presence and the absence of the dead—each name and set of dates doing its best to capture some small sense of someone's existence. No matter what words were etched in the stone, each spoke the same message: "Please remember me."

"I'm trying," I said, almost out loud. "I'm remembering."

I thought about my boyhood memories—of how our childish sense of adventure added something good and innocent to whatever else may have been happening.

Moving to San Francisco changed our perception of everything. Tim was never the same. None of us were, but for Tim, the move resulted in a wound to which no one tended. That childlike sense of adventure expired.

Our dad's ever-growing vision took us into some odd circumstances. I believe he meant well, but he was never very good at explaining what we were doing, where we were headed, or why.

My brother Doug seemed the most informed. He talked with Dad at length many times, processing ideas and possibilities. Tim and I were less apt to involve ourselves in those conversations.

We were left on our own much of the time. I was impressed with how well Beth adapted to the change. She developed a resilient personality but even so, the changes wore on her.

More memories flooded in—old stories of family and of friends, but I focused on the memories of Tim. The stories that came next brought to mind a time in which the two rivers of our lives flowed together as one.

Tim had always been both honest and happy. The honesty stayed with him into adulthood, but it wasn't long before the happiness was destroyed by an intruder—an invisible assailant who came into our lives and tried to steal Tim's mind. Its name was Chronic Undifferentiated Schizophrenia. It crept in slowly at first, adding an intensity to Tim's nature—a way of perceiving the world that confused him, causing unpredictable responses. Early signs appeared to be no more than an oddly timed statement, or a frown when others were smiling. But our move coincided with a critical time in Tim's development at fourteen years old. Tim felt overwhelmed by new people, a new school, and a new urban setting. Our new home, far different than anything previous, occupied our parents' attention. As a result, Tim's changes were seen as adjustments to growing up, when, in reality, they were more than that. He needed something no one knew about—not even him.

Later, the slow changes morphed into frightening psychotic visions, causing a string of chaos bombs, burying the formerly happy kid in ongoing fear. The nastiest part was that it made Tim himself look like the culprit. People feared and avoided him, but he wasn't the problem. He was being assaulted in mind, body, and soul by the illness.

Dad had a history of caring for wayward young men, but this was out of his league.

The joy-stealing intruder, that insane craziness that came and tried to kill my brother, found itself facing a challenging opponent whose name was Love. The love of several friends, along with the love in our family, however broken, would ultimately prevail. But there was something else too: something greater than our efforts, energizing the love—something divine. And even though Love was stronger, it had its own requirements. It could restore hope and perhaps even joy, but like a wise teacher, it wouldn't deliver its bounty without some work on our part—work that would leave us much stronger than it found us.

CHAPTER FOUR
1977 – 1983

Above all shadows rides the sun.

~ J. R. R. Tolkien

THE COMPOUND

I had just graduated from high school when we moved. I had no job yet and took advantage of my free time to explore the city and also to explore our new home, which was enormous. One day in one of the larger rooms, I heard laughter coming from one of the walls. I figured someone was in the next room. Nope. No one was around. More laughter. "Hey Dave!" shouted a voice from the wall. I looked around. "Up here!" Now it was coming from the ceiling. There was a wooden cupboard door built into the middle of the wall with a small ledge in front of it. It reminded me of a box office window. I opened it to find two ropes hanging in an open vertical shaft.

"Check this out!" called Tim, excited. "It's an old dumbwaiter." The voice was coming from above me inside the shaft.

Descending into the opening, a tiny wooden elevator came into view with Tim sitting cross-legged inside it. It was barely any bigger than he was. He had both ropes in hand, raising and lowering himself through the shaft.

"How did you even know I was here?" I asked. "Can you see through walls?"

"I saw you headed this way and set myself up."

"Okay," I laughed, looking up and down the dark shaft. "This old shaft is pretty cool."

This place was nothing like any of our previous houses. Dad was in the process of acquiring a large facility in San Francisco that was to be our home, and also home to many others. Of all the words that might characterize the place, the word "compound" says it best.

The fully gated property took up nearly half a city block. If you had entered by the main front door, you'd be standing in an old four-story building comprised of offices, classrooms, a chapel, a recreation room, two dining halls, a large commercial kitchen, and an attached three-bedroom home. The building was old, with beige walls and dark wood trim. Two worn, but once beautiful stairwells carried echoes of old-school carpentry.

That was just the beginning. Behind that building you'd find substantial room for parking along with two basketball courts. From there, you'd see another building with a large opening leading to an underground parking lot. Above that was a gymnasium with a stage at one end, fully equipped for concerts and other performing arts. The place was minimally landscaped, but nice enough for the most part. Past the basketball courts was yet another building, four stories with thirty-six dorm-style apartments that Dad had outfitted with desks and bunk beds he'd acquired from an old army base. That building also had other rooms and a garage large enough to fit the purple bus easily. The last stop on the tour would be another apartment building—four stories tall with about thirty-five family units and a series of rooms equipped as a childcare center.

After wild success in Concord, my dad's vision seemed limitless.

Our family lived on the third floor of the last building. Mom, Dad, and Beth had a two-bedroom apartment on one side of a hall. Doug, Tim, and I had one on the other. The apartments had no kitchens. All the residents ate together in a large dining room in the main building.

Several other families and couples moved into the compound with us, along with a few people from our church in Concord. The huge facility was still mostly empty, but Dad had a vision and was determined to see it through.

For me, the best part was getting to set up an art studio in the basement where I worked in various mediums—mostly clay.

For the next two years, more and more people moved into the compound. Dad's new vision was bigger than his last one. He pictured the place as a hub of ministry activity, influencing the city for good. He said he wanted to place a free Bible in every home in San Francisco (a project he would eventually complete). Teams of people systematically went out through the city distributing Bibles and other literature.

At one point we had nearly sixty people, which seemed like a lot, but there were still many empty rooms. Dad hosted luncheons for city leaders and gathered clergy from all denominations. Our new home was a center of much activity. The ultimate goal was a little vague to me, but I didn't think much about it. Dad was confidently moving ahead, and everyone seemed to trust him.

So, the walnut orchards and open environment of Pleasant Hill were left behind—the place where Tim had spent half his life. The days of hopping on his bike to go where he pleased were over.

THE CRUSH AND THE CRUSH

The most beautiful girl Tim had ever seen was Princess Leia in the movie Star Wars. On his first day at his new school in the city, that changed. He looked around, scoping out his new classmates and scanning the rows of desks.

His gaze riveted itself on a girl more beautiful than Princess Leia. His brain sort of froze, unable to make him stop staring. She wore a white linen jumper, had straight chestnut brown shoulder-length hair, brown eyes, and a face that left him in a state of such distraction that he could focus on nothing else. The teacher's mouth was moving, and there was sound coming out, but all he could hear was the five or six words he'd heard coming from that girl's gorgeous face a few minutes earlier.

"She must be the reason I had to move to San Francisco," he thought. Before the period was over, he'd heard her name: Becky. After class, he passed her in the hall and caught the loveliest delicate scent of her perfume.

Tim had had crushes ever since he'd been a little kid. First, it was Pam in kindergarten, then Princess Aurora from the Disney movie Sleeping Beauty, then Patty, Michele, Laura, Cheryl, and Carla. Of those who were not fictional characters, he never told any of them that he liked them. When it came to his crushes, secrecy was paramount, especially with an older brother like me, who would deride him endlessly if I found out. At least, that had been true when we were younger. Tim was now in the tenth grade, and I would have been more supportive, but his habits of secrecy were hard to break.

When Becky was around, Tim felt a sense of purpose, vague though it was. Images of her began to fill his mind, coupled with thoughts of how this uncomfortable life in the city would all make sense if they could get together. He never approached her and was at a loss as to how to initiate a relationship, but his thoughts of her provided a kind of comfort, even if it was imaginary.

Tim found his sense of hope in his imagination. He was relying on a crush to make sense of life. This was a little dangerous, but for the most part, it went unnoticed.

That school year was a very rough ride. For much of his life, he'd felt as if everyone else knew what was going on, while somehow he'd never gotten the proverbial memo. Now, in the unfamiliar environment on the sixth floor of a downtown building, that feeling was crushing him. The other students talked and laughed in the lunchroom while Tim felt disconnected and lost.

The new school was very different from his previous school, and much more academic. He felt ashamed for being a grade behind in math, so he talked the math teacher into letting him take second-year algebra without having taken first-year algebra. The teacher allowed it, and this mistake only added to Tim's sense of separation from the other students.

The one thing that made sense out of living in the city—the reason to continue in school at all—was Becky. The idea that living in the big city might be justified by meeting her was all he had to try and make sense of the move, which hurt much more than he revealed.

He did find some real joy in one other thing: he got to ride the cable cars each morning. He had ridden them before when visiting the city with our family. Back then, Mom rode with him and made him stay inside the car, but he wished he could stand out on the running boards, leaning out over the street.

Now he was on his own with no mom to tell him where to sit. He'd take a bus across town to Union Square, then catch a cable car up Powell Street. Tim found the regular cable car stops too crowded. The cars didn't move very fast, so he would jump on the moving car between the stops. The rules were more lax in those days and a person could ride as long as they were able to hang on. Sometimes he would hang on with one hand, squeezed in between people, leaning precariously around the front of the cable car. He enjoyed the freedom from Mom's protection.

At the top of the hill, by the towering Fairmont hotel, Tim jumped off and walked down the steep sidewalk to his new high school amid the skyscrapers. He tried to make himself feel good about the city—it was a world-famous destination after all—but part of each day involved deep sorrow and an inexplicable hunger for something he could not name. His sense of self was still in Pleasant Hill and life in the city felt like a bad dream. He thought about his childhood and felt like he was somehow betraying who he had been— like the kid in him was being crushed.

A NERVOUS KIND OF SLEEP

Our parents expected an unreasonable level of skill from my siblings and me. We were a do-it-yourself kind of family, and to my surprise, and perhaps a bit of horror, I would soon find out how far they would take that idea.

Soon after moving into the big compound, my dad brought me to a room he called the "sleep-watch" room. There was a bed and a desk. The desk was mostly empty— just some paper, a couple of pens, and a phone with a flashing light and a ringer.

"Dave, I'd like you to do sleep-watch two nights a week. It's important work, and each of us will need to take our turn."

I didn't want to do it, but I felt obligated. "What exactly do I do? I've talked with some of the others about this but I'm still not sure about it."

"When it's your duty night, you'll sleep here. If the phone doesn't ring, you'll just get a good night's sleep. However, if it rings, you'll need to answer it and talk with whoever is calling. When people call 'Suicide Prevention,' this is the phone they'll be calling."

Those four sentences were my training, and that phone rang several times each night.

"Dave, I don't know how you do it," commented Tim as we sat on the carpeted steps just inside the main entrance of our compound. "I answered that phone once and I hope I never have to do it again."

"You answered it once? Did Dad tell you to? What happened?"

"It was so embarrassing. No one else was around and I just felt like I had to answer it. All I remember was a woman asking me questions I didn't know how to answer. When Mom answered that phone she would sometimes say 'I'm a good listener.' So, I said 'I'm a good listener.' It was awful. The woman called me an idiot and hung up on me."

"People need help. I just try to be helpful," I said. "It's uncomfortable, but I feel obligated."

I recalled my first night on sleep watch. I tried to tell myself I was doing something helpful. I was eighteen after all—a real adult, right? I could do this. Such was my inner monologue while drifting off into a nervous kind of sleep as I listened to the sounds of the city outside and to the creaky building in which I found myself. The room was bare of any decor and felt like what it was: an old empty office. The living quarters were located in two other buildings on the compound. This building was administration and classrooms. I was on the third floor. No one else was in the building except a security guard downstairs.

Startled awake, I realized the phone on the desk was ringing. I had desperately hoped it wouldn't, but there it was, ringing and activating the flashing light.

"I don't know what to do." The woman spoke through tears, sounding both sorrowful and angry. "My husband got out of the hospital a couple of months ago, and I've been helping him nonstop. He was in there for almost a year. I thought I was gonna lose him for sure, but he kept pulling through. He made it, though, and finally came home."

"So what's the trouble? I'm here for you." I heard myself trying to sound like I knew what I was doing.

"He's finally getting well, and..." She faltered, sobbing. "He doesn't want to be with me anymore. He says he wants to..." More sobbing. "I can't tell you how hard I've worked for him. It's taken everything, and now he wants to leave me. He ignores me. He just goes out and parties with other men. How can I compete with that?"

"I'm sorry. That would feel terrible."

"I never expected this. I can't live with it anymore—I just don't know who I'm going to kill, myself or my husband." The tears yielded to anger, and her tone changed. "What do I do? I think about just killing myself, but I don't know, part of me feels like killing him. Damn, I kind of want to—I keep thinking about it."

And there I sat, in an old barren room, in an old barren building in the middle of the city in the middle of the night. I felt lost as I stared at the slightly textured beige plaster walls, but I needed to respond to this woman. I don't recall what I said, exactly, but I remember much of what she said during that hour-long call.

I finally hung up, got back in bed, and stared at the ceiling, dimly lit by the city outside. I thought of my bedroom in Pleasant Hill, now far away. I imagined myself lost in an alternate universe wondering if there was a way home.

The next day, Tim and I sat on the steps again, watching the traffic on Laguna Street.

"Do you like this place?" asked Tim.

"Yeah, it's great." I didn't know myself well enough to know how to tell the truth. I did like the place, but I constantly felt lost. I tried to be supportive of my family, but I never had a clear sense of what we were all doing.

Tim leaned forward with his chin against his knee, looking down, fiddling with his shoelaces. "I don't like the city. I miss Keesha. I miss riding my bike."

I felt for him, but I was caught up in Dad's momentum. "It'll be good. It'll work out great. You'll see."

I was doing to Tim what I did to the hotline callers— trying to say the right thing without any real understanding.

I answered that suicide line, off and on, for the next several years. By the time I stopped, I had spoken with hundreds of people in their moments of despair, grasping for someone, even a stranger, to help them find a reason to keep breathing. I felt important and maybe even necessary when answering those calls. But sometimes I felt like answering, "Hello, I'm a fraud, may I help you?" I was always afraid to reveal how little I knew, lest I cause more despair and endanger someone.

I had grown up enjoying the telephone. That joy was quenched as I entered adulthood. The sound of a phone ringing made me nervous after that, especially at night.

THE OTHER COMPOUND
DOWN THE STREET

I found a place up on the roof of the main building in our San Francisco compound. My seat overlooked a small sea of apartment buildings to the west. Just beyond that, I could see the Peoples Temple compound two blocks away. It was November 20th, 1978. I listened carefully to a small radio I'd brought to the roof. A body count was underway in Jonestown—as the Temple members called it—down in the country of Guyana. The group had purchased that land several years earlier and built a self-sustaining farm on which many of their members lived.

Peoples Temple was a church down the street from our place. The two ministries had several similarities. Both groups had large facilities from which they would conduct their ministry work. Both were outreach-oriented and focused on helping lost souls find a community in which they could belong. Another similarity I noticed was the names of the leaders. The pastor of People's Temple was a man named James Warren Jones. The leader of our community was James Warren Robinson, my dad. He went by the name Jim. So did Pastor Jones.

The body count continued. Those with the unfortunate task of counting had found several hundred people—church members—dead. I sat alone, trying to process what was happening. Guyana was a long way off, but these were not Guyanese people they were counting, they were San Franciscans. Many of them had been our neighbors, people I had spoken to on occasion.

I used to sometimes see pastor Jones on the sidewalk as I walked past his church. He always looked the same: black pants, a pale shirt, and dark glasses. He was a public figure known by many city leaders. I wondered if he was among the dead. I wondered what had killed everyone. The report changed by the hour, but the one thing that seemed consistent involved the words "mass suicide."

In the end, it was reported that 918 people committed suicide together. I wondered how many of them I had met. I recalled showing a man how to get to Jones' church after he had come to our place, mistaking it for Peoples Temple. Was his body one of those being counted now in a clearing in the South American jungle?

I had to tell myself to exhale. I couldn't stop picturing it in my mind—hundreds of dead people, most of them probably friends of each other, or family. I felt the horror penetrate me. Nearly three hundred of the dead were children, some of them very small. "Those little kids didn't commit suicide," I heard myself say out loud.

I could feel the bigger story beyond my own experience. This was the kind of moment people in the future would read about in history classes.

As it turned out, the entire population of Jonestown drank a poisoned beverage innocuously passed out in paper cups. That's where we got the phrase, "drank the Kool-aid," as a reference to someone who's been deceived.

The Peoples Temple tragedy wasn't the only body count that week. Just days later, city Supervisor Dan White killed two people. One was Mayor George Moscone, and the other was his fellow supervisor, Harvey Milk.

Dianne Feinstein took over as Mayor. Dan White was arrested. It was a confusing time—he'd always been considered one of the good guys—a soldier, a police officer, and a fireman. Now he was a murderer and a public enemy.

Our introduction to city life happened amid dramatic circumstances. The city itself was being wounded in ways no one knew how to care for. Even though I came off as a friendly, positive person, my experience of city life at that time created a private darkness inside me—a backdrop of fear. Tim was focused on different specifics at the time, but we shared that fear.

FULL HOUSE

"Well, it looks like we have to move," said Dad to several of us who'd been waiting for him to get off the phone in the front office. He tried to keep a good attitude, but he was obviously distraught.

After barely two years, Dad lost the compound in San Francisco.

The organization that previously owned the property had rotated its leadership. Agreements made with those previously in charge were now void including Dad's purchase agreement. There was some push-back on both sides but in the end, we had to leave. The place was enormous, so moving meant weeks of hard work getting everything into storage. Dad was convinced it wasn't over, so he kept everything.

Dad still owned our house in Pleasant Hill. Having no other place to go, we moved back into it.

After all the difficulty of moving away from Pleasant Hill, after becoming city dwellers, after saying goodbye to our friends and getting rid of our pets, here we were moving in again. This time, however, our family of six moved back into our old house with six more people. Dad tried to keep things going, however minimally, and was able to retain a staff who moved in with our family while they regrouped. In the meantime, it was communal living. In the house was our family, plus two other married couples and two single women. The house was very full, but everyone made it work.

I was nineteen years old. Tim was now in the eleventh grade and continued attending the private high school in San Francisco. To him, this seemed more backward than ever. Here he was back in the home he'd missed and never wanted to leave, but he had to commute into the city every day to attend a high school he wasn't interested in. On weekdays,

Doug, Tim, and I would cram ourselves into Doug's metallic blue Dodge Colt before the sun came up, commute across town through the Caldecott Tunnel in heavy morning traffic, and then across the Bay Bridge into the City to our respective destinations. Doug had enrolled in college courses, I had taken a job at a high-rise construction site, and Tim went to his high school.

Tim and I followed whatever opportunities came our way, but we didn't have any real plans. Conversations about the importance of further education were rare. Mom wanted us to attend a Christian college, but I didn't connect the idea to my own development—I just thought of it as something Mom was into, and I wasn't interested. Our brother Doug became engaged to one of the young women living with us. I found myself interested in the other one, but with no goals and no sense of my adult self, the idea of marriage frightened me. I avoided committing myself to anything long-term. My life perplexed me.

On Tim's first day back at school, he felt something inside stiffen when he realized Becky had moved to another school. He heard some of the girls talking about her, but he couldn't piece together where she had gone.

Now nothing made sense to him.

With Becky's departure, Tim felt no reason to continue school in the city. We were living back in Pleasant Hill anyway, so after finishing the fall semester, he told Mom & Dad that he wanted to start the spring semester at the public school near our house.

He finished the eleventh grade in Pleasant Hill, which was indeed pleasant. Public school was much easier after his struggle at the private school in the city. He said it felt more normal. Doug and I had both graduated in Pleasant Hill and it felt like a homecoming for Tim.

He signed up for a welding class, learning to use an acetylene torch to attach strips of steel.

"Dude, I'm going to make a shield!" he told one of his classmates, already picturing how he'd cut out 16-gauge sheet steel, put it through the bender to curve it, and then weld handles to the back. It would be the closest thing to his child-hood dream: a suit of armor.

"A shield? Man, that's so stupid!" the other student jeered.

He wanted to make the shield, but the ridicule stung. He scrapped the idea and never went back to it.

In his ceramics class, Tim learned to use a potter's wheel. Most students bought new, bagged clay from the class sup-ply room for their projects. The new clay was always ready to use—soft, clean, and consistent. Tim didn't have money, so he got his supply from the recycling buckets where used clay had been discarded. He would restore the used clay, and then work it on the wheel. He loved ceramics and became quite proficient.

A few years earlier, I had very much enjoyed the same class when I was in school there. We were both skilled and working with clay created an additional bond between us. It became something we both understood.

Tim also learned how to identify and locate planets. He got out the old telescope that Doug and I had purchased many years earlier in San Diego and enjoyed the night sky.

As a boy, he stared at pictures of the planets in books. Now here before his eyes was the real thing. To see the small yellow disk of Jupiter with its four star-like moons in a line, he felt like Galileo—he felt as if he'd stumbled across a long-lost treasure.

Tim's sense of life at that time was a strange mix. He was

no longer sure where his home was. He was away from the city, back in the house he loved, but there was no stability. Our house had twelve residents and our old family room was now an office. Dad saw the move back to Pleasant Hill as a setback and focused his energy on finding a way to get us back to the city.

WOW, YOUR BROTHER'S INTENSE

Halfway through Tim's senior year, Dad once again found a place in San Francisco. It wasn't a compound, just a house with a huge living room. So, we moved again. This time Dad sold the Pleasant Hill house. The money was certainly helpful, but he also said he wanted to "burn his bridges behind him."

Physically, the new place was our nicest house yet, but this time Tim lost all sense of home. He was allowed to stay with friends in Pleasant Hill during the week, then come "home" to the new San Francisco house on Friday. Doug had recently married and moved to a flat on Seventh Avenue in the city. I lived in the new house with my parents and my sister Beth, and of course Tim on the weekends.

"Dave, do you think Tim is alright?" Beth asked me one morning as we puttered around the kitchen.

"I don't know. I think so," was my response.

"He acts weird, and it's not just normal stuff. I think something's wrong."

Despite her seizures and possible brain damage as a baby, I had always found Beth to be wise beyond her years. She was eleven at the time.

We were interrupted when Dad and a friend named Joyce entered the kitchen. Beth and I left the room, our conversation sidetracked.

Walking back into the kitchen a while later, I found Dad sitting at the table going over some paperwork with Joyce, a friend and a supporter of my dad's ministry. They were talking over plans for some sort of upcoming event. Tim was leaning over in front of the open refrigerator, scoping out what he was about to eat.

As he set out a rather large snack for himself, Joyce made a comment about the food. "Wow, you must not have eaten for days!" Tim's response was an unfriendly glare, bordering on hostility. "I eat well," he said, looking overly serious. She thought he was kidding, and continued with a little banter, but as he walked out of the room looking stern and un-amused, she realized her mistake. When he was out of earshot, she looked at me. "Wow, your brother is intense."

"Yes," I said, feeling a little embarrassed. "He is. He wasn't always like that. He's changed. The word 'intense' fits for sure. A couple of other people have used that word about him lately too."

"Do you think he's alright?" Joyce seemed concerned— more than I expected. She shifted her attention from my dad to me, her dark eyes somewhat intense themselves. She was an interesting mix—mostly a put-together businesswoman, but with a touch of hippie thrown in.

"Uh, well, I don't know. I know the whole back and forth between Pleasant Hill and San Francisco hasn't been easy for him. But there's something else, too. I don't know what to call it. He seems preoccupied, but I don't know why."

Dad continued focusing on the paperwork in front of him. As was often the case, he looked like his mind was some-where else. Beth walked by, stopping to lean against the kitch-en doorway, listening. Joyce remained thoughtful. Tim came into the room at least two more times. Both times Joyce tried to engage him, but he remained aloof.

Later, I found him in the bedroom that he and I shared. "Hey Tim, what's with your reaction to Joyce? Don't you like her?"

"Like Joyce? What do you mean?"

"She was being friendly with you, and you seemed put off by her. I'm wondering why. I think she's a cool person."

Tim thought for a moment, "I don't know. I'm not into chit-chat."

I went back to the kitchen. Dad was still looking over the paperwork, but Joyce had gone. I asked him about Tim. "Did you notice how he treated Joyce?"

"What do you mean?"

"He was really rude to her."

"Oh? I didn't notice." He seemed unconcerned.

"Something's wrong with him."

Mom walked in at that moment. "I'll say something's wrong with him. We barely have enough food all week, we stock up the refrigerator on Friday, then Tim comes home and eats everything I was going to use for the weekend."

Many others who came through our house at that time made comments similar to Joyce's. Tim became known as intense, and interactions with him were unpredictable. We never knew if he was going to be friendly, hostile, or something in between.

At a gathering in our home, our friend Russ tried to start a conversation with Tim. Russ was known for his humor and jovial personality. He was somewhat short, had a round face, and a seemingly permanent smile. "Hey Tim, how come you're so intense all the time?"

"Intense?" responded Tim.

Russ leaned in close, lowered his voice, and spoke in a

friendly tone. "Yeah, you're intense."

"I'm not in tents, I'm in houses—two houses, one in the country, and one in the city." He was trying his best to be funny, but no one got it and Russ seemed to be at a loss for a few moments. Finally, he said, "Oh, in tents! I get it!" He then quickly turned away to another conversation.

Most people have occasional awkward moments and failed attempts at humor. But this was more than that. Tim's conversations became more and more peppered with odd references that were difficult to follow.

Mom and I were both in the kitchen one day. "Mom, don't you think Tim could use some sort of help?"

"What do you mean?"

"You see it, don't you? The way he interacts with everyone is way different than it was a year ago."

"Tim's approaching adulthood. We just need to give him space and trust the Lord."

"That's all? Really? This is more than just growing up. There's something else. He's not himself."

Dad seemed almost oblivious to the changes in Tim. He and Mom seemed to think that somehow all would eventually be fine.

FACING FEARS AND BREAKING BONES

"We're going to find something we're all afraid of, then face that fear together." The room fell into a kind of intrigued silence. Dad was leading a meeting of twelve ministry workers who gathered in our living room to brainstorm their activities for the coming summer. Several of them expressed that they were dealing with a bit of fear. It came up as a kind of theme.

Margo, an intern from Colorado, shifted nervously in her chair and fiddled with her short blonde curls. "How do we do that?" she asked.

Dad responded with a smile that quickly evolved into a smirk. "How many of you would be afraid to jump out of an airplane?" Dad asked the group. Several people expressed a whole lot of fear. Others said they would happily do it, but even those people expressed some apprehension.

By this time, Dad and Tim had both attended ground school with the possibility that one or both of them might go for a pilot's license. Planes had been on Dad's mind.

Dad failed ground school.

Tim passed.

Apparently, Dad had already made up his mind about how the group would face their fears. "I love this idea," he told them. "Imagine all of us parachuting from an airplane together. After that, we'll be revved up for anything!"

Some arguments followed as a few people thought it was a bit extreme, not to mention unrelated to why they were here in the first place. Of course, my dad just smiled, "See, this is perfect. We're clearly afraid of it. I say let's go for it."

The idea of facing fears together seemed good, but I knew my dad and his choice of activity didn't seem fair. He didn't seem to be afraid of it at all.

About two weeks later, the whole group found themselves at the Yolo Drop Zone for a morning of training with a guy named George, followed by an afternoon of jumping. George was very experienced, with about five thousand jumps already behind him. He spoke to the group about his planes and about parachuting. His rough face, uncombed graying hair, and stern demeanor held everyone's attention.

Tim and I were not actually on the team, but being

family, we took advantage of the opportunity. We weren't qualified anyway, as neither of us had any fear of the activity. We'd always wanted to do this. The only fear I experienced came later that day, during the one or two seconds when I exited the airplane.

The training lasted two or three hours and involved a whole lot of jumping off a platform about four feet off the ground. One at a time, we would each start by standing on the platform with arms outstretched in what they called an "arch." Then we'd each jump off, hit the ground—legs and feet together, knees slightly bent, twist the upper body, and roll on the ground, ending up with both feet sticking up looking rather stupid. This would all be done with a jumpsuit on, complete with a mock-parachute pack. Then you'd get up, wait in line, and do it again. And again.

After a lot of arching, jumping, and rolling, a chant was added. We each stood on the platform yelling slowly and rhythmically, like counting seconds, "Arch thousand! two thousand! check thousand! check thousand!" The chant was intended to create enough time for the parachute to open, and to make the jumper aware of it. When you got to the "check thousand" part, you would hopefully see your parachute opening. If you didn't, you'd pull the rip cord on your secondary reserve chute. I looked at George. "Will we be yelling this when we're up there?"

"Yes," he said. "You want to train yourself to expect something to go wrong, so you're not surprised when it does. Then, when it goes right, you can just enjoy yourself."

Eventually, the training was over, and we all spent a while brushing dust off each other. We selected jumpsuits, helmets, and other gear—a little like one might acquire shoes at a bowling alley, but more involved.

It was a beautiful, warm day in Yolo County. We relaxed and enjoyed lunch together. After a while, the little Cessna fired up its engine. The sight of the spinning propeller made it all suddenly very real.

We went up three at a time, along with the pilot and the instructor. That meant four or five flights to accommodate everyone.

Tim and I were on separate flights. "Tim is next," hollered George. He was in radio contact with the instructor on the plane, so he knew who was jumping next. I watched Tim, about four thousand feet up, hurl himself out of the plane. He wasn't much more than a tiny, human-shaped dot, but I could see him. His chute opened, his descent was smooth, and his landing was great—he rolled just like we'd practiced.

Dad jumped from the following flight. I didn't see it, as I was preparing for the flight after that.

Tim watched as Dad made his jump and descent. For the most part, all went well. Then, as he neared the ground, Tim could see Dad's legs swinging and relaxed. He looked like he was enjoying himself. Tim yelled as loud as he could, "Dad! Put your legs together!" He yelled again, moving to where Dad was about to land. "Dad! Feet together!" Dad seemed happily oblivious as he collided with the ground.

A few hundred feet away, my plane had just taken off. I sat on the floor of the small aircraft with my back against the back of the pilot's seat. The only seats were for piloting; the rest was bare metal. There was no door, just open air, the sound of the engine, and lots of wind. I was surprised how cold it was a few thousand feet from the warm day on the ground.

Margo was ahead of me. "Put your feet out!" yelled the instructor. Margo put her feet out, resting them on a platform no bigger than a salad plate. "Get out!" Margo got out, holding onto the wing strut, as she had been taught a little while earlier. "Jump!"

Margo disappeared.

I moved over toward the opening, taking in the landscape below us. The plane turned, revealing more of the view. We were circling the drop zone.

"Put your feet out!" yelled the instructor. I put my feet out.

"Get out!" I got out, both hands on the wing strut, one foot on the platform, the other dangling.

"Jump!"

What happened next confused me. I jumped, but I was still next to the plane as if I wasn't falling. I looked back into the plane, into the face of a disconcerted instructor who yelled once more: "Jump!" Apparently, I had "jumped" with my feet, but not with my hands. I was still hanging on to the wing strut with both feet trailing behind—like Superman, but with a plane attached.

I let go. "Arch thousand, two thousand…" I was interrupted by the tug of the parachute opening perfectly. The noise around me transformed into a quiet peace. I pulled down on one of the two toggles that controlled the angle of descent, swinging to one side. Pulling the other, I swung the other way. For a few minutes, I floated alone in the sky. Wonderful. I knew I would be doing this again.

The ground came on hard, nearly knocking the wind out of me, but it was totally worth it.

Tim met me not far from where I landed, still wearing his black jumpsuit. "Wait 'til you see Dad," he commented with a concerned look.

Dad was on the ground with his foot bandaged and elevated. "What did you do?" I asked.

"It's what he didn't do," answered George, the head

trainer. "Was I not clear? Feet together, knees bent—isn't that what I said? Did I not say that?"

Dad's ankle was broken pretty severely. He spent the rest of his life with pins and screws in his foot. His was the only injury. Perhaps he should have been a little more afraid.

Pots, Cups, and Castles

Dad once again set his sights on acquiring a large building. He seemed upbeat as he showed our family around the place he'd found. It was built in the 1930s but it was new to us. A long stairway, carpeted in deep red, led us upstairs where we found six rooms, one of which was quite large—there was probably room for about a hundred people. There were two fireplaces, one in the large room and one in a lobby area at the top of the stairway. Downstairs were six storefronts, two of which were in use: one was a bar and the other was a small cafe lunch counter. The place was much smaller than the big compound we'd left a year earlier, but it had Dad's attention, and he was set on finding a way to purchase it. Within a few months, he did. Once he set his mind on something, he seemed to have a special gift for making things happen.

What interested me most about the place was one of the vacant storefronts. I pictured myself setting up a clay shop there. While in school, I had spent a lot of time focused on pottery and ceramics. I loved working with clay. I had acquired a potter's wheel, a kiln, and some other equipment, but now it was all in storage. I wanted to put that equipment to good use.

A few months later, I made an agreement with Dad to rent the storefront. He was much more interested in the upstairs portion of the building.

I was hugely unprepared for running a business—I just figured I would make a bunch of clay stuff and look for somewhere to sell it. I started the business with a whopping eight hundred dollars in the bank and no specific plan. I went to the San Francisco Arts Commission to apply for a street artist's license and was granted one. For the next few years, I sold my pottery and other clay items at Fisherman's Wharf and the Embarcadero Center. I also found a number of stores interested in carrying my designs, which launched me into the wholesale business. Along with other, more standard items, I often made small-but-elaborate castles out of clay. Mostly they were just fun to make, but they also sold easily, always bringing a smile to people's faces. Those castles became the bread and butter of my business for a few years. I named the business The Clayhouse.

While working in the shop one day I looked up, distracted by the sound of a motorcycle very close. It was Tim. He removed his orange helmet and stepped inside.

"Dave, check it out—my own motorcycle!"

"Isn't that Don's?"

"Not anymore. He sold it to me for a dollar."

"Not bad!" I laughed.

Tim spent significant time with me in my shop. Many times, he came in, sat down at the wheel, and produced his own wares. He felt no pressure to sell them—he just enjoyed having access to the equipment and I didn't mind.

One day, as he worked away in my clay shop, he made a comment out of the blue.

"Dave, I'm worried that I could become the anti-Christ."

I continued with my work, assuming it was the beginning of a joke. Slowly I realized he was serious. I wasn't sure how to respond. "Um... That's a weird thing to say. Why would you say that?"

"It's like I'm trying to walk on slippery round rocks without falling. If I trip up, the devil will control me."

"What do you mean?"

"If he can control me, he'll make me into something horrible—the worst thing he can, which would be the anti-Christ."

"How is this stuff even on your mind to begin with? I don't know how to respond. It's ridiculous. You're not the anti- Christ and you never will be."

He was quiet after that, but he seemed preoccupied and troubled.

Strange comments like that became more frequent. Tim seemed very concerned that he might do something horrible—that he might be controlled by the devil. When he expressed such concerns, there didn't seem to be any resolving it. He might become quiet, but never relieved.

My new shop became a common hang-out for him, giving the two of us ample time for conversation. Tim highly valued this.

The shop became a hang-out for a few others as well. My sister Beth visited me there sometimes. We liked spending time together and enjoyed talking openly about anything. My shop became a sanctuary for conversations we didn't feel free to have at home.

During this time I also began to pursue theater, enrolling in a few performing arts courses. While in rehearsals for a local production, I met a young woman named Kate. She and I became good friends and spent a great deal of time together.

Tim was helping me with some work in my shop one day when I looked up from my work to see a small-statured young woman at the door. Her face was obscured by her curly dark hair and her hands, which were cupped around her face so she could peer through the glass. Then I recognized her.

"Hey!" I yelled, delighted to see Kate at my door.

"So this is your little factory," she said as she came in, transforming the shop's atmosphere with her blue dress, heels, and general loveliness.

"Yes. Welcome!" I gestured to Tim. "This is my brother Tim. He hangs out here a lot."

"I can see why. This looks like a fun place."

She returned a few days later, and before long she became another frequent visitor hanging out in my clay shop.

GREEN LIGHTS AND WHEELIES

After two weeks of false starts, Tim got up the nerve to dial all seven numbers of Becky's phone number. His body raced with adrenaline as he heard the ringing tone followed by Becky's voice on the other end. It was too late to back out. This was really happening.

Tim got her contact information from one of his teachers who knew her family.

"Hi, I'm not sure you remember me, but we were in school together. I'm considering different colleges and wanted to know how it's going at your school."

In reality, Tim couldn't have cared less about the college, but he had to come up with something. It was better than "I've had a raging crush on you since I first saw you in 10th grade."

He felt sheepish as he listened to her talk about her college experiences, but she was happy to share, so they continued on the topic for about half an hour. Eventually, they got onto other subjects and the call was going great. She asked him how old he was. Tim already knew her birthday—he'd heard her say it once in high school and never forgot it.

"You're older than me," she said, sounding dreamy.

He mustered more courage. "I'd like to meet you."

She agreed to go to a movie with him the next evening and they arranged to meet.

"It happened!" he thought, excitedly. "I actually had a conversation with Becky!" For Tim, this was huge. He felt like Superman.

The next day he was out riding his motorcycle, filled with joy at the thought of his date that night. He pulled up to a red light and stopped. When the light turned green, he spontaneously twisted the throttle and released the clutch, riding a wheelie across the intersection. He had imagined this day for three years.

Tim borrowed a friend's car and spent the afternoon thoroughly cleaning the inside, then washing and waxing the outside. He put on new clothes and set out toward her house.

There she was, standing out front with her dad, looking better than he'd imagined. She greeted him with a hug and introduced him to her father. "I'm pleased to meet you," said Tim, shaking his hand, but barely noticing him in Becky's presence.

Tim felt a bit stiff, but she was great. They enjoyed the movie, and then went back to her house. They ended up singing some songs they both knew at her piano. With some trepidation, Tim gave her a hug. "Thanks," was her response. They said goodnight, and Tim drove home.

He came in with a giant smile. "Dave, I had a date with Becky! We're good friends. It's happening!"

"Good friends? Didn't you just meet?"

"Well, yeah, but it's great. It's going great."

They got together again for a picnic. Tim felt a euphoric

peace as they hiked out over the hills, spread out a blanket, and set up their outdoor meal. Afterward, as they got back into the car, Becky reached across the old bench seat, attempting to affectionately rub Tim's back. Abruptly, he pulled away, creating a sudden awkwardness. She quickly withdrew her hand, looking surprised and hurt, and remained silent.

"What's wrong with me?" Tim kept wondering to himself. "I'm ruining everything. This is Becky! Why would I pull away like that?"

Tim could not answer his own questions, nor was he aware of his hurtful effect. After pulling away, he somehow felt the need to follow through with consistent behavior and remained aloof, spiraling into more awkwardness and anxiety.

The ride home was odd. Becky tried to make conversation, but Tim had trouble responding from within his anxious mindset. Of course, from Becky's perspective, his demeanor suddenly became cold, and she didn't know why.

He called Becky a few days later.

"Hello?" It was her mom.

"Hi, this is Tim calling for Becky. Is she around?"

"Hello, Tim. One moment, please."

Tim could hear the muffled voices as Becky's mom held her hand over the phone. "Becky, it's Tim Robinson. Do you want to talk with him?"

In the background, he heard Becky groan, not wanting to talk with him. At least, that's how he interpreted it. Then her voice came on the phone.

"Hi Brother!"

Tim wondered if her use of the word "brother" meant something—like maybe she was holding him at a distance.

Trying to be open, Tim only made it awkward. "I want to know you."

"I understand," she replied.

"I'm glad you understand. Goodbye."

He hung up the phone as abruptly as he had pulled away that day in the car.

He swallowed hard, but the lump in his throat remained,

Deflated and bewildered, Tim sat alone in his room. Tears welled as his disappointment grew into a deep longing for something, he wasn't sure what. He tried not to keep hoping for Becky, figuring he had destroyed any possibilities on that front.

He recalled occasionally hearing people talk about how God would sometimes talk to them. He wanted some guidance, so he experimented. Instead of just thinking, he listened, hoping to hear God.

"You will marry Becky," said a voice in his mind.

Two things happened in that moment. One was that he held onto the hope of a romance with Becky. The other was that he began to listen to the words that came into his mind, attributing divine guidance to pretty much whatever thoughts occurred to him.

YOU LIVE WITH YOUR PARENTS?

"You live with your parents?" asked Kate as we entered the deli to get some lunch.

I ordered first. "I'll have a hot pastrami on a soft roll with jack cheese and mustard."

Kate laughed out loud. "That's exactly what I was about to order."

We were both in a rehearsal for a small-time theater production and had run across the street during a break.

"As for your question, yeah, I do live with my parents."

The way she had asked the question sounded like it surprised her. I was twenty-three.

We grabbed our food and headed back to join the others at the rehearsal. Whenever she wasn't expected elsewhere that day, Kate spent most of her time at my side continuing our conversation. For a while now, I'd had the feeling she was interested in me, which was fine, as I had similar thoughts.

I later paid a visit to her house, where she introduced me to Bobo, her dog.

"I have to warn you," she commented, "Bobo's half timber wolf. You need to meet her on her terms. She'll wanna get behind you, and she'll bark a few times. Just let her do that."

"Bobo Lobo the wolf-dog," I said, smiling.

"That's her. Here she comes."

A medium-large dog, mostly golden colored with gray patterns on her back and a black, obviously wolf-like face ran to greet us.

She jumped up, gently bumping her nose against my face, making friendly noises.

"Wow, Dave, she likes you. That's so great. It usually takes her a while to warm up to people. You seem to be an exception. I like that!"

Five weeks and ten dates later, we sat in her car at the beach watching the sun slowly set. I thought about the recent weeks—dinners, lunches, hikes through the local countryside, acting opposite each other in the production, and through it all, long conversations that I hoped would never end. We talked about everything we could think of. Nothing seemed out of bounds, and it was always comfortable—like the feeling of coming home. I reached over and took her hand, interlocking my fingers with hers. She leaned her head over onto my shoulder and I leaned my head against hers.

The ocean slowly began to absorb the sun into its vast bosom, and the sky, filled with color just moments ago, now revealed starlight. Neither of us moved for a long time.

Suddenly she spoke up. "I could never marry a man who still lives with his parents."

Kate's comment that night stuck with me like gum on the bottom of a shoe—and no less annoying. "What's wrong with living with my parents?" I kept asking myself. But even as I asked the question, something inside me instinctively understood.

What was it with our family? That question dominated my thoughts. I knew my dad was sort of different, but I always thought we were a good healthy family. Now I was having doubts. And it wasn't just because of Kate's comment; I had already begun to feel something I couldn't name. Most of my friends were living on their own by this time. For Tim and me, it was different. We both lived in a situation that was home to more than just our family. We always had others living with us, and still more coming in and out of our house for various events led by my dad. These were people I loved and who loved being at our house. Our home was the place everyone wanted to be. There was no motivation to leave.

In our home life, no one offered much advice as Tim and I entered adulthood. No one explained the importance of planning for a career. All we had was a vague sense of helping with Dad's various projects. One possible exception was when Dad suggested I open my clay shop in one of the storefronts of the new building.

With those doubts on my mind, and without enough clarity to make a plan, I moved out of the house and turned the back half of my shop into a small apartment.

I was now on my own. I had left the nest. Sort of.

I enjoyed setting up my own space, but the conditions were poor, and I was still within reach of the nest.

Tim visited frequently. I gave him a key and he came and went as he pleased.

My new arrangement was good enough for Kate. We got married, and, along with Bobo the wolf-dog she moved into my humble home in the back of my shop. We decided we would live there for our first couple of years.

One morning Tim came into the shop. "Dave!" he hollered, oblivious to the fact that I was still in bed with my new wife.

I ignored him, figuring he would get the hint and go away. "Dave! Are you here?"

"Tim," I hollered back with an angry tone. "I'm married now. There will be times I can't answer the door!"

I could barely see him through a frosted plastic window between the shop and the apartment. He seemed to wilt with shame as he silently crept out.

I wasn't actually angry. I was trying to consider Kate's feelings, and for some reason, the result was harshness with Tim.

Kate and I enjoyed life together, but she was very uncomfortable living in my family's shadow, and I was afraid of truly launching out on our own—afraid of the future and of not being able to provide. I was accustomed to living in that large shadow. My fear was a constant companion, a threat hanging over our lives.

It turned out I was no more prepared for marriage than I was for answering that suicide hotline a few years earlier.

CHAPTER FIVE
1983 – 1985

Schizophrenia (skitsə' frēnēə, skitsə' frenēə), n. a mental disorder or... group of disorders... characterized by disturbances in form and content of thought (loosening of associations, delusions and hallucinations), mood (blunted, flattened or inappropriate affect), sense of self and relationship to the external world (loss of ego boundaries... withdrawal), and behavior (bizarre, apparently purposeless... activity or inactivity)... deterioration from a previous level of functioning.

~ *Excerpted from*
Dorland's Illustrated Medical
Dictionary 32nd Edition
by Saunders, an imprint of Elsevier Inc.

COMFORTABLE DRIVE

"Tim!"

Dad's voice was frantic.

"Tim!"

He banged on the window and yelled, trying to get Tim's attention. "Tim! Get a hold of the wheel!"

Mom, Dad, Tim, and Beth were traveling south on the seemingly endless Interstate Five that stretches through the length of California. They were all comfortable. Tim drove the pickup truck with its camper shell on the back. Under the camper shell, Mom, Dad, and Beth enjoyed napping on a mattress, leaving the driving to Tim.

Beth woke up, jostled by the truck's movement on the freeway. She peered through the small window that looked into the cab. The driver's seat was empty.

With the cruise control turned on, Tim sat on the other side of the cab, leaning comfortably against the passenger door, steering the vehicle with one foot stretched out from where he sat.

"Dad!" she tried to get him to wake up, which often took a while. "Dad!"

On the third try, Mom & Dad both woke up to see Beth pointing into the cab.

Dad sat up and got himself turned around. That's when he started shouting for Tim to get hold of the steering wheel.

Finally, Tim heard Dad yelling, moved back into the driver's position, and took the next exit.

Dad was furious. "What in the world were you thinking?" he yelled.

Tim looked confused.

"You could have killed us all."

More confusion. "Dad, everything's fine."

"No, it's not!"

Mom came walking around the truck, looking very stern. "Timothy, you scared us half to death! What were you thinking?"

Tim stood there silently looking at the ground, a dejected look on his face. "No one was in danger. Everything's fine. I'm sorry." He genuinely didn't understand what was wrong with what he'd done.

They had lunch in a restaurant near where they'd stopped. They didn't mention the incident again, but the atmosphere remained tense.

"I'll drive the rest of the way," Dad stated with a tone that did not invite discussion.

Tim watched the California landscape out the window as they traveled. He couldn't seem to get comfortable. They talked from time to time, but Tim couldn't shake the feeling of being in trouble.

FIX IT WITH SCISSORS

I parked outside my parents' house and went in to see how Mom was doing. I lived about two miles away, and such visits were common.

"Your brother wants to see you," she said. "He's downstairs."

I headed down. "Hey Tim, what's up?"

He called from the garage, adjacent to his room. "Hey Dave, just give me one second."

He was putting a shovel away.

"You've been digging?"

"Yeah, I buried those bones in the side yard."

"Bones?"

"You know those little bones we kept from the skeleton back on the Navy base?"

"Uh, yeah, I guess. We still had those?"

"Yes, but it wasn't right." He suddenly stood still with his brow furrowed, then spoke seriously. "I gave them the rest they deserved."

He stood still, thinking for a moment, then suddenly he spoke up, sounding excited. "I wanna show you something."

I followed him into his room where he grabbed an Astronomy magazine and opened it to a marked page.

"I'm gonna get one of these!" He pointed out a large telescope that had his attention. "This thing has a mirror over thirteen inches across, great optics, and it's affordable!"

"Wow," I responded. "That sounds amazing. How are you going to pay for it?"

At that moment, even though he was talking, I wasn't hearing his words. I was distracted by what I noticed in the magazine. There was an advertisement with two men standing next to the telescope. One of them had a hole in the middle of his chest—not in the image itself but cut through the page.

"Can I see that?" I asked, gesturing for the magazine.

"Sure."

Flipping through it, I found several other pictures of people with holes cut through the page. Each hole was positioned right in the middle of someone's chest.

"What's with the holes cut through the page?" I asked Tim.

He pointed to one of the images. "He had a bad heart, so I cut it out."

His tone of voice was casual and matter-of-fact.

My chest tightened. "He had a bad heart, so you cut it out?"

"Yeah."

"Tim, that's weird. And kinda scary."

"I took care of it. It's fine now. What do you think of the scope?"

I tried to keep my voice steady, but a disturbing feeling rose inside me.

"I like it. If you can find a way to pay for it, I think it would be an amazing thing for you to have."

"Yeah, I'm gonna get one of these," he said, still excited. "I've got some of the money, but I'm gonna need about five hundred dollars more."

"I hope you can get it," I commented. "I need to check in with Mom, I'll see you later."

Back upstairs, I found Mom. "How's Tim been doing?" I asked.

"Well, you know your brother. He's sweet one minute, then does something a little weird. I'm not sure what to do for him."

"Yeah, I know what you mean."

Driving away from the house, I kept thinking about the holes cut through the pages in that magazine, and his little burial of those bones. Tim seemed so casual, like nothing was amiss. I tried to tell myself I was overreacting, but I couldn't shake the feeling that something wasn't right. I was reminded of the feeling I'd had about five years earlier as I looked across all the apartment rooftops toward Peoples Temple—the feeling of looking across a divide at something frightening. This time it was my own brother across the divide. A dark mystery began to haunt my days.

EDUCATION

Don Burns walked in from his back patio to answer the phone. He was a good-humored guy, medium-tall with thick dark brown hair and a full beard. He and his wife Pat had become good friends to Tim and me. He was preparing to grill some burgers when his phone rang.

"Hey Don, I need to borrow five hundred dollars."

Don laughed loudly. "Well hello to you too, Tim. I gotta say, that's a bold way to greet someone. How's it going?"

"It's for my education."

Don laughed again. "Your education? What are we talking about?

"Five hundred dollars," answered Tim.

"That's a good chunk of change. What exactly do you need it for?"

"My education."

"Yeah, I guess you just said that. Well, come on over. I'll throw on an extra burger."

"Throw on two. I'm hungry."

More laughter, less from humor, and more from feeling taken-aback by Tim's bold forthrightness. "Alright, I'll see you in a few," he said, as he went back to the grill.

Tim had started attending San Francisco State University with no major and no particular goals. He chose whatever classes appealed to him, although if you had asked him, he might have said he was divinely guided. He had a few favorite classes. One was scuba diving, where he'd recently received his certification. But his all-time favorite was astronomy. He was enthralled with the stars and with deep-sky viewing. When he'd taken all the classes that interested him, he considered just dropping out.

About twenty minutes after Don had hung up the phone,

Tim walked quickly through Don's house to the backyard. "Hey, where's the food?" he hollered to the two couples enjoying the beautiful day. Steve and Alice had joined Don and his wife, Pat, for dinner on their outdoor patio.

Pat got up to retrieve a plate for Tim, the breeze blowing her wavy blonde hair as she entered the house.

Tim took her chair. "So, Don, how would you feel about loaning me five hundred dollars?"

"Hey, let's enjoy our dinner first, then we'll talk about it," responded Don.

"Sounds good!" replied Tim, enthusiastically.

Pat brought Tim a plate with two burgers on it, then went to find a chair for herself.

Steve spoke up. "Tim, what sort of education does five hundred dollars buy?"

Tim's mouth was full, but he replied anyway. "It will get me started in the world of astronomy. I've already taken two classes, and I want to get deeper into it."

"I don't see many 'help wanted' signs for astronomers," answered Steve, "but it's a cool field for sure."

After dinner, the others went inside, and Don and Tim remained awhile in the back yard.

"Tim, I don't have a lot of money. If I do this, I'll need it back at some point."

"No problem!"

"You're awfully excited about this."

"I am. Yeah, for sure."

Don wrote Tim a check for five hundred dollars.

"Thanks man!" said Tim as he left the house with a full stomach and a full heart.

A few days later, Tim brought home a brand-new telescope—a large one about fourteen inches in diameter and nearly five feet long.

"Now we need to set up a star party," he told me, excitedly.

"A star party?"

"Yeah, that's what they call it. You get a bunch of people out on a dark night and see what this telescope can really do."

The first star party included Kate and me, along with a few other friends, including Don.

"Wow," exclaimed Don. "That's one heck of a telescope! Did you borrow it from the school?"

"No, this is mine."

"Aren't these things kind of expensive?"

"Well, it wasn't too bad—with your help."

Don stood there with his mouth part way open. "Wait— this is what I helped pay for?"

"Yup."

"Tim, you said the money was for your education. Are you enrolled in classes?"

"Well, not exactly. But I will be for sure, at some point."

Don's thumb and forefinger fiddled with his beard, his mouth still part way open. He was not enjoying the moment. "Tim, man, you misled me."

We all stood there not sure what should happen next. Don looked at me. "Dave, did you know about this?"

"I knew about Tim wanting the telescope, but I didn't know he used your money."

I watched Don walk away shaking his head while everyone else followed Tim's lead getting the telescope set up for viewing.

Tim showed us Jupiter and its moons. He showed us Saturn. He showed us spiral galaxies, and he showed us the Orion Nebula. He was excited, but I noticed something more than that. He showed a passion that seemed like something more than a passing interest. He loved this.

Don returned and motioned for me to walk with him. "Dave, do you think this is really part of Tim's education?"

"I'm not sure. He's really into this. He'll probably take every astronomy class he can, eventually."

"I wouldn't have loaned him money for a telescope, but maybe it's a good thing. I don't know how to gauge it."

"I'm not sure I can help with that. He understands he needs to pay you back, right?"

"Yeah, well, we'll see how this goes."

We walked back to the others.

"So, Tim, can I have a look?" asked Don.

"Yeah, what do you wanna see?"

"The moon, but it's not up yet. You decide."

Tim and Don spent a while staring through the telescope into the deep night sky. After about an hour of viewing, Don looked a lot happier. "This thing's amazing," he said with a smile.

Don came along on many star parties after that. He enjoyed Tim's passion, and in spite of Tim's previous conniving, he genuinely enjoyed the telescope.

Tim built a special wooden box for the large parabolic mirror and painted it white. "That's so cool!" he exclaimed when he opened the box after putting the mirror in it, He smiled, seeing his face reflected—illuminated and enlarged to four or five times its usual size.

THREE WEEKS WITH A PRY BAR

"Dave, you gotta check this out." Tim seemed both earnest and excited. "We'll need at least an hour."

"For what? Can't you just tell me?"

"I'd rather show you."

We drove down to Ocean Beach. "Okay Dave, head south. Go all the way to the cliffs down past the zoo."

"Really? There's not much down there."

"There is now. I've been busy."

After parking, Tim led me down the beach and up a trail to the top of the cliffs to the south. We were forty or fifty feet above the surf as it crashed on a small strip of sand below us.

"Okay, here's the spot. I'm gonna climb down right here. You wait until I yell for you. This is gonna be cool—I promise."

Tim scrambled down the face of the sandstone cliff feet first. At about ten feet down he disappeared, but I could still hear his voice.

"Okay, come on down!"

Following his path, I climbed backward down the cliff. No Tim. Puzzled, I looked all around, seeing nothing but sandstone and ice plants. It seemed I was alone.

Suddenly I was surprised by a voice very close to me. "In here!"

Laughing, Tim stuck his head out of an opening about two feet wide.

"Come on in!"

"Whoa—there's room for you in there?"

"Yup. Like I said, I've been busy."

It took a minute for my eyes to adjust to the shadowy interior. The small hole penetrated the cliff, going in about three feet, then opened into an area where two or three people could sit comfortably.

"Wow. What's this?"

"Welcome to my cave. I've been doing a lot of digging!"

"You sure have! Dang, man, this is something."

Tim had always been into digging. Seeing this brought

back several memories of the underground forts he dug when he was a kid.

"How do you know this is safe?" I asked.

"It's gotta be safe. This ground seems really solid."

"Hmmm… I'm not so sure, but it is kinda cool."

We hung out there for a long time, looking out at the ocean through the round cave entrance that was now our window.

"You actually dug this?"

"Yup. I dug the whole thing with a small spade and a pry bar—mostly the pry bar."

"How long did it take?"

"I started three weeks ago."

"Man, Tim. This is wild. Nobody tried to stop you?"

"How would they? You can't see it unless you're down on the small part of the beach, and even then, you can't tell what it is. A couple of people saw me when I threw a bunch of dirt down the cliff, but they didn't do anything."

We sat in there for a long time talking about all sorts of stuff. It was a great place to hang out.

"Dave, I think I'm done with S.F. State."

"Already?"

"Yeah. I've already taken the good classes. There's not much else for me."

"What will you do now?"

"I think I'll work full-time for The Movers."

Our dad, ever the entrepreneur, had started a moving company called The Movers. Maybe the name was brilliant or maybe it wasn't, but it was easy to remember. Tim already helped out part-time. Our brother Doug managed it, our mom did customer relations, and Tim did a lot of heavy lifting. This was in addition to the ministry work Dad already did.

"I don't have a major," Tim continued, "And I don't plan

to graduate. Besides, it's a great workout. I'll get pretty buff moving furniture all the time."

For months, Tim and I visited his cave and had many conversations.

One day he crawled down from the cliff top for some quality cave time, only to see someone's foot sticking out of the opening. He backed off, deciding to let someone else enjoy the spot. In the end, however, his cave had become a tomb. A man had climbed in, apparently for shelter, and died there.

The Park Service removed the man's body and filled in the cave. No one ever found out how it was created, and Tim never went back. "I don't wanna hang out where that guy died," he commented. "It's ruined now."

———————

"Come on, you guys. We gotta do this!" Tim insisted.

Don, Steve, and I looked at each other. We were interested, but cautious.

Tim continued. "I've wanted to do this for a long time. I know we can find the place if we look."

The place to which Tim referred was the Black Diamond Coal Mine. It had been abandoned long ago and Tim wanted to find and explore it.

"You really like caves, don't you," commented Don.

"I sure do."

"And how do you propose we find the place?" asked Steve.

Tim's face lit up with a big smile. "Well, I already found it, sort of. I know where to look."

A week later, the four of us stood on the side of a hill in front of a gaping hole about fifteen feet across and eight or nine feet tall. It was known to local hikers as Whale's Mouth. We stepped into the darkness, turned on our flashlights, and descended into the earth, down a steep embankment of broken rocks.

About eighty feet down, we found a network of tunnels stretching out in all directions, including further down. There was an odd smell to the air. The dim remnant of daylight was far above us.

Tim looked happy and a bit sobered. He loved going underground but he'd never been this deep. The air was cool, quiet, and perfectly still. Since this was Tim's adventure, we let him lead and stayed until he felt satisfied.

"That was so cool!" exclaimed Tim after we climbed back up into the sunlit afternoon. "People say it's dangerous in there, but it's great."

Two weeks later, Don showed Tim and me a newspaper article about four young men who had climbed down into Whale's Mouth just a few days after we did. One of them wanted to celebrate his birthday with an underground adventure. As four young men ourselves who had just done the same thing, we understood completely.

All four of the young men ended up breathing coal vapors. They died in those tunnels, absorbed into the dark stillness.

Once again, something that brought Tim joy was thwarted by death. "Oh, man," said Tim, looking profoundly disappointed. "What a drag. Why does that have to happen? Why do all the cool things get ruined?"

THE VOICE IN THE PALACE PILLARS

A group of seven or eight of us had decided to spend a few hours at the Palace of Fine Arts, relaxing and enjoying the gorgeous day. Tim was with us, but no one had seen him for the last twenty minutes or so. We were hanging out under the Greco-Roman-style dome, a remnant of the 1915 World's Fair in San Francisco. Around the edges of the dome stood a circle of enormous pillars, easily forty or fifty feet tall, holding up the circular roof.

Walking into the space under the huge dome, our friend Caleb began making clapping sounds with his hands, struck by the amazing echo chamber the dome provided. Caleb had recently moved into Mom and Dad's house as an intern working with our dad. A young woman named Marilyn had moved in as well, so there were six in their house: Dad, Mom, Tim, Beth, Caleb, and Marilyn.

Soon, all of us were listening to the effect of our claps. Clap once, and you could hear many rapid claps, diminishing over a few seconds. Under the dome, sound played tricks on anyone listening. When a person spoke from the edges, near the pillars, they could be heard on the opposite side, but a person standing in the middle might not hear them. When a person spoke from the middle, their words bounced back to them, louder than they seemed to those on the edge.

Our conversation was constantly interrupted by echoes of whatever had just been said. This, of course, was the whole point: to play with the sound created by the shape of the giant structure towering above us.

A single voice seemed to echo above all the other sounds. At first, no one noticed, but after a few minutes it became eerily obvious. Several in the group kept asking, "Whose voice is that?" Others who were busy talking didn't hear the question.

At length, there was enough silence that the mystery voice could be heard. Then, as if on cue, the whole group resounded in a chorus of the same phrase: "Whose voice is that?"

Everyone stopped. Everyone listened. There was only silence. Then, from what seemed to be very close, definitely under the dome with us, the voice spoke again. It was casual, not loud at all, mocking our bewilderment.

"Hey, how's it goin'?"

The voice and its close proximity must have been too much for Marilyn, who suddenly exclaimed, "I'm freaking out!"

"It's not worth freaking out over," said Caleb, to which Marilyn replied, "Yes it is. Look!" She pointed to the top of the pillars that held the giant dome. There, at the top, far above us, sat my brother Tim, wedged between two huge concrete pillars. I say "sat," because he was positioned as if he were comfortably sitting with his legs outstretched. There was nothing beneath him. He held himself up by sheer pressure, with his back against one pillar, and his feet against the other.

He spoke calmly, his voice aided by the dome next to him. He was obviously enjoying himself.

We all stared for a long moment. He had climbed the entire height simply by pressing on the two pillars, one at his back and the other at his feet, with enough pressure to prevent a fall that became increasingly deadly as he ascended.

About half the group started yelling for him to come down, saying it was too dangerous to be up there. This was not a good idea. Not only did it pressurize Tim's already deadly situation, but the yelling produced a massive, echoing cacophony, impossible to understand.

"That's really foolish," commented Caleb to me quietly. "Is he trying to get attention?" Caleb was a level-headed guy, and this sort of thing annoyed him.

For me, this was a familiar kind of moment. Tim had developed a strong social independence which caused him to do things like this without considering the effect he might have on others. He made decisions based on what he might enjoy the most, without consulting anyone. I frequently found myself covering for him.

"Tim's an amazing climber," I responded, loud enough for everyone to hear me. "Let's give him some peace, and he'll get himself down soon enough."

In truth, I was fully aware that his life was in jeopardy, but he'd got himself into a situation where there was no way to help. Tim would not be able to hold himself up long enough to wait for professionals with appropriate equipment, even if he chose to. And he would likely choose not to.

Once again, I felt like I was viewing him across a divide, as if he'd somehow moved into a space—a mindset—in which no one could join him. Tim's choice to put himself in that position with such a relaxed attitude troubled people, which caused them to view him as odd and distance themselves from him. That left him feeling isolated. He was the cause of his feelings of isolation, but he couldn't see that.

MESSING WITH GRAVITY

"I'll just hang out here for a little while," said Rich, as he steadied himself on the cold steel platform.

Rich Travis was a good friend to both Tim and me. He was a striking young man with dark hair, and physically fit from years of rock climbing.

He slowly stood up, taking in the vast three-hundred-sixty-degree view from the top of the seven-hundred-foot tower. Tim stood near the platform taking in the night. The lights from the city were familiar, but he had never seen them from this angle before. Very few have.

It was after midnight, which meant it had been his birthday for about half an hour. Tim was now twenty-one. He chose this location to celebrate, which meant getting there in secret, and including just one or two people. Our friend Rich was the perfect companion, or perhaps I should say accomplice. He was an experienced climber who was also experienced when it came to trespassing for the sake of a good adventure. He would be undaunted by the boundaries they would need to cross to reach the top of the monolithic structure.

Tim had invested significant thought over the previous several months, determining whether this was even possible. After some very sneaky reconnaissance, he decided it was doable.

"Hey Rich," Tim spoke into the phone. "We can totally do this."

"Did you find a way up?"

"Absolutely. There's a rocky cliff next to the concrete foundation. We can reach a vertical pipe from the rocks and climb from there. It's a stretch, but I know we can do it."

From that pipe, the two of them would have to squeeze between a chain-link fence and the giant cable. That cable was the big ticket—three feet thick, and, as long as they didn't fall, it would take them all the way to the top. The fence, of course, was intended to keep people like Tim and Rich off of it.

"Let's go for it!" stated Rich with resolve. "If you're right, then there's nothing in our way. We can get on the low end of the cable and we're home free, except for the authorities. We've gotta keep a good lookout."

"Yeah," said Tim. "If we get arrested on the way down, that's fine, but we have to make it to the top first."

This was the night. Rich drove down a small access lane off the main road to a utility yard with several large spools holding suspender ropes and cables. There was no sign of anyone on duty. Parking in the least noticeable place they could, they worked their way up to the area Tim had scoped out earlier. They both made it to the vertical pipe and began the climb. "Whoa, that's a long way down," commented Rich, looking at the rocky ground below them. "Yeah," responded Tim, but he was focused on getting to the fence above them. He had estimated correctly. They squeezed past the chain-link fence and onto the top of the huge cable.

The night was cool and humid, which meant the cables were wet and slippery. They brought no safety equipment of any kind, just strong hands and bold hearts. Holding onto the small cables positioned on either side, Rich led the way, moving quickly along the giant cable. He was an avid rock climber accustomed to heights. They weren't clipping in with any safety equipment, which helped them move quickly. The textured, grainy paint provided some traction on the wet surface as they moved upward.

"Whoa!" shouted Tim suddenly, as his feet slipped. Fortunately, he had a good hold on both smaller cables. Rich reached the top first, followed by Tim, and there they perched, like two satisfied owls in the night.

Lightning flashed over Angel Island. It was a beautiful sight to the two human lightning rods taking in the view, oblivious to the danger.

"So cool!" shouted Tim. Rich just smiled and nodded from his roost atop the magnificent structure. The red glow from the aviation marker illuminated his face, then off again, then on again. Cool, indeed; Tim's hopes had become reality, and here they were at the very top of the north tower of the

Golden Gate Bridge.

After a satisfying experience, they began to descend the great cable, looking five hundred feet down to the traffic on the bridge deck on one side, and seven hundred feet to dark seawater on the other. "This really charges my batteries!" yelled Rich. The two young men moved carefully, deeply sobered by the fact that going down is more difficult and more frightening than going up. They moved down the wet surface of the cable, vividly feeling their height, having to look down in order to climb down.

They managed to retrace their steps, shimmy down the same vertical pipe, and run back to Rich's car without being seen.

I stopped by my parents' house the next morning to wish Tim a happy birthday. He seemed thrilled about something— elated. When he told me he had climbed the Golden Gate Bridge during the night, I wasn't sure if I should take him literally, or if his words were somehow metaphoric. Then Rich walked into the room and confirmed it. It was real.

In a way, Tim seemed better than usual, almost like the experience had brought his best self to the surface.

I'm not sure what our parents thought about it. They were probably glad not to have known ahead of time.

Tim often struggled with intense fear, but then had no fear at all of climbing the bridge or jumping out of an airplane. Many people would call it a "crazy" thing to do, but I'm not so sure.

Tim fulfilled a life-long desire that night and did so with a friend. It was dangerous, illegal, and perhaps unwise, but not necessarily crazy.

It scared me a little to think about Tim and Rich up on the wet cable in the cold night, but another part of me felt like wildly applauding. I felt proud of my brother, and secretly, maybe even a little jealous.

VOICES AND MESSAGES

"I'm not so sure about that," muttered Mom as she folded the clean laundry she had spread over the dark brown couch. While listening to a Christian radio station, she had just heard the voice of a preacher making a dogmatic proclamation: "God does not speak to people today; reading the Bible is the only way to hear from God."

Tim heard the radio preacher and also Mom's comment. Tim, Mom, and our sister Beth were in the room. Caleb was downstairs out of earshot.

A voice in Tim's mind spoke plainly: "You want to hear God through the Bible? Pick it up and open it."

Finding a Bible was not difficult in my parents' house. He picked one up, opened it, and his eyes fell immediately on these words: "Your ears will hear a voice behind you saying, this is the way, walk in it." [2]

To someone unfamiliar with the Bible, this may seem unremarkable. But verses that make that sort of statement are not common. Out of hundreds of pages and over thirty thousand verses, that's the first one he saw.

That small experience greatly complicated Tim's life. He heard a voice in his mind telling him to open it, then the voice seemed to be affirmed by external reality—the page in the Bible—when he saw the verse.

"I should listen to that voice," he thought to himself. "It must be the voice of God." He looked at Mom. "God spoke to me," he commented.

[2] ISAIAH 30:21 (NIV)

Beth had come into the room by that time and heard him.

"And what did God say?" asked Mom.

"I need to keep listening," he answered.

"Are you sure it's God?" she asked, slowly realizing her predicament. She was the one expressing a belief that God speaks to people, but she had massive doubts that whatever Tim heard was actually divine.

From then on, anytime he heard voices in his mind, he felt constrained to let them guide him. While fantasizing or daydreaming he began to assume that the thoughts and images in his mind affected the external world. If he imagined something evil and then imagined good overcoming the evil, he no longer thought of it as happening merely in his imagination. He thought he was influencing the world for good. This became hugely troublesome as he could not always control the outcomes in his imagination. He determined that a good outcome in his mind meant that he was acting from faith, while a bad outcome showed he had a lack of it. With such a mindset, his emotions swung like a pendulum between joyous highs and depressing lows, based on what was happening in his daydreams.

Visualizing himself as an armored knight jousting against evil, he tried to imagine vanquishing it, believing he was actually removing evil, little by little, from the universe. Everyone close to him knew something was wrong, but we didn't know what it was or how to fix it.

Tim's growing obsession with following the voices in his mind was especially concerning to our sister Beth. She was fifteen, with long brown hair, a friendly countenance, and a generally positive attitude.

She confided in Mom one day while Tim was away. "Mom, Tim scares me."

"How so?"

She spoke hesitantly. "I'm afraid if he thinks God tells him to do something, he'll just do it. I don't trust him. I don't want to be alone with him."

Beth was not alone in these feelings. An increasing number of friends were feeling it, too.

Don't Worry, God Told Me to Do It

The ride home was dismal. Tim peered out the window of the city bus at the traffic, the businesses, the people on the sidewalk, and the ever-present advertisements. He heard the muffled roar of the bus engine as it pulled away from the stop and continued up Van Ness Avenue. The memories of the previous twenty-four hours kept replaying in his mind.

Most of his thoughts focused on Bernice, a woman he'd grown close to, and had just seen at church the day before.

"May I kiss you?" Tim had asked Bernice after they shared a lingering hug.

"No!" She quickly reacted, although her face betrayed mixed feelings.

Our dad's ministry work included a public church gathering each Sunday. Tim made a point of talking with Bernice whenever he had the chance, and each conversation started and ended with a hug. For some reason, his usual awkwardness around young women didn't come into play. He was confident and self-assured. Hugs were common among people at church, so Tim's attraction to Bernice didn't stand out.

Bernice was married. Her husband Joel didn't attend with her, but he had become a casual friend to several of us, including Tim.

I noticed her sitting alone after the gathering that day. I

was behind her, but her brown hair, fully three feet long, was unmistakable. "Hi, Bernice. Everything alright?"

"Hi, Dave. Yes. Um, well, I think so."

"I've noticed you and Tim connecting a lot. Everything alright on that front?" My question sounded blunt, but she didn't seem bothered.

"Well, that's what I was just thinking about actually."

"Yeah?"

"I feel very conflicted. I love my husband and my kids, but he won't come here with me. Then there's Tim, always ready with a warm hug."

"There's a lot of hugging around here. Forgive me if I'm off on this, but I don't think hugging by itself would leave you feeling conflicted."

"No, you're right. It's the way Tim listens to me. I share how I'm feeling, and he makes me feel seen and appreciated. But it's more than just that. Part of me is lonely and then there's Tim. I feel distracted by him."

"Hmm..." I wasn't sure how to respond. "I appreciate your honesty. Do you want me to talk to him?"

"Oh, I don't know." She sat looking across the room. "I don't know. Maybe."

I spent the next twenty minutes talking with a couple of other friends, and then Tim approached me.

"Dave, can I talk to you?"

"Sure."

The church met on the second floor of the building our dad had acquired, above my shop and the other storefronts. We sat down at each end of a couch in the foyer at the top of the long stairway.

"I want Bernice to experience God's love, and I'm supposed to show her—to reveal it to her."

"Um… That sounds a little weird. What do you mean?"

"God told me to love her, so I'm doing that, but I'm also attracted to her."

"Okay."

"She's married, obviously, and I'm not willing to do anything wrong, but I'm supposed to love her."

"What do you mean by 'supposed to?'"

"At home, when I was alone, I heard a voice in my mind say, 'Love Bernice.' It was God talking to me and guiding me."

"Man, I don't think that's it." I felt irritated. "Bernice said she feels conflicted about you. That doesn't seem right."

"She told you that?"

"Yes. She's having trouble with this. She likes you, but she's also confused about you."

Tim went on to say something, but I was distracted by my own thoughts. He wasn't the only one who thought he had heard God's voice. Bernice had previously told me that when she prayed about Tim, she heard God say, "He's a gift from my hand." When she said the words "gift from my hand," I found myself cringing a bit. It sounded too churchy to be God.

I suddenly realized I hadn't been listening. I focused again on Tim.

"Dave, do you think God might set up a special case, where he might bend the rules?"

I've always welcomed questions. But Tim was hugely stressed out. He was trying hard to make sense of what made no sense.

"I don't know how to answer that," I responded. "I think rules can be really important, but following them in and of themselves won't necessarily result in something good. We need to have a vision of life that's more than that."

"I think I'm an exception. God is setting up a special situation for me."

"Hold on, Tim. What are you talking about?"

"Bernice. I am a conduit for her to experience God's love."

I was concerned for Tim, but I was also getting perturbed. "Man, that just sounds dumb. You're attracted to a married woman and you're looking for a way to make this work for you. This is not going to end well."

Tim's expression was one of pain. He genuinely couldn't seem to discern the difference between God's guidance and a stupid idea. At least that's what I was thinking. Then he said it himself: "Dave, I can't tell if I'm expressing faith, or losing my mind. I know it seems like a bad idea, but I keep hearing God tell me to show love to her. I think God is testing me to see if I have faith."

"Tim, man, you've got to communicate with other people more. Compare notes, you know. Get help processing your thoughts rather than going it alone."

He looked down, frowning. "But then I fail the test. God is asking me to trust him and act on faith."

"That doesn't sound like faith to me. It sounds foolish and a little weird."

To me, it looked like Tim wasn't allowing himself to hear what I was saying. He appeared to be so deep into the idea that God was guiding him that he wouldn't change course.

"God's telling me I should tell Joel about this."

Joel was Bernice's husband.

"Man, Tim. I don't know about that."

The next morning, Tim caught a bus downtown to where Joel worked and asked if he could talk with him. Joel came out. He was thin, had a full head of red hair, and wore fashionable clothing.

"So, what are we talking about?"

"It's important."

They stepped away to talk in private.

Tim went straight to it. "I don't think I should be friends with your family unless you and I can hang out too."

"What are you trying to say?"

"It's the desire to get closer."

Tim wasn't making sense. He was trying to tell Joel he had inappropriate feelings toward Bernice. He thought if he spent more time with Joel, it would somehow help.

"Tim, what are you talking about?"

"If I'm close to Bernice, I should be close to you too."

"That's weird. What do you mean by 'close to Bernice?' Is there something going on between you?"

"God told me I have to love her."

Joel looked at the ground for a moment, then back at Tim.

"Don't blame God if you've got a thing for my wife." He began shaking his head with a resolute look on his face and started walking back to his work. Then he stopped, shifted his weight a couple of times, slowly shaking his head again. He suddenly walked back to where Tim stood.

His voice shook a little with anger held under the surface. "This wouldn't be the first time she found another man at church. The last guy had a similar story."

Tim was dumbfounded. "I didn't know."

"That guy said he wanted to kill me."

"Kill you?" Tim was flabbergasted.

"Yeah. That guy ended up in a mental hospital."

"I'm talking about real love," responded Tim.

Joel looked incredulous. "Christians have left a bitter taste in my mouth."

He walked back in, shaking his head, obviously disturbed.

Tim's bus ride home felt like the sun went out in his life. He felt the weight of having done wrong after convincing himself he'd been doing right. His friendship with Bernice ended that day.

THE SMILE THIEF

Tim seemed oblivious to his odd behavior. From the inside, his thoughts seemed to flow normally. He knew he was passionate and intense, but he couldn't see that his thinking was sometimes irrational.

Tim continued to wage imaginary battles in his mind believing he was doing good and ridding the world of evil. And even though these battles were fought in his imagination, he began to lose some of the imagined jousting matches. These internal battles weren't going the way he wanted, and he became discouraged. He felt that he might be on the wrong side in these mental battles, and if he was on the wrong side, then perhaps he was evil. If he was evil, then he needed to distance himself from people so he wouldn't be a bad influence. More and more, he grew disconnected from other people. A few of us could feel his struggle, but no one knew his inner experience or how terrified he was.

One evening at a friend's house, he felt aware of ugly and malicious spirits outside, peering in the window at him, trying to get in. He knew they weren't physical, but he thought they were real in some way.

One day at home, he walked into the hall where he saw Caleb and Marilyn smiling about something. He smiled at them. They nodded, but both faces turned serious. Sometimes he would look at smiling people, but when they returned his eye contact, they stopped smiling. Tim assumed that after looking at him, they began to feel the same fear he felt, causing their smiles to vanish. This even happened with our parents and our sister. Sometimes Beth would see him, and her mood might change as she became sobered by his presence. When that occurred, Tim thought his own fears were somehow getting into her. This was not the case; she simply felt nervous about his unpredictable behavior. Others felt the same.

He grew increasingly fearful, believing he was stealing people's smiles. After a while, he could no longer produce a smile of his own. He could make the corners of his mouth turn up, but a real smile flowing from a good mood or inner happiness became impossible. He no longer experienced good moods. He worried that his non-smile was contagious. He feared that it would spread fear everywhere, sucking up the world's joy.

He often misinterpreted events around him. One day while he was working with Dad carrying boxes for a woman who was moving, he felt a sudden rush of fear. Immediately the woman started screaming angrily at someone. Tim thought his own inner feelings had sparked her rage.

Another time, on public transit, he suddenly felt terrified inside. Seconds later, a woman stepped onto the bus shouting something about going to hell. Tim thought his feelings were causing these events. He felt he must control his fears and feelings, or terrible things would happen.

I've wondered if he was actually picking up on the feelings of others empathically, mistakenly seeing himself as the cause. I don't know.

His inner terror sometimes immobilized him, leaving him barely breathing.

While talking with others, Tim would often start a

sentence and not finish. He would hear a voice in his mind refute what he was about to say before he could say it, causing him to avoid speaking.

"Dave," he told me one day, "I'm so afraid to tell Mom and Dad what's in my mind. The fear is so contagious. I'm like a falling rock. If they start to fear, it'll be like an avalanche."

By this time, he should have been under some sort of psychiatric care, but—unbelievably—it never occurred to anyone in our family. I think our parents' religious convictions clouded their awareness of Tim's psychological needs. They prayed for him, but he needed something else as well. I felt he needed help, but I made the mistake of thinking I had time to deal with it later.

CHAPTER SIX
1985 – 1986

---

*"There are times when the mind is
dealt such a blow it hides itself in insanity.
While this may not seem beneficial, it is.
There are times when reality is nothing
but pain, and to escape that pain
the mind must leave reality behind."*

~ *Patrick Rothfuss*
The Name of the Wind

MY BROTHER'S BLOOD

I began to stir, my bed feeling extra comfortable as I awoke to the sound of the phone ringing. I tried to ignore the sound, listening to the sleepy logic that always prioritizes more sleep. It was very early in the morning, too early for a casual call. When I answered, my mother's voice revealed her heartache. There was something else, too—shock, maybe.

"We don't have Tim anymore."

I tried to understand what she was saying. "What happened? What do you mean?"

She was shaken and not speaking clearly: "There are pieces of him all over the floor. He cut off his hand. We don't have Tim anymore."

My brother was dead.

"I'm coming over," I said, the news cleaving my mind in two: part welling with sorrow and another part rapidly making decisions.

I roused Kate. We threw on the nearest clothes and headed for the door.

The phone rang again. It was my mom's voice, still shocked and broken. "He's alive—he's still alive. He—we called an ambulance."

The house was just two miles away, but the drive seemed long. I kept trying to imagine what he'd done. I couldn't quite picture the injury itself. Mom said he'd cut off his hand, but she must be mistaken. He must have cut his wrist. I couldn't accept that he'd actually dismembered himself. Although, it was also somehow believable given his intense mindset.

Tim and I had been at a friend's house the night before. I thought about the expression on his face as he said goodnight at about nine-thirty. He was obviously experiencing some sort of inner pain as he looked at me questioningly. I had seen that expression many times; it was the look of a soul dissolving into deep uncertainty while simultaneously resolving to stabilize itself without help. I figured he had probably been up all night dealing with whatever it was until something just caved in.

I suddenly noticed my tears—free flowing careless tears that I couldn't control and didn't want to. I heard my own sobs like they were coming from someone else. It wasn't grief I was feeling. It was horror. I kept imagining what he'd done. "How could a person cut their own hand off?" I asked Kate, knowing she couldn't answer. But the injury, however severe, was not the worst part. The feeling of horror came when I thought about Tim himself, having to experience it.

At the house, Tim was already in the ambulance which was just about to leave. Inside, the atmosphere of shock, chaos, and fear hung like a rank fog. Dad was there, but he was lost and unreachable. I spoke to him, and although he looked at me, he didn't seem to hear. He was walking to and from the kitchen as if on a mission, but effectively doing nothing. "Oh God... oh Tim!" he wailed repeatedly. The whole household had awakened to the shock. Mom was in the living room crying and praying. Beth and their housemate Marilyn stood on the long stairway leading upstairs, a bewildered look on both faces. I didn't see Caleb.

The paramedics offered Dad the opportunity to ride with Tim in the ambulance, and he accepted.

Kate went into the living room and sat with Mom. I went into the kitchen where they had found Tim. That's when I found Caleb preparing to clean up the mess so the others wouldn't have to. When he had moved in a few months prior, I'm sure he could not have imagined this would be part of the experience. His choice to clean the kitchen that morning could only be called an enormous act of love. He left the room, saying something about needing a bucket.

I immediately understood the atmosphere in the house. Blood dripped from the countertops, the cabinets, the walls, and some from the ceiling. This was my little brother's blood—Tim's blood. The thought of him lost in this horrible experience pounded and throbbed in my mind, forcing me to bear it.

Feeling like I might collapse, I sat down on the floor next to the vacancy that had been my brother: a pool about the size of a man, with a yellowish liquid separating from the coagulating red which seemed to sort of pile up here and there.

"My brother." I wept, staring into the crimson pool as if he was in it. My mom's comment about "pieces of him all over the floor" made sense now.

My throat locked up. My mind still echoed the sound of my dad's wailing. My mom's whispered prayers were audible from the other room. The smell of blood made the house feel unfamiliar. I wanted to rescue Tim, but it was too late. It was as if he'd been killed. Somehow, the experience of that much blood made it difficult to remember he was alive—so much of him was still in the room. But he was being rescued and was on his way to the hospital.

Caleb reappeared with a large sponge and two buckets. He filled one with water from the bloody sink and soberly began the terrible job. He had a second bucket for himself in case he needed to throw up. "Dave, are you sure you want to be in here?"

It was difficult to speak, but I choked out a reply. "Yes, I'm sure."

Caleb was not immune to the horror, but he managed to

show compassion. "When I came in, I went to stop the bleeding, but it had already stopped. I thought he was unconscious, but then he spoke to me."

"What did he say?"

"He mumbled at first, then said, 'Caleb, is this real?' I told him it was."

We both sat there on the kitchen floor for a minute, then I got up, and leaving the horrible mess to Caleb, I drove to the hospital.

My dad was useless to the doctors who were asking him questions. He was still in a state of mind that was hard to reach. He had suffered his own traumatic injury that morning. He was injured in mind, and while that injury wasn't bloody, it, too, was severe.

I recalled the time Dad killed that rattlesnake when Tim was three years old. Mom had asked Tim if he was afraid. "Daddy was there" was his response. Back then, Dad's presence was enough to prevent fear. Now everything was different. Dad was afraid.

A doctor came and sat next to me. "I'm Dr. Schecter. Your dad's having a lot of trouble right now. May I talk with you?" His voice was all business, but his face was kind.

I was having trouble too, but I was able to converse. "Please. Yes. Of course."

"I've got a number of doctors on their way here for reattachment surgery. We probably won't do that, but it's standard procedure to prepare for it." He looked at me closely. "Is there any chance in hell your brother will do this again?"

Compared to my dad, I must have seemed clear-headed. "With help, I don't believe this will ever happen again. Tim can follow through with commitment once he sets his mind on something. Obviously."

The doctor thought for a moment. "This surgery is a lot of work and will take all day. I need to decide in the next few minutes whether to send the other doctors home and close up Tim's wound or to begin reattachment."

I was adamant. "If you can put his hand back on, you have to do that."

I didn't mean to sound demanding, but I knew that's what had to happen. "I will be there for as long as it takes. He will never do this again."

He asked me a few more questions, looking at me intently, then wrote something down on a pad. "Well… we may go ahead with reattachment," he said. "I wanted to have the testimony of a family member. Thank you."

I went into the room where they had Tim lying on a gurney. When he saw me, he seemed lost, horrified, and a little embarrassed. His handless forearm stuck straight up with a tourniquet still in place. I grabbed the air where his hand would have been as if I were clutching him by the hand. He gave his arm a small shake, responding.

"Dave, I couldn't die."

"Good. That's a good thing."

He spoke slowly, without energy, like a person exhausted. "Something was trying to invade me. I couldn't stop it. It got into my hand, and I couldn't let it get into the rest of me."

"You'll get through this. Think about something good."

"Like what?"

"I don't know—trees—flowers—anything." My comment felt stupid, but that's what came out. It's all I could think of.

He spoke slowly. "I kept picturing myself attacking Mom and Dad. I had to stop the evil. I had to protect them."

His hand was in a small tub filled with ice, a nurse periodically moving it around in the tub keeping the ice loose. Her warm dark hands contrasted sharply with the pale hand and the ice. Even amid horror, her work was beautiful— tenderly caring, treating her charge, not like a severed hand, but like part of her patient. And her ministry to Tim ministered to me as well, holding some of the darkness at bay.

His skin was pale and wrinkled. New blood dripped slowly into a tube, then into his arm.

"I'm so thirsty."

The nurse wouldn't let him drink, but she allowed me to put a piece of wet gauze in his mouth, which I did, getting it wet again and again.

They spent twelve hours operating. The sounds and images from the house haunted me as I waited. The scene in the kitchen superimposed itself over everything else I could see—the waiting room floor, the people around me, the clock on the wall. I knew it was all in my mind, but everything I looked at seemed to start bleeding.

In the midst of the horror was something good—a blessing oddly placed. A team of highly trained doctors was reattaching Tim's amputated limb. How many people in the world would be given such a gift? I pondered this as I stared at the floor feeling the faintest light in the sick darkness.

Tim's injury had bled until it stopped before they got a tourniquet on him. It began to dawn on me that people don't survive such things. Even a slit wrist can cause death, and Tim's was far more than slit. As I became aware of the miracle, it began to give me hope. The only reason for the team of doctors and nurses to invest in this surgery is that Tim's life had value. His future had value. I already knew that, but now I felt it. I resolved to keep my word to Dr. Schecter. I would do whatever it took. Tim would never do this again. And beyond that, he would learn to live again and to find joy. I knew I had no control over Tim's future, but I could throw myself into my resolve.

The afternoon slowly made its way toward evening. I felt the old familiar presence, but differently. There was something else—a grief greater than my own—as if some divine sorrow mixed its tears with those already on my face.

NIGHTMARES AND DAYMARES

Dr. Jones, a hand surgeon, came into Tim's room, followed by a team of doctors. He smiled at Tim. "How are you doing today, friend?"

Tim stared back at the doctor, wishing he could return the smile. Dr. Jones' smile faded, and the cheerful tone of the group seemed to fade as well. They spent a short while examining his hand, then left the room. Tim was convinced that his non-smile was contagious and incurable.

He began to recover physically. The reattachment surgery worked, and his hand showed strong signs of life. But his mind was tormented by the knowledge of what he had done and seeing the horror it caused in those around him. Unfortunately, he was seeing through a psychotic lens.

From his deluded perspective, he thought he had done something helpful when he cut his hand off. Specifically, he thought he was protecting our parents. The night he did it, he had been haunted by visions in which he brutally attacked them. In injuring himself, he thought he was cutting off something evil in order to protect them. He thought people would be grateful. In the days that followed, it was impossible for him to clearly understand what he'd done and why it horrified people the way it did.

The only thing he felt clarity about was the fact that something was terribly wrong and he couldn't seem to do anything about it. He felt that something evil was coming through him and trying to get to others and he couldn't stop it. He was saturated with fear. His struggle with sanity was already an issue, which now combined itself with an emerging delirium as the medical staff sorted out which antipsychotic medication would work best.

I walked into the Intensive Care Unit to his bedside. His reattached hand was elevated on one side and his other one strapped down to prevent him from harming himself.

"Hey, Tim."

He looked very sober and kind of lost. "Hey, Dave."

"What's today like for you?"

He glanced up to his right hand, loosely strapped to a stainless-steel frame. He spoke softly: "Give my finger a squeeze."

"A squeeze? What do you mean?"

"Just squeeze one of my fingers and watch. I won't feel anything."

I gently took one of his fingers between mine and gave it a squeeze.

"Now let go."

I let go. The finger was pale where I'd squeezed it. Then it filled in with color as the blood returned to the spot.

He didn't smile, but he sounded positive for a moment.

"See? My hand is alive."

"Yes, as are you."

"It's super hard in here." He spoke in an earnest tone. "Last night I had a nightmarish urge to try to pull my hand off again. My left hand is strapped down, so I kept imagining pulling it off with my teeth."

"I'm sorry, those sound like horrible thoughts. Thank you for not trying that."

Several days later, I was once again at his bedside, this

time in a regular hospital room.

"Dave, thanks for being here. I'm sorry it's so terrible."

"It doesn't matter," I said, "This is where you are."

"Yesterday they gave me some medication, but it was the wrong stuff. Everything was fine at first, but then I thought the wall was the ceiling. At the same time, all my muscles started moving against my will. They said it was caused by the medication they tried, but I can't tell. I keep thinking I'm becoming possessed."

"Possession... psychosis... wrong medication, who cares? Those things suck, but we have to live anyway. We have to keep breathing. We have to live into the next thing and find ways to make it better."

Tim started crying, just for a moment, then looked out the window. "Dave, did you see my blood?"

"Yes."

"Did Mom clean it up?"

I paused for a moment. "No, Caleb did."

Tim was quiet for a while, his chest and shoulders shaking intermittently with the tears. "I guess Caleb is my best friend right now."

"Maybe so. Don't worry about that. Your job right now is to help your hand recover, to keep communicating, and to keep breathing. Believe it or not, this will actually pass."

"Thank you, Dave."

"Of course."

"I'm gonna try to sleep now."

I stayed in the room for a while, looking out the window. I was well aware that Tim was off balance mentally and I knew he'd been experiencing delusions. Even so, our conversations continued to keep us connected.

✧ ✧ ✧

FRANK'S FRANK SMILE

A psychiatrist named Dr. Wolf stopped by Tim's room just as I arrived for a visit. "Are the good guys winning or are the bad guys winning?" he cheerfully asked.

The look on Tim's face made it obvious that the question disturbed him. He felt the psychiatrist was making a joke about something Tim was deeply concerned about. Of course, Dr. Wolf was merely using a simple metaphor to ask how Tim was doing, but the wording wasn't helpful. After a brief conversation, Dr. Wolf left the room.

Tim still looked disturbed.

"How are you doing?" I asked him.

He lay on his side, staring at the wall. "Tortured."

"What are you thinking about?"

"I don't know how to keep my balance in my mind."

"How do you mean?"

"It's like I'm balancing a ball on the tip of a cone." He paused awhile. "You know Sisyphus, the guy in the Greek myth? I feel like him—destined to roll a boulder up a hill forever, only to have it keep rolling back down."

"Just relax. Let it roll down. Don't worry."

"My un-smile is contagious. It makes everyone else unhappy. It's like I'm under a spell that makes everyone else lose their joy."

Just then, Frank walked in. He was older and was a friend of our parents. Frank's life seemed to be connected to an inexhaustible well of joy. As a person who had himself suffered, his joy was more than the happiness that comes from pleasing circumstances or a good mood. His joy had depth. He greeted Tim with a warm smile. "Hello, Tim."

Tim understood that people who cared about him wanted to come see him. But he also found it very difficult to receive visitors. He felt pressure to greet them and talk with them, but he wasn't up to it.

Frank just stood there smiling at Tim. He looked perfectly at ease, without any awkwardness. "It's wonderful to see you, Tim."

Tim looked back through his own joyless countenance, anticipating awkwardness, waiting for Frank's smile to fade.

It didn't.

Frank was the kind of person who could generate joy and spread it around. His smile only lit up more. He loved our family and truly was delighted to see Tim alive and recovering. "Tim, may I give you a hug?" he asked.

Tim reached out with his left arm, responding to Frank's affection. Then Frank gently touched Tim's elevated right hand, and mumbled a simple prayer: "Lord, please bless this hand and bless the man attached to it."

"Well, I can't stay, but I very much wanted to come by and say hello.

Tim, you're doing great." With that, Frank left the room, still wearing a genuine smile.

Tim and I sat for a while in silence.

"Dave."

"Yes?"

"I still can't smile."

"That's alright."

"Did you see Frank smiling when he left?"

"Yes."

"He was still smiling. After he looked at me and talked to me, he was still smiling. Frank broke the spell."

"Yeah," I said, "Your un-smile isn't contagious."

THE DEEP END

"Man, I don't know, that's pretty far," William commented as we sat in his living room.

We had just been talking about what Tim had done to himself. I had come over to talk with William and his wife Audrey as I knew them to be level-headed and straightforward people, and I needed that amidst all the drama. They were about ten years older than me.

William spoke courteously and slowly. "Dave, when you say he cut his hand off, that's an exaggeration, right? I mean I get that he cut himself badly, but it wasn't literally all the way off, right?"

I sat there unable to respond for a moment. Images of Tim's blood assaulted my mind, along with his handless arm. I pictured the emergency room nurse caring for his hand in the tray of ice.

"Six feet away," I responded.

"'Six feet away?' I'm not sure…"

"His hand was about six feet away from his arm."

"Oooh!" William squirmed with realization. "I'm sorry. I thought he'd cut his wrist, and everyone was just being dramatic. I'm sorry. I'm sorry."

"Well, I'm not sure what to say. It's hard to get your mind around what he did. I can see how it would seem like an exaggeration."

William shook his head, still kind of squirming.

Audrey spoke up. "Dave, that is horrible. That is so severe. I don't think he'll be coming back from this."

"What do you mean?"

"That's pretty far gone," she said, with some concern in her voice, but also sort of matter-of-factly. "Some things are just too severe, and people don't recover."

"I'm not sure what to do with that," I responded.

"I'm sorry Dave. I'm not saying to give up on your brother, I just don't see what anyone can do for him at this point. He's too far gone."

"Too far?" I questioned. "I can't think that way. He's still my brother."

That's when William commented, "Man, I don't know, that's pretty far. He's gone off the deep end."

I realized in that moment that the Tim I knew had become obscure to others. They couldn't understand. To them, Tim was a hard case—a friend, but one in whom they wouldn't have invested much given his mental illness. They thought in terms of how well or how poorly he might be doing at a given time. It was different for me. I thought only in terms of who he was, and I knew he was always the same guy no matter what his condition.

"How did they stop the bleeding?" William suddenly asked.

"They didn't. Nobody was there yet. Tim let it bleed until it stopped on its own."

"Oh God. Wait. What?" exclaimed William with complete incredulity. "Are you sure? How is that even possible?"

"That's what happened. He bled out. Their house-mate Caleb was the first to check on him but it had already stopped. I gotta say, when I saw the amount of blood, I was beyond shocked. My first thought was, 'I didn't know there was that much blood in a person to begin with.' And he was still conscious. I've been thinking about this quite a bit. It seems miraculous to me."

"Oooh, man," said William, squirming again. "Yeah, I'd have to agree with you. That seems miraculous."

Audrey had stepped out and returned with a tray of tea. We all fixed ourselves cups in silence. Then William spoke up again.

"So that must have been a hell of an expensive surgery. Is Tim well-insured? How will that be paid for?"

"Yeah, um… interesting question. As it turns out, the hospital has an endowment for this sort of trauma. It's covering Tim's surgery completely. There's a celebrity whose family benefited from the trauma center there. They set up finances to cover state-of-the-art surgeries, which Tim's was."

William half smiled. "Another miracle if you ask me. That's really cool."

"Yes. Very."

William looked very thoughtful. "I notice miracles. They remind me not to depend entirely on what I may or may not understand. Maybe Tim's pretty far gone, but I'm not giving up hope. Not at all."

MOVEMENT

It was a quiet ride home from the hospital.

Tim sat looking out the window watching the city go by.

"Dave, I never meant to hurt people."

"I know."

"I thought I was helping everyone."

"I know."

"It seems like I hurt everybody."

"Yeah, well, people love you."

Tim held his right hand out the car window. "I feel the wind on my arm, but not on my hand."

He wore a contraption on his arm that held his hand in place. Long metal rods protruded from the space between each knuckle. Those rods went all the way through his hand into the bones in his forearm.

"My skeleton is part metal now."

"Only for a while. Those things will come out. And you'll eventually feel your hand again."

"It's so weird. I know it's my hand, but it feels like a foreign object attached to my wrist."

"It's not. It's your hand." I paused for a bit. "Actually, it's my hand."

Tim looked at me. "Your hand?"

"Yes. Dr. Schecter put it back on because I insisted on saving it. So, you threw it away and I saved it. Finder's keepers, bro. It's mine now."

We both looked straight ahead, thinking for a minute, then I continued. "Yep, it's mine now, but I don't have a place for a third hand, so you'll need to take care of it for me."

We rode the rest of the way hearing only the city around us. Everything looked so routine—people coming and going, the usual traffic—just another day running another errand. Ever since I was awakened by Mom's phone call three weeks earlier I had felt like I was outside of the world—like I was in orbit. I would eventually need to experience re-entry.

Mom greeted us in front of the house. "Welcome home, son," she said warmly, tentatively offering Tim a hug.

"Hi, Mom." His response was also warm, and his hug also tentative, for different reasons. I think she felt fear whereas he felt shame.

"I've got your room all ready for you," she said with a smile. Her optimism was real, but she carried more pain than anyone realized.

I came by to see him again the next morning.

"Dave, I didn't sleep at all. I'm so tired."

"At all?"

"No, not at all."

He lay in bed with his hand elevated by a strap hanging from a rolling rack.

Each night for weeks he craved sleep, and it would evade him. His doctors prescribed powerful sleeping medication, but it seemed to have no effect. A dull aching misery pretty much ruled his days and nights. Every time I saw him it was the same.

Finally, I came by one morning to find him smiling, just slightly.

"Dave, I remember a short dream I had this morning. That means I was asleep."

"Excellent. That's encouraging."

As the weeks passed, his aching depression slowly began to recede.

"I moved my thumb!" Tim shouted to Mom one evening.

It was just a tiny bit, but Mom always expressed gratitude and affirmed every small evidence of healing.

Mom continued to offer care, always expressing optimism, which was great for Tim. Many of her feelings she expressed in private writings.

I discovered a poem on her desk. The ink was practically still wet.

> *My Dear Son,*
> *troubled,*
> *broken,*
> *I lay at God's feet in shards of what was*
> *or could have been*
> *jagged edges cut within*
> *memories as bitter water*
> *pain seared eyes,*
> *released in moans*
> *and sighs even in my sleeping dreams…*

I put down the piece of paper just as Mom entered the room. She saw what I'd read and without a word walked over and put her arms around me with her head against my chest. I could feel her beginning to shake as she released her tears.

"David, I want to believe he'll be alright. I'm not accustomed to hopelessness," she said between sobs. She stayed there for a while then went back to waiting on Tim.

I had always thought of my mom as strong, but in that moment, I realized it was something else. She lived from hope more than strength. Regardless of her strength or lack of it, she chose to continue on through whatever came, never giving up. She could do this because her sense of hope was strong. She believed that life was good and she wanted to say "yes" to whatever it offered. I think that's how she put her faith into action. She trusted God. She allowed for whatever came her way without trying to control it or run from it.

Dad had not yet recovered from that shocking morning. He went about his routine, but his energy was flat and he seemed to have no passion. He had a lot of difficulty connecting with Tim.

My parents' conversations about Tim became much more sober. Before his injury, they sometimes mentioned how they looked forward to Tim doing better. Those thoughts were gone now. The severity of his condition had become obvious, and he had now shown everyone just how deep his destructive thoughts could go.

Eventually, Dad drove Tim back to the hospital where a doctor removed the metal rods protruding though the skin between his knuckles. Mom had consistently applied antibacterial ointment to the area around the rods and the wounds closed up and healed cleanly.

At the occupational therapy department at the hospital, they fitted him with a special device with five long metal braces, each one positioned above each of his fingers. From those, elastic bands wrapped around each finger holding his hand open. The contraption would also help him exercise his hand once he could feel it again.

Dr. Schecter, accompanied by several colleagues entered the room. "Hi Tim, how are we faring today?"

"Okay, I guess."

"Let's have a look at this." They examined his hand carefully. "You won't get full use of your hand, and your wrist won't move freely, but it's looking good. Take care of it, and you'll be using your hand again for sure."

They examined each finger, squeezing and poking. As they touched his middle finger, Tim felt something in his index finger. "Hey, you messed up my nerves," he exclaimed.

Three doctors responded instantly. "No, *you* messed up your nerves!"

Surprisingly, Tim laughed, and it was genuine. Somehow his humor pushed past his shame, and they shared the medicine of laughter.

"Okay, that's it for today, buddy. Remember, take your medication every day!"

Tim's physical needs were being well cared for, and antipsychotic medication was prescribed, but he was not under any regular care for his psychological needs. Those were still not adequately addressed, and Tim didn't see himself as mentally ill. All six of us, as a family, met with a counselor for several weeks, but we thought of the sessions as merely helping us deal with the trauma of what Tim had done. Astonishingly, none of us realized the kind of care Tim needed long-term.

✧ ✧ ✧

THE TRUTH IS TOO WEIRD

Slowly, the nerves in Tim's hand revived, and feeling returned.

Interacting with people in public was very difficult after the surgery. He had to wear a hard plastic wrist brace to stabilize his hand, and sometimes he wore the larger contraption with the elastic around each finger.

In the days since climbing the Golden Gate Bridge with Tim, our friend Rich became engaged to be married and asked Tim to be the best man at his wedding. He understood Tim's difficulty, but Rich wanted Tim in that role, and Tim was willing. Aside from the brace on his hand, everything appeared to be normal.

During the reception, Tim encountered a new struggle when interacting with old acquaintances and friends, like Rob, a vivacious young man, a friend of Rich's who remembered Tim from several years earlier. "Hey Tim, what's goin' on?"

"Rob! How's it going?"

Rob extended his right hand for a good shake, then saw the contraption on Tim's hand. "Whoa, dude—what happened to your hand?"

Tim stared across the room at nothing, suddenly feeling exposed. He tried to hold his smile, but his self-consciousness took over, leaving him socially lost.

"I cut it off."

Rob stared at Tim, now also lost. "What?"

"It's okay now, it's healing." Tim struggled to regain the moment.

"Accidentally, right?" asked Rob, assuming his question was rhetorical.

"You could say that," I said, entering the conversation.

"Oh, hey Dave!"

"Hiya Rob."

Tim looked relieved, but his face was very sober.

Rob looked back at Tim, the question still hanging.

"Tim's injury is not easy to talk about," I suggested. "Ask about it some other time."

"Oh, sure, no worries."

About fifteen minutes later Tim asked if he could talk with me privately. "Dave, what do I say to people? The truth is too weird."

"It depends. You probably don't need to give the same answer every time. And there's nothing wrong with telling people you'd rather not talk about it. That's totally fine."

"I heard Rob tell someone I was mentally ill."

"And that bothered you?"

"That's ridiculous. I'm not. I have a hand injury—that's it."

Tim's mental health was a point of concern for all his family and friends, but aside from a few moments of openness, he generally refused to acknowledge the problem.

Rich walked up at that moment. "Hey, Best Man—you ready to give a toast?"

Tim looked at me with uncertainty. "Here goes…"

"You got this bro. No problem."

Tim proposed a fine toast to Rich and his new bride and everything he said was appropriate—no small feat for him at that time.

DISTORTED REFLECTION

Alone in his room, Tim opened the white wooden box containing the thirteen-inch parabolic telescope mirror. His face gazed back, greatly enlarged and illuminated by the reflected light. Then he heard Mom's voice calling from the kitchen.

"Timothy, it's time for your medicine."

Closing the box, he walked into the kitchen.

"Mom, I need to get off this medication. It's not for me."

"Son, you need to take it. It's very much for you."

"I can't stand the stuff. It makes me crazy."

Mom didn't know how to respond to that. The reality was quite the opposite.

Whenever Tim stopped his medication, he would hear "divine guidance" through the thoughts in his mind. This made him antagonistic about his medication. From his perspective, the meds prevented him from hearing the voices he had come to value. He couldn't see that living under that "guidance" was the very thing that was off-putting to people and caused the personal isolation he so feared.

Without the medication, he lived in a universe filled with messages. He believed he was being guided—shown how to open his mind so he could discern the messages. The unfortunate result was that he tended to believe whatever occurred to him. Any thought at all might be taken as guidance.

Wanting to keep Tim occupied, Mom arranged for him to spend his disability income attending a private college in San Francisco. He enjoyed having some structure in his life. This was his second attempt at college.

He particularly enjoyed Dr. Ken Harold's classes on ancient cultures and Hebrew poetry. Dr. Harold was good-looking and young for a professor. He gave Tim personal attention, which was meant to encourage him, but Tim misconstrued what it meant to study under someone. At the same time, he also decided to stop taking his medication. He began to see Dr. Harold as a sort of glorified being, an elder deserving of reverence.

"Dr. Harold, you are a true elder," said Tim, his admiration bordering on worship.

"I'm not sure how to respond to that, Tim."

"That's because you're humble."

"You have another class, and I have things to do. I'll see you later."

When Tim heard the words "I'll see you later," he took the words literally, like an invitation.

Tim went home and returned to school that day, having changed into his three-piece suit, but instead of nice shoes, he wore slippers. He brought the white wooden case containing the heavy thirteen-inch parabolic telescope mirror and waited for the perfect opportunity. Eventually, he saw Dr. Harold headed for his office. Tim followed.

Entering Dr. Harold's office, he placed the box on the professor's desk. The top of the box was now adorned with the words "Ken, the Son of God." Dr. Harold looked at the box in front of him. Tim expected Dr. Harold to open the box, and when he did so, the professor would see his reflection in the parabolic mirror—glory radiating from his face, causing him to be revealed as a majestic celestial being. Tim was beside himself with anticipation.

Dr. Harold did not open the box. He was, of course, put off by the weird gesture. It was unsettling and creepy.

"What is this, Tim?" he asked, trying hard to remain professional. He was more than put off. He was also afraid, even if only a bit.

"It's a glorious moment. You are a true elder—a wise man—a god."

"No offense, Tim, but you're talking nonsense. This is not a glorious moment. In fact, it's an inappropriate gesture, and indicative of a mental imbalance." He spoke to Tim straightforwardly, feeling nervous and unsure of what was happening.

"Are you on your medication?"

"I don't need medication. You are my teacher, which is all-sufficient."

"I'm a professor and you're one of my students. I'm your teacher in that sense, but that's all."

"You should open the box. You'll feel the joy," said Tim.

"I believe you have good intentions Tim, but please take the box away."

Wanting to please Dr. Harold, Tim carried the box back to his car and returned to the building. He noticed a stairway leading up and ascended the five stories to the roof. He walked to the edge where a short wall encompassed the flat roof. Stepping up onto the wall, he walked along it until he stood on the corner of the building, the toes of his slippers sticking out over the fifty-foot drop.

The motion caught the eye of some students on the ground, who stopped and watched. "You need to get back. You could fall!" one of them shouted.

A crowd of students and faculty gathered, watching, wondering if he meant to jump. Dr. Harold saw him from his office window and even though he was tempted to ignore it, he headed for the roof.

"Tim, you need to come down from there." He spoke matter-of-factly, not wanting to upset Tim.

"At once, my elder!" shouted Tim, walking back across the roof in his suit and slippers.

It was decided that Tim would not be allowed in class again until he could be psychologically evaluated.

Several evaluations followed, all with similar results and advice: whatever Tim did with his life, he needed to do it on medication. This disturbed Tim. He felt a strong self-stigma at the thought of taking psych meds. He couldn't see the enormous difference between the times he was medicated and the times he wasn't.

I'M GETTING MARRIED!

Tim's illness sometimes involved radical mood swings. Sometimes he was overly happy. Other times it was the opposite. One might think that Tim's "happiness" would be easier to be around than the more somber or depressing moods, but that was not necessarily the case. His positivity could also be disconcerting.

Sorting through my keys, I grabbed the one for the front door of my parents' house and reached to open it. I could hear laughter coming from inside. Normally, the sound of laughter would be a good thing, but not today—not this laughter. The word maniacal came to mind. "I'm so tired of this," I thought to myself, changing my mind about entering the house.

Instead of going in, I sat down on the front steps to think for a bit. I heard Mom's voice inside saying something to Tim, but I couldn't hear the words. The laughter continued. It was laughter without joy. Tim seemed hugely elated, as he often did, but I still thought of it as joyless because of the way it affected the people around him. True joy begets more of the same, whereas Tim's extreme laughter just made him seem weird, and it often scared people.

I felt for my mom having to deal with the psychotic behavior as part of her daily routine. How exhausting it must be. Her love for Tim was huge, and that fact carried her through many crazy-filled days.

Thinking about Mom got me to my feet. The door wasn't locked, and I put my keys back in my pocket. Tim and Mom were standing in the foyer having exactly the kind of conversation I expected. Mom was trying to make sense of what Tim was saying, but she couldn't. She stood, committed to the conversation, but her face looked heavy, like someone who hadn't slept.

Tim turned to me very excited. "Dave, I'm getting married!"

On many such occasions, I would try to meet him partway, letting myself get somewhat excited so as not to bring him down. In that moment I had no motivation to try. He stood there, arms spread exultantly, exclaiming that he was getting married. I knew there was no particular woman on his mind. This announcement was not about a real engagement.

A few days earlier, he'd told me that he needed to commit to a life of celibacy. I guess he had a revelation later that resulted in a different conclusion—one that he found very exciting. Regardless, I wasn't excited with him, which troubled him. From Tim's perspective, he was honestly trying to share good news and it wasn't being received as such. From my (and Mom's) perspective, this was just another crazy moment to get through.

Mom thanked me for coming by, saying she needed to attend to something else, and went to another part of the house. I figured she needed a good nap. I heard her talking with Beth in another room. I felt for Beth. Developing through her mid-teens in a house with Tim was not easy. She loved him, but she also feared him.

When Tim saw that I wasn't excited for him, his laughter stopped, and a tormented look came over his face. Tears began to flow, and he leaned forward, hands on the front of his legs, and began to sob. He looked at me entreatingly. He often got himself stuck in a mindset where he thought if he could just stay excited, he could experience the things he was excited about. Consequently, if he lost the excitement, he felt doomed to lose those things. He saw it as a manifestation of faith, or a lack of it. If he could maintain excitement about getting married, it showed that he believed it, and it would happen. So, when he began to lose the excitement, he experienced it as losing faith, and the imagined blessing would pass him by. We had many conversations in which I, and others, would show him how that kind of thinking made no sense. But, in the end, the wrong thinking ruled the day. Many friends bowed out and stopped trying to communicate, unable to deal with him. This was understandable to most of us, but not to Tim. When someone avoided him, he felt hopeless, like he was too far gone to love.

This was the kind of moment where remembering to show him love especially mattered. I was caught off guard, already tired of the insane nonsense, and I just wanted to leave. For me, faithfulness meant staying connected, despite my feelings. I looked at my brother standing there, sobbing big tears, just as dramatic as the laughter only moments ago.

"I hope you get married, Tim. I want you to have the fun and romance you want." He stood back up, listening. "I think it's going to be a long time before that happens, but when it does, you'll remember the desires you have now, and you'll experience real fulfillment. You'll get there, but I don't think it will be soon."

I didn't really know what to say, but I felt the need to speak anyway. That moment, like many others, required what felt impossible. I couldn't promise him he would be married someday, but it felt wrong to discourage him when the discouragement could so easily lead to some sort of destructive behavior. And after seeing the level of destruction he was capable of, I was afraid of saying the wrong thing lest I stimulate another horrible event.

Underneath all the crazy was a perfectly normal desire. His emotional expressions were bizarre and poorly timed. Nevertheless, they were still expressions of hope and faith. Those things are healthy, but he was processing them through damaged thinking. It was difficult to encourage his hope and faith while having to navigate the crazy thoughts at the same time. It was difficult, tiring, and often weird, but I believed that somehow it would be worth the effort.

I'M GOING TO MARS!

While hanging out at my parents' house the following week, I heard Tim's voice calling me from his bedroom.

"Dave!" He stood there with his wide eyes darting back and forth busily sorting through some apparently amazing thought. "I can read my own mind!"

"Uh, yeah, I suppose you can. Is that new?"

"Wait," he said, suddenly looking surprised at whatever had crossed his mind. "There it is! I know every word I'm thinking!"

The absurdly comedic moment notwithstanding, I tried to show some support—or perhaps mock support might be more accurate. "Congratulations, Tim, you now know what you're thinking. This is truly amazing."

Fortunately, my sarcasm didn't do any damage. He saw how he was coming off and I was relieved to hear him laugh with genuine humor, which got me laughing as well.

It was a nice moment, but short-lived.

He'd been looking at pictures of Mars—recent shots from NASA's Viking project.

"Dave, I can't wait to let you in on this." He spoke sincerely with a tone of excitement. "I'm going to Mars!"

A couple of moments of silence passed. "Mars?" I was surprised by how disconnected he was from reality, even for Tim.

"Yes. I've decided. I'm going to be among the first visitors to Mars. I've been uncertain about what to focus on— how to apply myself, and this is it!"

I had already checked with Mom about whether Tim was taking his medication. She assured me he was.

"Well, sending people to Mars may happen at some point, but I don't think it will be soon. I don't mean to discourage you, but there are probably a lot of years between now and whenever that happens. Besides, you'd have to be in perfect physical condition."

Tim seemed unaffected by my words. "I know it sounds far-fetched, but I've given it a lot of thought. If God wants me to go, then nothing can stop me."

"I wish you wouldn't play the God card like that. It's like cheating in a conversation. When you say that, no one can argue with you."

"That's perfect. No one should argue with me. Why would someone want to argue with something so cool?"

"Tim, going to Mars is a cool idea. I get it. But I'm not going to go along with something that's just going to end up being another weird thing to be embarrassed about."

His face remained confident but also revealed a slightly tortured look.

"Dave, think about it. How could going to Mars be embarrassing?"

I found myself beginning to retreat. "I wish you could hear yourself," I said. I'd had many such conversations with Tim. Sometimes continuing a conversation caused him to end up talking with more sense, and other times he seemed headstrong in his delusions. Why couldn't he be excited about something normal, or even something fringe?

Mars?

Really?

SILENCE

The rear-view mirror was black, reflecting the absence of any would-be traffic behind us as Tim and I drove out Highway Four into the Central Valley. There was a spot on this highway that I particularly loved when traveling at night. I recognized it by a fork in the road which served as a personal landmark. At this spot, I would sometimes pull over and stop late at night, the later the better. I loved it for its simple offering of silence: no traffic, no streetlights, no human sounds—just silence and stars.

I pulled off the road, stopped, and turned off the head-lights. Without a word, Tim opened the passenger door and got out. He stood and stared upward, absorbing the night sky. I got out and leaned against the car, taking in the stillness. This sort of moment brought a simple kind of joy, and with it, a simple kind of sanity.

Tim pointed upward. "Scorpio looks huge."

"Yes," I said. "Beautiful."

The mental illness didn't damage the beauty of the sky. For a few minutes, Tim seemed normal, and life was good.

NUMBERS, COLORS, AND DECODING THE UNIVERSE

During his psychotic episodes, I tried to follow Tim down paths of strangely connected thoughts as he strained to communicate what he was experiencing. The unreasonable nature of the illness made it impossible for me to fully understand. The common cold can be understood. Even cancer can be understood. But this was an illness of insanity. It would not allow anyone to understand it. He was isolated, living in a world apart. When he tried to communicate from that isolated place, he sounded crazy, frightening people and driving the isolation deeper.

Tim walked into The Clayhouse loaded with confidence. "Dave, do you know where that pot is that I made with the lavender glaze?"

"Um… I think you made several pots with that glaze."

"Yeah, I need them."

I rummaged through the back room trying to recall if the pot was there. It was a nice piece—a deep bowl shape nearly a foot tall with gorgeous glaze patterns on the sides. "I guess he won't be making more of those," I thought to myself. No one knew for sure, but I didn't think his reattached hand was up to using the potter's wheel again.

"Ah, cool! Yes, here it is." I brought out the pot and handed it to Tim who immediately put it in a large paper bag.

Before I realized what was happening, he set the bag on the concrete floor and struck it hard with a hammer I hadn't noticed before. The pot shattered inside the bag.

He stood up, beaming. "Four down, two to go!"

"What? What are you talking about?"

"I'm destroying everything I made with that glaze. I realize now that lavender is evil."

I looked at the broken pieces inside the paper bag. A kind of sorrow came over me as I felt the loss of the beautiful piece of artwork that was now irreplaceable due to the condition of Tim's hand.

"You said 'Four down, two to go.' Is that how many

lavender pots you made? Six?"

"Yes, but I'll soon be free of them." His face still shone with something like joy—but not. It was always difficult to respond when he got this way. If I showed disapproval he might swing to the opposite end of the emotional spectrum. "It's just pottery," I told myself. "It doesn't matter that much." But I didn't believe my own thoughts. He was destroying something beautiful for a crazy reason.

Over the next few weeks, Tim declared some colors good and others evil. And it didn't stop with colors. He also began to see various numbers as evil and tried to avoid them. "One," "three," and "seven" were good numbers. In conversations he did his best to be the first, third, or seventh one to speak, regardless of whether he had anything pertinent to say. This became awkward when someone asked him a question. He wouldn't speak until his "number" was up but no one else knew why.

Eventually, his relationship with numbers cascaded into a full-fledged sort of numerology guiding his decisions and interactions.

I learned much of his perspective on numbers and colors. We always talked openly and there was just enough consistency in his thoughts to provide something to follow. My efforts may not have been wise—I've never been sure. I was able to keep communication open, but I was also participating in a delusion, inadvertently affirming the very thoughts that were causing problems.

One night we talked again in the clay shop, after I'd closed up for the day.

"Dave, I think I'm beginning to understand everything." He looked at the floor, pondering for a moment before continuing.

What he said next sounded a little like comedy, but he was completely serious. "Three redeems two. Two, which would normally be a bad thing, is justified by the presence of three.

So, there are two of us here, right? But it's okay because we're here." He pointed to the door that led out onto the street. "The number—the address on the door is "111" which is also three. That three, combined with the two of us is five, which is the number of man. We are two men, which is two fives. We are together. Two fives together equal ten, which if you ignore the zero, is a one. So, we are one!"

I sat there not knowing exactly how to respond.

Conversations like that became increasingly common. He came to believe he was on the verge of a breakthrough of understanding. He saw hidden meaning coded into every color, every musical note, every number, every sign, and every piece of art.

Not long after the conversation in the clay shop, I sat with him in his room.

"Dave, God is showing me the meaning of it all. It's like a spiritual genetic code of the universe written in the physical arrangement of everything. We can learn to sense it and understand it."

Many people assumed he was on drugs, though he never was. He made judgments about people based on the colors and numbers he associated with them. The resulting social awkwardness got him ostracized more than once, which had its own cost—leaving him feeling rejected. The cause of the rejection may have been somewhat imaginary, but the rejection was real, nonetheless.

Tim's need for regular professional help with his mental illness should have been obvious. It's a bit shocking in hindsight, but most of the people in his life, including me, didn't realize how much he needed psychiatric help as part of his regular routine. I don't know if it was denial or simply obliviousness—probably some of both.

THE CREEPS

Tim walked through the Academy of Sciences in Golden Gate Park. The museum was closed but he was on his way to a meeting with the San Francisco Amateur Astronomers Club which met in the building at night. He passed through the African Hall where the work of taxidermists was displayed in African scenes. He noticed a hippopotamus and a warthog behind the glass. He felt as if malicious demonic spirits haunted the stuffed animals, causing an atmosphere of spiritual oppression.

The next night he attended a church-related meeting at the home of a family friend. It involved a Bible study followed by a time for prayer. It wasn't formal, just a simple time for anyone to pray about anything they wanted to. He was quiet for the most part, but when the praying started, Tim sort of took on the role of God. Each time someone prayed, he responded as if they were praying to him. One woman felt bad about something she'd done and prayed for forgiveness.

"I forgive you," said Tim in a somber tone followed by an awkward silence.

"Thank you Tim, but I wasn't talking to you," she replied.

The meeting shut down early as it was difficult to continue with Tim present. He thought he was helping but he was giving everyone the creeps.

Soon after that, Tim spent a couple of hours transforming his bedroom into a special "royal throne room." He draped green velvet fabric over everything in the room until the chairs, bed, floor, and everything in the room was covered entirely in green.

I don't know where he got all the fabric.

In the middle, he placed a large chair on top of a wooden box, all covered in green velvet. Next to the chair was a small table. On the table was a chalice holding some sort of drink.

He then went into our parents' room. "Dad, come and be exalted."

Dad looked bewildered. "Exalted? Tim, what are you talking about?"

"Come and see."

Dad followed Tim to his room.

Tim gestured to the chair. "Sit and drink, oh king!"

Dad stood there looking around the room, even more bewildered.

"What did you do to your room?"

"This is to honor you. Sit and drink."

This was too weird for Dad. Tim didn't know it, but in that moment, Dad found himself recoiling inside. He looked at the cup and all he could think was that it was poison. He thought that for some deluded reason, Tim was trying to kill him.

"No thank you, Tim," replied Dad. "I think you should put your room back the way it was."

Since Tim's hand injury, Dad had a very difficult time connecting with Tim. He thought Tim's odd behavior was merely a matter of Tim needing to make better choices. He didn't understand that Tim was ill. The lack of connection was hard for Tim, and beyond that, Dad began viewing himself as a failure, which was no help to himself or to Tim.

A few days later, Tim was once again on his way to the Amateur Astronomers club meeting. And once again, he walked through the African Hall while it was closed. He looked at the hippopotamus and the warthog, still standing unmoved. He felt the same dark presence, but this time he decided he needed to take the upper hand. He pictured the animals alive again.

Most of the displays and dioramas were behind glass but at the end of the large hall, the biggest scene was blocked only by a railing. Tim ducked underneath and stepped onto the fake grass of the African Savannah. Touching and petting the giraffes and zebras, he believed he was bringing them back to life and giving them freedom.

He was not alone that night. Others from the astronomy club watched with a mixture of incredulity, amusement, and concern.

THIS IS GONNA GET WEIRD

Davies Symphony Hall was filled with a fascinating crowd—one that had not been there before and would likely never be again. The 2,743 seats were almost all occupied by the faithful, the curious, and those who dared to hope for what seemed impossible.

A fairly well-known faith healer was to take the stage that night. He would do what he often did—declare what illnesses were present, and, if the spirit moved him, he would also declare healing, and people who arrived sick would go home well.

That was the idea, anyway.

I wandered through the aisles as the crowd gathered, never quite settling into a seat. I overheard people telling each other stories of dramatic physical healing—an aunt here, a cousin there.

In the Bible, there's a moment in the life of Jesus, when he said, "The lame walk, the blind see, and good news has come to the poor."[3] Many who came into the concert hall

[3]MATTHEW 11:5 (PARAPHRASE)

that night were believers: those who saw themselves as lame, blind, or poor, hoping for a miracle.

Tim wanted to come to the event, and my dad and I had come with him. He wore a very nice pinstriped suit that Dad had given him as a gift about a year earlier. The general attire in the hall was for the most part on the casual side, but Tim seemed to think he should wear the suit. He said he was dressing for a special occasion and that we would be thrilled when we found out.

"What's the special occasion?" I asked.

"You'll see," said Tim, with an odd smile. "Tonight is the night. Today is the day. My time has come."

I sighed, frustrated, but chose not to respond.

My dad found a seat, where he remained, while I continued wandering the hall. Tim disappeared.

This sort of crowd always left me feeling embarrassed, and guilty for feeling so. It was like a trap. On the one hand, if I joined in the wave of belief that filled the hall, I could fully participate in the event, and, who knows, maybe I'd see a miracle. Maybe my brother would be restored, or at least get a little better. On the other hand, I would be giving over to the weirdness that I felt embarrassed about.

My faith has never embarrassed me, but certain religious experiences have. And there seemed to be a cultural milieu at this gathering that had "embarrassing" written all over it.

I paused in a doorway where three ushers also paused. They were not part of the crowd; they were Symphony Hall employees who happened to be working that night. Each of them was quiet. They were obviously struggling, trying to remain courteous and helpful, while also appearing nervous about what the evening might entail. I couldn't read their minds, but they each looked somewhat bewildered. Then I heard one say quietly, "This is gonna get weird."

I understood. Culturally, this crowd would seem foreign to most people. A healing service, complete with shouting, praising God, seeing a minister put his hands on someone only to then see the person fall over and lay on the floor awhile, then get up and dance. It was all very strange, and yes, embarrassing. I kept thinking, "Why can't God just heal people without all the show? Why does it have to be so weird?"

Finally, someone appeared on stage, and the crowd grew quiet. "I hope you're all ready to meet with God in an amazing and powerful way tonight!" The voice was dramatic—sort of cheerleading the crowd. Several other leaders took turns at the microphone. Then I heard music, and the whole crowd started singing, led by a recording artist well known for his gospel music.

During all the activity, Tim had wandered backstage, seeking out the featured minister. He found him and asked him to pray for the healing of his now-crippled right hand. The man met with Tim very briefly, but he found this unplanned one-on-one session to be distracting and sent Tim away.

I found a spot from which I could see everything and stayed there, leaning against the wall near one of the exit doors. Some of the music moved me, and I watched the leader, listening to his voice: strong, authoritative, and also melodic and soothing. He stood at the front of the large stage.

An arm emerged from the curtain at the back of the stage, followed by a well-dressed young man, walking tall and confidently toward center stage. The crowd could see him, but the music leader could not. Suddenly, I recognized Tim.

"Of course," I thought, as Tim approached the leader from behind. He opened his arms wide as he approached the guy, then threw his arms around him in a happy embrace—still from behind. Tim wasn't thinking about what the other man would be experiencing. The singer was pulled backward by the hug, causing him to flail his arms wildly to avoid falling. Having no idea what was happening, and no longer able to sing, he tried to free himself as Tim persisted in hanging on. Half the crowd continued singing, and the other half watched, trying to understand what was happening. Several men rushed onto the stage, grabbed Tim, and escorted him out a side door.

"They just threw Tim out of the building," I thought to myself. I glanced up to where Dad was sitting. He was walking now, looking very disturbed. The crowd seemed oddly divided. Some people continued to sing, while others stopped, distracted by what just occurred. The music leader recovered, continuing the song along with those who were still singing. I intercepted Dad. "I'll go look for Tim," I said. "I'll see if I can find him and bring him back."

"Oh boy," said Dad, distraught. "I should have known something like this would happen."

I hurried out of the building, making for the area where Tim would have found himself outside. He was probably experiencing feelings of rejection and could easily slip into a suicidal mindset. Finding the correct exit door, I scanned the area, walking, looking in every direction. Putting myself in his shoes, I tried to determine what he would do. There were several high-rise buildings nearby. "If he decided to, I'm sure he could get himself up to one of these rooftops and jump off," I kept thinking to myself. I felt my reaction was extreme, but I knew Tim, and extreme was his style.

Twenty-five minutes later, having found no evidence of Tim, I returned to the concert hall to find Dad. Entering the building, I heard the music still going full throttle. During breaks in the music, the minister declared that he sensed a number of people being supernaturally healed. Some of those had come up near the stage, and some were apparently still in their seats.

I found Dad in his seat, still looking disturbed. I sat down next to him.

"Anything?" he asked.

"Nothing."

We sat together, frustrated and feeling at a loss.

As the healing service continued, I watched the blind remain blind and the lame remain lame, while those with invisible troubles, like diabetes or back pain, experienced dramatic healing—apparently. As for the schizophrenic, they not only remained so, but they got kicked out of the building. My faith was not encouraged. I could only imagine what Tim must have been feeling.

As it turned out, Tim was not suicidal at all that night. After being removed from the concert hall, he wandered the streets for about an hour, then returned to find the meeting over, although hundreds of people were still milling about the hall.

Tim's original plan that night was to announce to the crowd that he was the second coming of Christ, which is why he walked onto the stage. His plan didn't work, but he remained in a state of elation, believing that he was Jesus and that he would somehow manifest himself as such.

Walking through the crowd toward the stage, a thought occurred to Tim, "Since I'm Jesus, I have to die." So, he collapsed onto the floor right there in the middle of one of the aisles.

Having chosen to be dead, he decided he could no longer

move. A few people from the crowd tried to help him up, but his body was limp, and he wouldn't sit up or stand. Assuming he was paralyzed, someone called an ambulance.

That's when I found him—surrounded by a small crowd trying to help him. I tried to get him to get up and come with me, but I could see that wasn't going to happen. A young man about Tim's age was holding Tim's hand, consoling him. "He's been injured," said the young man, showing me Tim's right hand. I didn't feel like explaining anything. I just wanted to retrieve Tim and get home.

Some concerned onlookers found a wheelchair. I wasn't sure exactly what I should do. "This is nuts," I kept thinking. "I just want to take Tim home." But how was I supposed to handle him when he was completely paralyzed? I knew he wasn't really—he kept moving his head, talking, and even helped a little when they got him into the chair. I was tired of dealing with crazy. Lifting him into the chair, they quickly began wheeling him out to the street to meet the ambulance. I followed.

A woman who worked for the symphony hall also followed, watching the little crowd as the ambulance pulled up to the curb.

The paramedics were experienced. Within moments of beginning to examine Tim, they questioned his paralysis. "He's not paralyzed," I said. "We just need to get him home." My comment confused the others gathered around us.

One paramedic spoke up, sounding upset. "I've got a heart attack victim waiting for me on the next call. Do I see to him, or do I take this guy to the hospital?"

"Go. See to the heart attack." I stated with conviction. At the same time, I noticed Tim saying the same thing. It was a weird moment. He didn't want to take the ambulance away from helping someone else, but he didn't seem to mind sitting there slumped in a wheelchair "paralyzed" and causing a scene that had him surrounded by a small crowd of people trying to help him.

With the help of a few others, my dad and I lifted Tim out of the wheelchair and into Dad's car. Tim managed to sit up in the car just fine.

The woman from the symphony hall looked relieved to see we would soon be gone. "Everything okay now?" she asked, agitated, but trying to remain professional.

"Yes. And thank you for being patient with us," I said. "Pretty ironic, an ambulance having to come after a healing service." I was trying to come off as normal, but it was too late. She probably wished she didn't have to be there dealing with us. Her demeanor was cold.

It wasn't her fault. I recalled the usher's comment earlier about the evening getting weird. It did. And, like it or not, I had become one of the embarrassing people.

I CAN'T BE CRAZY, I'M GOD

Back at home, we tried to lift Tim out of the car, which was awkward as he was still choosing to be paralyzed. As we tried to stand him up, he fell in a heap into the gutter.

"Oh, brother. For pity's sake, Tim!" shouted Dad, getting increasingly upset. Tim was lying in the gutter, sullying the beautiful suit Dad bought for him. He remained limp, so we carried him into the house and laid him on his bed in the back bedroom. Dad looked angry and fed up with Tim's behavior. Tim lay on the bed, obviously capable of movement, as he was subconsciously gesturing with his hands as he talked. Dad had had enough, and as Tim lay there on his back, Dad gave him a hard, open-handed slap on the stomach, trying to get him to move. That got a momentary reaction, but then he went limp again. I understood Dad's feelings, but I thought he was being too harsh.

I was at a complete loss but felt we had to do something. Perhaps the spirit of the healing service had influenced me, I don't know. "Let's take Tim down to the church," I said. "We'll gather a few friends he trusts, and just spend time with him. We can talk, pray, and just see if we can get through. I don't want to leave him here like this."

It's difficult to admit this, but calling a hospital didn't occur to us. Perhaps the do-it-yourself attitude of my family had no boundaries at all.

Dad stayed home, which was probably good, as the night only got worse. Soon after parking at the church building, Tim "miraculously" sprang to his feet and jumped out of the car. I was already standing on the sidewalk.

"Dave, I'm Jesus!" declared Tim, as he grabbed me by the head and kissed me haphazardly on the face. Then he sprinted up the long flight of stairs like an athlete.

Four friends showed up: Bart, Don, Andy, and Caleb. We were all prepared to spend as much time as it took to reach Tim. Adding to the drama, the power went out unexpectedly just as we were settling in.

There in the dark, Tim started in with the crazy. "Elohim," he said, in a somber tone, followed by "I am Yah." Both terms are ancient names for God. In Tim's mind, he was referring to his friends as gods, and naming himself as the true God, letting us know that he (God) was with us.

After his annoying proclamation, he expected the lights to come back on, but nothing happened.

Andy spoke up assertively. "Tim, we're here, and we're

going to stay as long as it takes to help you get your feet back into reality." Andy was a minister from the church. He and Tim weren't close, but he had joined us out of a sincere desire to help.

Tim looked at him as if he'd been speaking an unknown language, and Tim's response seemed like pure nonsense. "Yes, you are here, I am here. I am. We are here."

Andy meant well, but his thoughts about helping Tim get his "feet back into reality" were not realistic. I was finally beginning to see this myself. I had always been able to get through to Tim, even if only enough to help him through the next hour. Tonight was different. I was beginning to see that he was falling into a state of mind that simply wasn't reachable.

We all sat there like a band of idiots. Caleb had found some candles and a large flashlight, so we could at least see each other. After his experience cleaning up the kitchen after Tim's injury, Caleb had kept a distance from Tim. I knew that and was grateful for his presence.

Bart chimed in. "I don't believe you, Tim!" Bart wasn't prone to anger and the sound of it in his voice was new. "I feel like I'm losing a friend. What happened to you?"

Tim looked concerned. Bart had become a close friend of Tim's, and Bart's anger surprised him. "You don't believe in me, Bart? You've always believed in God."

"You're not God!" yelled Bart, fully releasing his anger.

The disjointed conversation continued for the next thirty or forty minutes. The whole time, Tim was trying to reveal himself as God, thinking the rest of us would be delighted once we understood. He wasn't messing with us; he believed what he was saying.

The power eventually came back on, and we had lights again.

Talking was getting us nowhere. We prayed for a while. We were, for the most part, church people, and praying was normal for us. At one moment I watched Don put his hand on Tim's shoulder as he prayed for him. It was a rough hand, from a formerly rough life—gently and lovingly squeezing Tim's shoulder. If we accomplished nothing, at least love was being expressed, which is not nothing.

Don sat close to Tim, and leaned in, speaking to him. "You make a great human being. There's no reason to think of yourself as supreme or divine. Why burden yourself? We just need you to be you."

Praying seemed as fruitless as talking. Tim was lost in delusion and nothing we said or did made any difference. Nevertheless, we continued talking with him.

Eventually, Tim began to feel pressured. He started to back down and try to change his mind. On the one hand, he believed what he was saying, on the other hand, everyone was so sure he wasn't God. He began to feel doubts. He also began to feel miserable. "I just want out," he said at last.

"That's good," I said. "Maybe we can help you."

As ridiculous as it sounds, we stayed up all night having this bizarre conversation. As the sun was coming up, I drove Tim home figuring he'd go to bed after being up all night, but instead, he went to the College to try to attend classes he'd been missing.

A few hours later, I came by Dad's office to see how he was doing. "How did last night go?" he inquired.

"I don't know," I said. "As a whole, I don't think we were helpful."

Then something happened that changed everything. Dad called a doctor to talk about the previous night's experience at Davies Symphony Hall.

This was the first time any of us had sought out psychiatric help. I don't know what we were waiting for. Dad spoke with me after the call. "Tim needs to be hospitalized," he said, sounding a little disturbed. "I didn't want to think of Tim as being mentally ill, but it's pretty clear he is. I don't know what I've been thinking all this time."

That same day, Tim discovered he was not allowed to attend classes without submitting to a psychological evaluation. He was eager for the two psychologists to interview him as he felt sure they would conclude he was of sound mind.

It was the opposite. They directed him straight to Langley Porter Psychiatric Hospital at UCSF Medical Center. His days at that school ended right there.

RED DOG MOST HIGH

"Wow," commented Dad as we headed back to the car in front of Langley Porter Psychiatric Hospital. "I was feeling pretty bad about putting Tim in there, but man, as soon as we did, I realized he fit right in." Dad seemed to be feeling a strange mix. He was a little relieved that we'd found an appropriate choice of action, but he also seemed sort of depressed as he began to come to terms with the fact that Tim's condition wasn't going away.

After an evening at Langley Porter, Tim heard the staff say they decided to move him to Mt. Zion Medical Center.

He couldn't help but notice the Biblical name Mt. Zion and assumed he was being sent there for some lofty spiritual reason.

They strapped him in a wheelchair by the waist, wrists, and ankles. "God's throne has wheels," he thought to himself, vaguely aware of a biblical reference about such things.

Instead of feeling humiliated, he felt honored and great. A man wheeled him up a ramp into a white van and locked the wheelchair in place. As they drove across town, Tim conversed with the driver.

"Where are you taking me?"

The driver responded matter-of-factly. "Well, where did they tell you?"

"Mt. Zion."

"Well, there you go."

While strapped in a wheelchair, being taken from one hospital to another, Tim believed he was the Son of God, on his throne, carried in honor to the biblical Mt. Zion.

He may have been lost in a delusion, but that didn't mean he wasn't skilled or clever. During the drive, Tim focused on the straps around his hands, noticing the way they were tied. For several minutes, he worked with his fingers, puzzling through the restraints until they restrained him no more. Once his hands were free, he got his ankles unstrapped and released the belt keeping him in the wheelchair. He suddenly appeared up front in the passenger seat, surprising the driver.

"What the hell?" exclaimed the driver, muttering a number of other expletives as well. He pulled the van over and strapped Tim back in the "crazy" chair, where he remained.

At Mt. Zion, a psychiatric nurse asked Tim if he was hearing voices.

"Just yours," he replied. Tim wasn't ready to share his actual thoughts.

After three days, they transported him to The McCauley Institute at Saint Mary's Medical Center. I saw him there soon after he arrived.

"I've been sent here to free these captive patients from their enslavement," he said, with a quirky seriousness.

Once again, I felt I was looking at Tim across a divide. Even when I touched him, I felt the distance between us.

As the days passed, he began connecting with some of the other patients. Bruce, who became one of his friends while he was there, walked into the day room calling out: "Five-five-five, one-two-one-two, can you tell me what to do?"

555-1212 was the standard telephone number for out-of-area directory assistance. Tim, having already worked out his own original system of numerology, interpreted meaning in the number.

"Red Dog, calling Red Dog," Bruce called out to no one in particular. The words "Red," and "Dog," had symbolic meaning to Tim as well.

Tim answered deliberately, and with authority:

"Five—five—five—one two—one two, I can tell you what to do."

Bruce approached Tim. "What's your name?"

"I am Red Dog Most High," responded Tim.

Trembling, Bruce took Tim's hand in both of his, while energetically whooping and yelping. Bruce believed in Tim, and Tim became like a little cult leader with one follower.

Tim also made friends with Adam, a young man who was missing several of his fingers. Given Tim's hand injury, I suspected that Tim might have in some way identified with him.

Tim and Adam stood face-to-face, their noses just inches apart, loudly chanting simultaneously. Adam chanted song lyrics or poetry about being "faster than the grave," while Tim passionately recited the Lord's Prayer.

Deciding that Tim was too unpredictable, the staff put him in what they called the Quiet Room. This was a locked room with a bed—a place intended for isolation. Patients were sometimes locked in the Quiet Room to cool down when they became agitated or violent.

Locked in the Quiet Room, and still believing himself to be Christ, he thought, "This must be like the tomb Jesus was put into, and like him, I must rise again." Stepping back to get a running start, he crashed against the locked door. Then he did it again. And again, repeatedly hurling his whole weight to break out of his tomb. Before he succeeded, six staff members opened the door, rushed in, and tied him to the bed, wrapping him up with his arms at his sides so he couldn't move. They left him there and locked the door again.

When they finally let him out into the day room, he began the self-appointed job of straightening up the place. He sorted the books, organized disheveled piles of art paper and craft supplies, and straightened out the chairs and tables. One of the staff encouraged him: "If you could get out of here because of good behavior, you'd be on track. Unfortunately, that's not how it works."

Tim leaned against the nurse's station, elbows on the counter, gazing at one of the nurses. "How come you're so sexy?" he asked.

She stared at him, blank-faced.

In this stage of Tim's illness, he seemed free from self-consciousness, but he had no sense of what was socially appropriate.

She blew smoke from her cigarette and went back to work. Yes, smoking was allowed in the ward. Patients could ask for free cigarettes, and they would be given up to three a day.

Remarkably, Tim enjoyed his stay at The McCauley Institute. But enjoyment would not bring healing. Like a happy drunk, Tim was high on his delusions, having a good time, but always at the expense of those around him.

Our friend Steve joined me for a visit to the ward one

Sunday afternoon. Tim had a big smile on his face as he approached Steve and hugged him. "Steve, I'm getting happy."

"Don't get happy, get better," responded Steve.

The doctors at McCauley diagnosed Tim with Chronic Undifferentiated Schizophrenia.

By the time they released him, stabilized again on medication, he had been there for forty days. The number of days had no particular significance, but Tim was excited, attributing meaning to it, since many biblical stories reference a period of forty days.

Once back home, his self-identification as Christ gradually faded. What was odd was that he never noticed. As the medication took effect, I expected him to say something like, "Wait, I'm not Christ. What was I thinking?" But that didn't happen. He couldn't tell the difference between schizophrenic thoughts and normal thoughts until years into his recovery. That inability to discern whether thoughts might be sane or not became a point of connection for Tim and me. He would sometimes tell me what he was thinking, then ask me if it sounded crazy. I learned to answer him straightforwardly as well as I could.

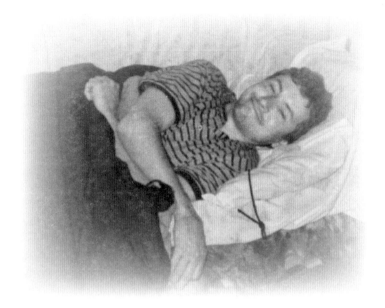

CHAPTER SEVEN
1986 – 1988

---

*"You must learn to be strong in the dark
as well as in the day,
else you will always be only half brave."*

"To try to be brave is to be brave."

~ George MacDonald

BACK IN THE SWING

At home, Tim turned out to be too much for Mom. Even on medication, his odd behavior was too draining for Mom to cope with effectively.

Dad and our brother Doug had plans to rebuild our aunt's house in Kansas. Doug traveled there independently, so when Dad left, he took Tim with him and made a road trip out of it. The two of them traveled through Southern California, then across the Southwest. They stopped at Palomar Observatory in the mountains east of San Diego—a favorite of Tim's when he was a kid, and part of what inspired him to get into astronomy. They traveled through the desert to Carlsbad Caverns, revisiting another of Tim's childhood memories. They took the three-hour walking tour to the bottom, seven hundred feet below the desert floor. Dad was patient and kind despite all the stress Tim put him through over the preceding year. Now that he understood that Tim was mentally ill, he treated him as someone to help, and he didn't seem nearly as frustrated.

Tim enjoyed revisiting the southwest. The desert was beautiful, and it brought back familiar feelings of a happy childhood. Sadly, his medication made him drowsy, and he missed many of the views.

Finally arriving in Lawrence, Kansas, Tim took up residence in Doug's vintage camping trailer in the driveway of our aunt's house now under reconstruction.

He stayed in Kansas from spring until mid-summer, helping Dad and Doug as they worked on the house. Although, he may not have been much help—frequently sneaking off to lie down in some corner, hoping no one would notice. He stayed on his medication, but it made him sleepy, and while Doug and Dad tried to keep him busy with construction cleanup,

Tim found it torturous. Most of the time he just wanted to lie down. To make matters worse, after being tired all day, he was often unable to sleep at night.

The three of them went to church on Sundays, where Tim enjoyed making new friends. He also became good friends with the next-door neighbor's two cats—especially the calico, Tiger. On warm summer nights, Dad and Tim sat on the front porch swing—the same place Tim sat when he was small, visiting our aunt on family vacations from San Diego.

On one such night, Tim found Dad in the porch swing crying—very uncommon for our dad.

"Hey Dad, what's wrong?"

"Oh, I miss your mom."

"Me too."

"And I guess it's more than that. This house brings back a lot of memories. I sat right here on this porch looking at this same street when I was a kid."

Tim sat on the swing next to Dad. Dad put his arm around him. For the next twenty minutes, the only sound was the soft rhythmic creaking of the chains where they swung from eye-bolts in the porch ceiling.

On such occasions, when they were quiet, Tim began to feel a longing to be normal. He thought about what it would be like to have a real job. He imagined being employed somewhere, feeling respected and doing work that actually accomplished something—contributing to other people.

SWALLOWING DARKNESS

Tim held the phone to his ear, hoping his friend back in San Francisco would answer. After four rings, he began to wonder if he'd missed him. Then he heard his friend's voice.

"Hey Tim, how's it going?"

"Hi! It's going well! I'm doing great, how's it going with you?"

They talked for a while, both of them sounding upbeat and positive. When the call ended, Tim looked out the window, enjoying the moment.

Dad walked in from the adjoining room, paint on his clothes and tools in his hands. "Tim, I heard you say you're doing great. You are not doing great."

Tim didn't know exactly what to say. He looked at the floor, his body tightening. The brief moment of freedom was supplanted by a sudden crushing feeling. He stood there, head down, Dad's declaration echoing in his head.

Tim tried to survive on a combination of positivity and denial. He would muster his energy and try to make himself look and sound upbeat to counter the stigma of mental illness. Dad's comment made it difficult. Dad may have come off as cruel in that moment, but he was probably trying to help Tim stay grounded in what was real. He probably hadn't known what else to say.

In Tim's mind, the thing to do was to quit taking his medication to prove to Dad and everyone else that he was doing well.

One simple fact demonstrated itself repeatedly: When Tim took his medication consistently, his life became more ordered, and his relationships more enjoyable. Somehow this simple fact eluded him. He continued to feel a self-stigma when on the meds, no matter how much they helped. "If I can just show everyone that I'm alright when I'm not medicated, they'll understand," he thought to himself.

He made plans to fly back to San Francisco to live with Mom and return to school—this time City College of San

Francisco. He registered to enroll in a business program. Dad spoke with Mom about it. She was doubtful, as was Dad, but Tim was headstrong and insistent. Against her better judgment, Mom said he could return home and live with her.

He arrived back home very unsettled. He hadn't had his meds in several days. The first apparent symptom was insomnia.

Insomnia is hard on anyone, but for Tim, a schizophrenic off his meds, it was torture—bizarre, disconnected thoughts chaotically ricocheting through a broken mind—the opposite of rest.

He would buy food, then not be able to eat. The insomnia and the fear of more insomnia paralyzed him.

Mom called Dad. "Honey, I don't know what to do with Tim. He's not sleeping, and I'm just so afraid he's slipping backward again."

"Well, I guess I'm not surprised. I'm sorry to leave him with you like that. I'll see about coming home right away."

Dad stopped his work and hit the road. He drove the two thousand miles to San Francisco to pick up Tim and drove him all the way back to Kansas.

As they drove through the desert vistas, so beloved in his youth, they seemed empty now. Tim saw only desolation accompanied by feelings of dread.

Dad found a room at a small-town motel. That night, Tim lay awake trying unsuccessfully to stop the fear. In his mind, God came near him, trying to free him from the clutches of evil. He then heard a voice talking back to God.

"F*ck you—you're the devil."

In the absence of anyone else, Tim assumed the voice was his own.

"I'm sorry," he mumbled from his bed.

The voice continued to argue with God until the sense

of God's presence disappeared, leaving him with the slander-ous voice, which then told him something very clear: "If you kill yourself now, you will go to hell alone. But if you delay, you'll drag your loved ones with you."

A dark agony overwhelmed him. He saw himself as a sort of "ball and chain" dragging his loved ones down. Through all the horrible experiences, he'd always had someone around who showed him love. Now he couldn't allow that. He had to end his life before it was too late. He saw himself as a danger; he figured he'd already sealed his eternal damnation, but he still held out hope for those he loved.

Tim lay in a crumpled wad of anguish as Dad slept soundly a few feet away.

Finally, the light of day returned through the window. They loaded up and got back on the road. In Tim's mind, he kept seeing an image of a fuse, burning shorter and shorter.

Despite Tim's attempts to conceal his feelings, Dad was well aware that Tim was struggling hard. As they traveled the highway at seventy miles per hour, Tim considered jumping from the car. He tried to figure out whether it would do the trick, whether jumping out would be enough to kill him. Dad was able to perceive what was happening and tried to be vigilant, but neither said anything about it.

It was dark when they arrived at the house in Kansas. Tiger, the cat from next door, came to greet Tim. Tim felt a deep gladness at seeing his furry little friend, but he was also still struggling with fear. Tiger sensed something amiss and withdrew. Tim felt relieved. For no apparent reason, he was afraid he would somehow harm the cat.

They unpacked in the house.

"I'm going to take a bath," Tim mentioned to Dad.

"Okay, buddy."

A few minutes later Tim filled the tub with water and tried to drown himself. It surprised him how difficult it was. He thought he needed to die, but his survival instincts were still working. He was unable to make it happen.

Dad's question through the door was straightforward. "Tim, are you trying to drown yourself?"

Tim's exhausted voice responded. "Yes."

For the most part, Tim had a compliant nature, and he stopped when Dad told him to.

The following morning Dad, Doug, and Tim ate a simple breakfast together and got to work on the house. Dad asked Tim to measure and mark lumber which they would later cut. When he finished, he found Dad and Doug talking. He stood around the corner, listening.

"I don't know," said Dad. "I think if we can just get him working—get a routine going, it'll do him good."

"That's impossible," Doug replied. "He can't do it. He's too preoccupied."

"Well, what do you suggest?"

"He needs to be hospitalized."

"Maybe so, but they won't just admit someone based on our suspicion."

As Tim listened, he spied a rectangular can of paint remover on the floor near where they were standing.

"If I can get that and gulp it down quickly enough, I can end it right here." he thought. But he knew he couldn't pull it off with the two of them standing right there. The fact that they were standing where they were may have saved Tim's life in that moment.

The voices of Dad and Doug faded into the background as Tim stood there pondering how he might kill himself. Then, another part of his mind stepped in, wanting help. "I'm so miserable," he thought.

He stepped into the room. "I think you should take me to the mental hospital."

He didn't really want to go, but in his delusion, he reasoned that he might at least isolate the evil to the hospital alone. After some discussion, Dad and Doug drove him to Kansas State Hospital in Topeka.

THE LOST SHEEP

"You seem terrified," said the doctor during his initial interview with Tim.

Dad made sure Tim was back on the medication before leaving California, but the doctor told Dad it wasn't working, which, by this time, had become obvious.

They admitted Tim that day, and he checked into the ward in Rappaport Hall. That August evening, in the main room in front of the nurse's station, he tried to choke himself to death with his bare hands.

The doctor tried another psych medication. It was the same one they tried after his hand surgery, and they got the same result. Tim's muscles contracted against his will, and fear consumed him. They gave him a shot to suppress the reaction, drove him to a medical hospital for tests, and eventually, they found a more effective medication.

After a few days, a doctor at the facility had a conversation with Dad. "I believe Tim needs to be hospitalized for psychiatric help long term,"

"Well, I guess I'm not terribly surprised to hear you say that," responded Dad.

"He'll need to appear before a judge to have him committed involuntarily."

"Oh?"

"Yes. And unfortunately, he'll then be taken to the hospital in a police car. And he'll be handcuffed."

"Handcuffed?"

"I know it's probably not necessary, but it's required in situations like this."

"Oh boy. I don't like the sound of this at all. I'm afraid he'll go berserk if they handcuff him."

"I'm not sure what to say. That's how it's done."

Dad thought seriously for a while. The sheriff was an old high school classmate from long ago. Dad looked him up and paid him a visit. He explained Tim's situation. They had a good conversation and by the time Dad left the sheriff's office, he had been deputized and allowed to drive Tim to the hospital after seeing the judge.

The judge was a kind woman with a gentle demeanor. "Tim, tell me about your recent suicide attempts."

"I can promise not to do it again. I'm trying to live, but I..." He faltered, not sure how to continue. "My family doesn't understand that I'm trying to protect them. I'm endangering them. I might need to die so they can live."

The judge asked Tim several other questions, which he answered as best he could. In the end, her decision was clear.

"Tim, you seem like a fine young man to me. It's important that you receive the care you need. With that in mind, you'll be committed to Topeka State Psychiatric Hospital until the medical staff there decide you should be released."

After the hearing, Dad drove him back and left him in their care. It was the beginning of August.

Unlike his stay at the McAuley Institute back in San Francisco, this hospital stay was not fun. They didn't let him into his dorm room to lie down until ten o'clock at night, then they burst in and roused him at six o'clock every morning. He and his roommates slept on plastic-covered mattresses which made enough noise to wake him up whenever they turned over or shifted during the night. Aside from the noise, he often dreaded going to sleep because of the nightmares he would experience.

From Tim's perspective, his life was destroyed beyond recognition. Even tears would have been sweet, but he felt only deadness and anxiety inside. He described that time as "Blandness blended into bitterness—dry dust and gray ashes in an empty room."

"I feel like a candle that has been snuffed out," he told a nurse.

"That's a good word picture for depression," she replied.

He still believed in God, but he had lost all faith and hope. He felt a new kind of loneliness. He was surrounded by other patients, and while they shared mental illness in common, it didn't make for an atmosphere of good fellowship.

Dad drove out to see him every other day, but with each visit came a deeper realization that Tim was still exhibiting crazy thinking and now dropping into depression as well.

Tim turned twenty-four in Rappaport Hall. He remained at the Topeka State Hospital for four months. His earlier diagnosis of Chronic Undifferentiated Schizophrenia was affirmed, and another diagnosis was added: Passive Dependent Personality Disorder. The additional diagnosis put a name to Tim's frequent inability to make decisions on his own without clear approval and encouragement from those around him.

He thought about how just three years earlier he was standing on top of the Golden Gate Bridge celebrating his twenty-first birthday with Rich. Three short years ago he had never felt more alive. Now here he was, locked up and put away with the other crazies, unfit for mainstream society.

Dad's visits continued. Sometimes he would just sit with his arm around his lost son, sharing the depression, saying nothing for whole stretches of the afternoon. He stopped trying to figure out what should be done and instead chose to simply offer his presence.

Dad listened as Tim mumbled something barely audible, loosely quoting a verse from the Bible. "The good shepherd leaves the ninety-nine sheep and goes looking for the one who is lost." [4]

"That's right buddy."

"Dad, I'm still me. I'm still in here."

Dad felt his emotions lodge in his throat, barely managing to gently choke out a response. "I know buddy. I know."

Dad Has a God Moment

Tim sat in one of the vinyl-covered chairs in the main room at Kansas State Hospital waiting for Dad. He expected Dad to come by and sit with him as he had done for the previous several days. The visits were good in a basic sense— better than being alone. But as much as he tried to help, Dad's own despondence often left Tim feeling discouraged. Until today.

Dad walked in with a spring in his step, sporting the face of someone truly enjoying life. "How's my dear son today?" he asked, arms outstretched for a warm embrace.

"Okay, I think."

"Good. That's great, Tim."

---

[4] LUKE 15:4 OR MATTHEW 18:12 (PARAPHRASED)

Dad was different. They sat together near a window, Tim looking out at the world as he listened.

"Something happened, son. It's like God touched me. I can't explain it, but I feel new confidence in you."

"In me?"

"I know you'll recover."

Tim let out a long exhale. "Really?"

"I don't know the details, or how long it will take, but I just know that at some point, you'll be free of this."

It had been a long time since Tim had seen Dad looking hopeful. It felt good.

"Dad, I don't believe it, but if you do, maybe it's true."

Back in California, Mom was also experiencing a new sense of hope. Like Dad, she felt an inexplicable faith begin to take hold. She had always been one who prayed, and in this instance, she began to feel heard.

Prayer is an interesting thing. In one sense, it's like doing nothing—talking to the air hoping someone's listening—effecting an emotional catharsis, perhaps. But in another sense, it seems productive; it gets results that seem otherwise impossible. What her prayers may or may not have accomplished, I can't say, but I knew Mom and her newfound hope was definitely connected to her prayers.

Tim was encouraged by Dad's new hopeful demeanor, and he began to feel somewhat hopeful himself.

On the psych ward at McCauley in San Francisco, Tim got over his belief that he was God. During the months at Topeka State Hospital, he got over his horrible fear that he would harm his family and drag them into hell. The insanity slowly dissipated once he got stabilized with proper medication, but he still had a long road ahead.

✧ ✧ ✧

FACING THE MUSIC

The morning sun shone in through the hospital windows as Tim sat in one of the familiar vinyl-covered chairs.

"Tim, I have your medication ready." The nurse on duty smiled and spoke kindly.

He got up and walked across the room. "Thank you," he said, actually feeling some gratitude. It's amazing what a kind tone can do in an otherwise dismal environment.

He sat down again, staring at the pills as they lay there in the palm of his hand. The nurse was still watching. Usually, he hated this, but for some reason, he didn't mind this time. Her eyes on him felt different than usual. Not only was this nurse kind, but she reminded him a little of Mom. She didn't look like Mom, but there was something in the way she watched him, as if she were supporting him in his choice to take the pills. It reminded him of the way Mom had supported him when she made him take that awful-tasting pinworm medicine when he was a kid.

"That horrible medicine Mom made me take when I was a kid," thought Tim, "It tasted terrible, but it was a good thing. It got rid of the pinworms. Schizophrenia is definitely worse than pinworms. Maybe these pills are a good thing."

He swallowed the meds, and as he did so, a new experience presented itself. He found that he looked forward to the effects of the drugs. He considered genuinely, for the first time, that having the medication might make his life better.

After taking the pills, the nurse smiled and asked if she could get him anything else.

"No thanks," he answered. And as he did, he felt something new—a greater connection—a sense of good fellowship with the nurse as they cooperated with each other. This was his first glimpse into recovery on a social and relational level.

Right there on an otherwise average day, the stigma began to be displaced by hope.

Tim was released from Kansas State Hospital and into Dad's custody in late November. He took Tim to the house he and Doug had been working on for so long. Tim was impressed with the work they had accomplished, but in spite of his improvement, he was afraid to allow himself to feel any joy in it. He felt hope, but he didn't trust it yet.

By this time, he had no illusions or stubborn pride telling him he was not mentally ill. He was ready to try anything to live again. And with that new attitude, real recovery began.

It was snowing when Dad and Tim pulled out of the driveway to begin the trip home to California.

SHAME AND CLARITY

Tim had been back with Mom in San Francisco for two days. I'd seen him the day before, but I dropped by again just to check in. After talking with Mom for a while, I sat in the living room in solitude. Tim came in, red-eyed and somber.

"Dave, do you remember that guy I told you about on the BART train that I offended?"

"Um…"

"It was several years ago. He was talking to me about his relationship struggles and I told him he was 'all twisted up inside.'"

"Hmm…maybe. Was it the guy who was part of a Catholic order?"

"Yeah, that guy. I've been thinking about him today. I wish I knew how to find him."

"Why?"

"I keep thinking about him, and other people, too. I can't

believe how rude I was. I verbally abused a guy who'd done nothing but share a friendly conversation. I wish I could go back and tell him I'm sorry."

"You're feeling ashamed."

"Yeah."

We sat in silence for a while.

"Tim, you don't have to feel guilty for being sick."

"But that guy didn't know I was sick. I didn't even know I was sick. I was so judgmental. I really hurt people."

"Yeah, what can I say? That's true. But listen to yourself right now. You're doing well."

"I still feel bad."

"I think that's good. Feeling bad might be part of healing. I don't think you should feel bad long term, but if it leads you to change and grow, that's probably good."

"I'm still afraid most of the time, but my thoughts are clearer."

"That's for sure. Right now, you seem completely normal, guilty feelings and all."

After another long pause, Tim spoke up again. "I think I'm starting to understand the medication."

"How do you mean?"

"The meds stabilize me. That stability provides opportunities for growth."

"Yes, exactly."

"I guess I understood that already, but it's not just that. Improvement isn't automatic; the meds don't make me any wiser and they don't improve my abilities."

"Ooh, that's well said. That makes huge sense."

"And they don't alter my circumstances. I still have to figure out how to make a life for myself."

"Wow, Tim, I suppose that should all be obvious, but it

strikes me as super insightful. Can you put all that together into one statement?"

"I think so. Give me a second." Tim sat quietly for a few moments before he spoke.

"The meds stabilize me, but they don't make me wise, they don't improve my abilities, and they don't alter my circumstances. I still have to choose to grow and to make a life for myself."

I grabbed a pen to write down what he was saying. "That may be the best way I've ever heard that put. It's so clear."

"Yeah, it's getting clearer. It feels good to be back here with Mom. I don't feel much hope, but I don't feel terror either."

That summer Tim went to work for Carlos, a friend of the family who owned a cleaning and painting business called Casa Limpia. Finally, he had a real job.

Carrying on with life required him to navigate around his distracting thoughts. Most days at work, his mind raced with a host of loosely connected thoughts and voices. Sometimes it was as simple as a commercial jingle getting stuck in his head, but constantly changing into new words. Other times he found his thoughts ricocheting between God's voice comforting him, and then God telling him he was becoming the anti-Christ. He now knew it wasn't God he was hearing, and he knew he could reject the voice—but it still tormented him. He tried his best, but he could only do a relatively small amount of work before he would become exhausted, mostly due to his racing mind, not the job itself.

Carlos was always gracious.

"Carlos, are you making any money off my work?"

"Well… I'm breaking even," responded Carlos with a chuckle in his voice. He understood that he might be helping

Tim more than Tim was helping him.

"I'm grateful," said Tim. "I want to work—to help."

That Sunday Tim listened as Dad spoke at church about a passage in the book of Matthew. In the text, judgmental religious leaders asked Jesus why he spent so much time with the outcasts of society.

"It is the sick that need a doctor," replied Jesus.

Of course, those religious leaders were just as "sick" as anyone else, but they weren't ready to receive help.

It hit Tim like a ray of light breaking into a dark room. I saw him later that day.

"Dave, I'm starting to get it. I don't have to stress about the help I need. It's okay to relax and receive it. I need help and that's okay." I feel hope inside—like a little sprout—like I'm back in real life again."

Tim's recovery still had a long journey ahead, but it was happening. He had embarked on the journey.

NED'S RANCH

Dad and Tim crossed the Golden Gate Bridge and cruised along the highway all the way up to Mendocino County. Tim bought a six-pack of iced tea for the three-hour drive and drank all six cans by the time they arrived at Ned and Jean's ranch where they planned on staying for a couple of days. My dad had known these people for many years.

The ranch was great, as were Dad's friends. Ned had a kind face with a contagious smile. Jean was observant, thoughtful, and hospitable. They gave Tim a bed out on the wood deck for the night, which suited him fine; he loved sleeping outdoors.

But Tim got no sleep that night, despite medication for

that purpose. In the morning, he was quietly distraught.

"Tim, my friend, how did you sleep? Did you enjoy the night out on the deck?" Ned's friendly way made Tim feel better, but he was disturbed by his lack of sleep.

"I like the deck, but I didn't sleep well at all."

"Oh, I'm sorry to hear that," responded Ned. "We'll see if we can help you fare better tonight." He turned his attention to Dad.

"So, Jim, how was the drive up here? Everything go smoothly?"

Dad laughed. "Well, Tim put away six large cans of iced tea on the drive up. I couldn't believe how much he drank!" Dad was just making conversation.

"That's a lot of caffeine," said Ned, looking at Tim knowingly.

"Oh, man, maybe that's it!" declared Tim. "I never even thought about that."

Ned's wife, Jean, went over to sit with Tim who had placed himself on the other side of the room.

"What are you hearing in your mind?" She asked him matter-of-factly.

Something about Jean made Tim feel safe speaking openly about what the voices were saying. He liked these people.

"Not much right now," he replied, "I was just thinking about how silly it was to drink all that caffeine and then complain about not sleeping."

"Oh, you weren't complaining," said Jean. "It's all good."

Privately, Jean told Dad she wanted Tim to stay. This was why they were there—to see if their ranch might be a good home for Tim.

Dad drove back to San Francisco.

Tim settled into life on a horse ranch.

Ned found Tim sitting on the deck. "Hey Tim, let's go for a little hike together."

"Sounds great."

Ned gave a loud whistle, and Shawna, a German Shepherd, appeared, eager to join them.

They walked by Ned's pond—three acres of beautiful water situated between pine forest and open meadows. They both stood on the earthen dam overlooking the pond on one side and meadows with horses on the other.

Ned took off his hat, looked out over the water, and said, quietly, but boldly, "Thank you Lord for Tim being here with us these few days—"

Few days? Tim gulped, beginning to give into a sinking feeling—but Ned continued...

"Weeks..."

"Months..."

"Years..."

When he said the word "years," Tim's heart gave an internal jump for joy. He felt something he hadn't felt in a long time: safe.

Tim went on many early morning hikes with Ned, usually accompanied by Shawna, and sometimes by Mustard, a yellow-orange cat that Tim also enjoyed. Ned would share encouraging wise thoughts with Tim. His kind acceptance and willingness to instruct and guide changed the trajectory of Tim's life. Ned became his mentor, and even though Tim already had a father, Ned was another one—of a sort that Tim needed.

After a month of joy, dark thoughts returned, and Tim once again found himself troubled by voices that left him feeling condemned.

Ned and Jean's daughter Nancy lived next door. Tim

liked her and was impressed with her deep and sincere faith. He found the courage to tell Nancy about the voices and about his feelings of terror that sometimes felt like they would take over.

Her compassion and cheerful laughter diffused the dark feelings. He had started to think of drowning himself in the pond, but Nancy's kindness erased that from his mind.

"Nancy, I know it's only been a few weeks, but I think I'm getting better."

Nancy smiled. "Of course you are." She paused, thinking. "You know, it may very well take ten years to really recover."

"Ten years?" he groaned. That idea was hard to take.

"Nancy, what's it like to be normal?"

"It's peaceful."

He was delighted to be able to talk with people who weren't frightened when he revealed his thoughts.

He still had a great deal of fear around a few specific things, one of which was the idea of the devil or evil spirits. He cringed whenever the devil came up in a conversation. Over the years, Tim knew people who tried to be helpful by telling him that spirits don't exist. This never helped, as he had lived with waking nightmares for years and felt plagued by a terrifying darkness.

Ned and Jean took him to visit a friend of theirs, an older man named Jack.

Jack seemed like an average sort of guy. He sold insurance, drove a decent car, and came across as humble and unassuming. He also happened to be known for his spiritual wisdom. He had helped a number of people experience healing from deep personal wounds.

Jack was easy to talk with. Something about him brought an inexplicable comfort to Tim.

"Can you help heal my schizophrenia?"

"Oh, I don't think so. I don't know much about schizophrenia or mental illness. What I do know about is spiritual freedom, and therefore something about spiritual oppression as well. Part of what you're experiencing may well be spiritual in nature, aside from whatever illness. I can help with that part."

"That sounds great."

His session with Jack involved some deep personal conversation and a few very pointed questions. Then Jack directed Tim through a series of specific prayers. In less than an hour, the results were obvious. After a second session a few days later, Tim's fear of devils and demons was gone. Much of his recovery and healing was still ahead of him, but that one specific area of fear never returned. Tim enjoyed the sense of peace and relief that Jack facilitated.

Part of Tim's recovery involved simplicity: learning to be consciously present with ordinary aspects of life. Helping around the ranch provided ample opportunities for such things.

Ned, Jean, and their daughter Nancy demonstrated wisdom and showed tremendous patience and care for him during those ten months at the ranch. A few months into the stay there, he was calling them "Dad" and "Mom" and sometimes referred to Nancy as his older sister.

Ned was an example of a man who valued true joy. Our dad had exemplified vision, hard work, and commitment, but often at the cost of joy. Tim benefited hugely from Ned's joyful outlook. Tim loved the people, the animals, and the land itself. It was a context and a routine he came to deeply enjoy.

Each time I saw Tim at the ranch, he seemed a little more at peace. On one visit, we sat out by Ned's beautiful pond. The sun shone through the pines, reflecting off the water in front of us.

"Dave, I feel like I won the lottery, but it's better—it's the lottery of the things money can't buy. I've never met a more honest and positive-minded person than Ned."

Tim spoke thoughtfully, "It feels like the lights are coming on. It's gradual and incremental, but I can relax. I feel hopeful."

"That's so great, Tim. It shows. You seem to be absorbing the healthy atmosphere of this place."

"I was thinking about my time in the hospital."

"In Kansas?"

"No, before that, with my hand."

"Oh." I paused, remembering. "What have you been thinking?"

"You saved my life that day, as surely as Dr. Schecter and his team did. If they had left me with just a stump and a prosthetic device, I would have been too discouraged to try to recover. You insisted they do the surgery."

We sat in silence for a few moments.

"Thanks for saying that. I appreciate it."

"And you know what?" Tim's tone quickened slightly. "As much as I hated living in the city, the truth is, it saved my life too."

"Seriously? I can't believe you're saying that about the city."

"If I had done what I did somewhere else, like if we lived in Pleasant Hill, they probably wouldn't have had that world-class team of surgeons or that unique funding they had ready at S.F. General."

I let out a big sigh. "Man, you're probably right. That's a good point."

"I hope saving my life means more than just keeping me alive. I want to be able to contribute. I feel like I'm headed in a good direction. I hope so."

"Man, it sure seems like it."

"I hope someday I can have a real career. I'd like to have a trade, and maybe even my own business."

"Way to think! That's so cool to hear. You may have to be patient, but those are great things to work toward for sure."

"This place is so great," Tim replied. "Today's a good day. It's confusing, though, sometimes," he continued. "I might be feeling like this, then the next day it's like the lights are fading again. I know nothing has changed except my feelings. How can I know I'll be okay even when I can't feel it?"

"Well, for the moment, I think you should just enjoy this place. Keep listening to Ned, Jean, and Nancy. Their influence seems like good medicine."

I looked up into the sky,
the brightest stars still visible
in the early dawn.

✧ ✧ ✧

PART THREE

RECOVERY WITH NO CURE

The sun was not yet up, but the birds in the cemetery were now wide awake, filling the Kansas prairie with their jubilant declaration of a coming new day.

Memories continued to float through my mind. I thought about the unexpected twist in our lives, how Tim gained stability right when my own life seemed to unravel. I recalled how he encouraged me when I lost all sense of future; how hard he worked to gain solid footing in life, and how inspiring that was. Mostly, I found myself thinking about how far he had come from where he started. He had camped for a while at the gates of Hell and lived to tell the tale.

My brother's journey was heroic, an odyssey fraught with mines and riddles triggered by his broken thoughts. It's one thing for a person to do well throughout their life, but it's another to wipe out in the ditch of mental illness and then make a comeback, especially when there's no real cure. Tim navigated the illness, learning as well as he could, falling and getting up again repeatedly—improvising his way through recovery.

The journey had been difficult, weird, and embarrassing, but a sense of purpose marked our path, teaching us to grow through the heartache, transforming it into something else.

I looked up. The stars had all but vanished as the night yielded to the arrival of daylight.

CHAPTER EIGHT
1988 – 1998

---

*"The medication stabilized me,
but it didn't make me wise, improve my
abilities, or alter my circumstances.
I still had to choose to grow and
to make a life for myself."*

~ *Tim Robinson*

TIME TO GO TO WORK

After a good long stay at Ned's ranch, when the time seemed right, Tim moved back in with Mom and Dad in San Francisco. Beth was now away at college. Life was simple. They let him sleep in every morning until he was fully rested. This was a big deal for our dad, who always valued rising early and accomplishing tasks in the morning. I felt proud of my dad for that simple grace he showed Tim. It left me feeling like Dad was growing and learning too.

Mom and Dad were on the lookout for something Tim could do—a job that would be stress-free enough for his recovery, and also something that would be a real contribution in some way. Mom had an idea.

The three of them sat at the table over breakfast. Mom reached across the corner of the table toward Dad, who reached out and took her hand in his. They both looked at Tim. "Tim," said Mom, "I think you're doing well enough to take on a simple job. I know you haven't driven a car much lately, but for the most part, you're a pretty good driver."

"Except for that time on Highway Five when you were driving with your foot," interjected Dad with a smirk.

"Oh Honey, let it go," responded Mom, squeezing his hand.

Mom hadn't driven for years, due to a condition that caused her to experience many tiny stroke-like events, sometimes involving momentary lapses of consciousness. She still had a driver's license, but never used it as she didn't feel it was safe.

"How would you feel about being my chauffeur? I could get a lot more done with my days if I had someone to drive me from place to place."

Tim's face lit up. "Yeah, great. I can do that."

Tim's new job as Mom's driver was a simple life, which was perfect. He didn't need to plan anything or make decisions about where they would be going. He just started up the car and followed Mom's directions. Routines like this helped him face a difficult recovery without feeling over-whelmed by people's expectations. He enjoyed being Mom's driver; it was a way he could truly contribute, and still main-tain a fairly stress-free level of responsibility.

Driving became a favorite pastime. He not only worked for Mom, but he also acquired his first car, an old Honda with a standard transmission. He loved the car, and it provided him with additional freedom. Tim drove that old Honda on many visits to Ned's Ranch which gave him a sense of continuity as he transitioned from life on the ranch to life in the city again.

Mom went along on one of those trips to the ranch. "Tim, I notice you're speeding a bit. I'd like you to observe the limit."

Tim made the rest of the three-hour drive at exactly the speed limit. This turned out to be important, as he generally had trouble maintaining consistent discipline. He discovered that observing the speed limit provided something to focus on that left him feeling successful.

After they came home, I visited Tim one day. He shared with me how he was doing.

"Dave, life is good, but it's hard."

"I agree, on both counts."

"I'm so glad I got to live with Ned. I love what he said about anxiety and doubt: 'Life is ten percent what happens to us, and ninety percent how we respond to it.' That leaves a lot of room. I'm learning to make room in that ninety percent to choose a good attitude, and not to feel victimized by what-ever is happening."

Those words from Ned, along with many others, became part of what sustained Tim. He also attended a group for people with mental struggles called Recovery International. The group offered recovery methods that Tim found very helpful. In the group, he discovered the writings of Dr. Abraham Low who wrote the book, *Mental Health through Will Training.*

"The group is great," he said, and told me about the mental tools he'd picked up from the group—tools for dealing with anxiety, like: "feelings are not facts, they are merely present or absent." Or another good one: "When I experience a string of fearful thoughts, I can simply acknowledge that my imagination is wildly active."

"So, I've got another job idea for you."

"Two jobs? I don't know…" said Tim, with a big smile. It was obvious he was interested.

"How would you feel about working at The Clayhouse part-time?"

Tim had enjoyed ceramics classes in high school and at San Francisco State. His face lit up.

I had been learning the art of mold-making, something I'd talked with Tim about before and knew he was intrigued with it.

"I think you and I would make a good design team. I have sculpting skills and you've got good ideas."

Tim held out his hand to shake on it. "Let's do it!"

"Alright!"

We shook hands. As we did, I could feel the stiffness of his wrist, which no longer rotated, but his grip was strong, and I could feel the warm life in the hand I was shaking.

My visit was cut short when Mom entered the room.

"Are you ready to go?" she asked Tim.

"Yup!" He jumped up and the two of them headed for the door: Mom and her new chauffeur.

Tim's work at the The Clayhouse gave him a healthy, productive routine in which he flourished. That flourishing happened slowly at first, but it happened. I also financed some counseling sessions for Tim with a therapist named Bob who had been helpful to me.

Tim walked into the shop with a big smile on his face. "Hey Dave, according to this, I should become a Land Surveyor."

"Really? According to what, exactly?"

"Bob gave me a career aptitude test. The results say I could be a Land Surveyor."

"A Land Surveyor. That's interesting."

"When we were kids back in Pleasant Hill, my friend's dad was a surveyor. He was a Survey Party Chief, which always impressed me."

"Well… I'm not sure what to say. That's a good trade, for sure. You've always liked math, which couldn't hurt."

"Yeah, that's exactly what I want to do. I would love that," he said, as he got his work area set up. He tried to attend to his work in the shop that day, but he was distracted by this new idea.

He continued driving for Mom and also working in the shop with me. In his off hours, he took remedial algebra, geometry, and trigonometry at City College, and with that math foundation, he went on to take surveying classes. For the first time in his life, Tim had a career goal. He later passed the California Land Surveyor-In-Training test.

Tim's surveying professor spoke to him in earnest after class. "Tim, there's a good program at Fresno State you should look into."

"Fresno State?"

"Yes. I can see you're serious about surveying, and they've got what you need. I've got a pretty extensive brochure here.

Take this and read through it."

The next day Tim brought the brochure to the shop with him. "Dave, look at this. My professor thinks I should go to Fresno State."

We stopped and both looked over the brochure.

"Man," said Tim. "The students in these pictures look so grown-up and sophisticated." He felt nervous after so many years outside of mainstream culture and had trouble seeing himself as a real adult. He felt intimidated, but he also felt interested.

"I'm going to pursue this," he said. And when he said it, something inside him shifted. Standing in our shop that day, we both somehow knew this decision was real.

THE CLAY SHOP BECOMES A FACTORY

"Dave, you need an investor to take this thing to the next level." Ron spoke with a smile and a look of keen interest. Ron was a clean-cut, business-oriented, mainstream kind of guy. He also had money, which made his comment sound like more than mere small talk.

"Why? You interested?"

"Maybe."

Ron was an acquaintance I'd met through some mutual friends. He stopped by The Clayhouse that day to ask if I wanted to join him for lunch. I gave him a tour of the small shop and then we went to a local diner. His comment about an investor kept echoing in my head.

"So, you might be interested in investing in my little company?"

"I don't know, but it looks like you've got more work than that little shop can handle. Am I right?"

"It often feels like that. Sometimes I make my wholesale customers wait longer than they expect. I can't always get their items fired in time. My two kilns are the bottleneck of course. It doesn't matter how much stuff I make if I can't fit it all in the kilns. I've got room for one more but they're pretty expensive."

Ron and I talked regularly after that, and three weeks after our lunch at the diner, my shop sported a third kiln, greatly expediting production.

"Thanks, Ron," I said as we stood in the shop one day. All three kilns were full of ceramic ware waiting to go out the door. "This is amazingly helpful."

Ron's response surprised me. "Let's get together Thursday morning and go look at warehouses. We need to find a place that's a lot bigger than this."

I stood silently for a bit. "Seriously?"

"It can't hurt to have a look, right? You need to be making as many items as you can sell. Am I right?"

"I don't know. Maybe you're right."

That night I talked with Kate about what Ron had said. "Wouldn't it be great to move the business to a big facility? We could finally make this thing grow."

She looked sober. "I don't know. It's a great idea, but I'd wait till you've outgrown the shop you're in before taking on the expenses of a big place."

"Well, I think we may have outgrown it already."

"I don't know. It seems a bit rushed."

"Or maybe it's an opportunity to take advantage of. I think we should go for it."

Slowly, Kate got on board, but I was caught up in the moment, not fully considering her doubts.

Over the next few months, Ron's investment moved us

from the little eight-hundred-square-foot storefront to a five-thousand-square-foot warehouse equipped with four kilns, one of which was enormous, and all manner of equipment made to fit the size and scope of the new shop.

We hired several workers, so instead of making things out of clay, I now found myself teaching others how to do what I had done.

Tim flourished in the new environment. I even experimented with leaving him in charge for short spells. The future looked bright.

Late one afternoon after everyone had gone for the day, I stood alone under the skylight in the eighteen-foot ceiling admiring the new place. It was a great set up and I deeply enjoyed creating a productive system out of all the new equipment. I had turned off the lights, so the late afternoon sun in the skylight filled the space where I stood.

"A lot of changes at once," I thought. I would now be running a much bigger business and managing more employees. But that wasn't all. My family was also making big changes. My sister Beth had recently married and was settling into her new home about five hundred miles away. Mom and Dad, along with Doug and his growing family, were in the process of moving to Kansas. Dad had an idea about building a retreat center there. The only family left in the area would be Tim and me, working together in this new place.

"I hope I can do this," I muttered under my breath. That night I took Kate to dinner to celebrate the growth in the business.

"Well, Sweetie, the new shop is awesome. I think the business is going somewhere. Pretty exciting huh?"

"That's great, Honey. I'm super excited for you."

"Thanks. And I'm excited for both of us. With Ron's

investment, we may stand to really make some money."

"We'll see. I've got my job at the hospital, so I'm covered if it doesn't work out."

Kate had a good job at a local hospital. She found the clay shop to be financially unreliable. She thought of it as a high-risk experiment.

Several months later, walking into the The Clayhouse office, I sat at the desk and answered the phone. My dad's voice sounded energetic on the other end.

"Hey buddy, can I come out there and be your employee for a week?"

"My employee? I'm not sure. What do you mean?"

"I'd just like to come out and work for you for free. You could just treat me like another member of the crew. I think it would be fun."

We talked for several minutes, and I ended up inviting him to come join the team for a week. He'd never offered anything remotely like that before, and I wasn't sure what to make of it.

Tim was ecstatic. "Dad's gonna work here with us? That's so cool!"

A few days later, Dad and I sat in my office talking about the business.

"Well, buddy, you've come a long way since starting out in that little storefront. What was that, about fourteen years ago?"

"Yeah, that's just about right."

He sat looking at the floor awhile, then made another comment.

"Dave, it looks like Tim is doing well here."

"Yeah, it's been difficult at times, but totally worth it. He's capable of pretty much running the place at this point, except for connecting with customers. But as for the shop itself, he can do everything."

"You've done well too, Dave. You've grown a lot as a person."

This sort of personal affirmation from Dad was new. Deep inside, I felt a mysterious tension relax just slightly.

"And you're not the only one," he continued, soberly. "I've learned a lot myself."

"Yeah?"

He just nodded, looking at the floor again.

The week with my dad was enlightening. He worked hard alongside the others in my shop. The morale that week was positive—even fun. I had never seen this side of him before. By the end of the week, I began to suspect that his presence and his work were simply an expression of love.

✧ ✧ ✧

A TASTE OF YOUR OWN MEDICINE

Tim mustered some courage and spoke plainly. "Adam, here's the deal: You take your meds, and we can be friends. But if you don't take them, I can't do it."

He hated talking that way, but that's what he needed to say, and what Adam needed to hear.

Tim met Adam during his first hospital stay at the McCauley Institute. They liked each other and both wanted to remain friends after their release. Adam was tall and dark-featured. He had a number of scars and homemade tattoos, and the four fingers on his right hand were mostly missing.

"Brother Tim, if you insist on taking your drugs and remaining crazy, then I will be patient and allow you to be my friend."

"Adam, that didn't make any sense. My meds are helping

me live normally. Yours do the same thing, and you need to take them if we're going to hang out together."

"Doctor-induced insanity; that's what you have, brother." Tim just stood there feeling stressed. "I can't do this."

"No, not until you embrace the freedom from drugs."

"I like you Adam, but I need to be alone for a while. Can you leave now?"

"I'm off to see the wizard!" said Adam, and he headed for the door.

Just a week before that, Adam had come over to Tim's place and shared a simple meal. Tim had made "spaghetti" with ramen noodles and a can of tomato sauce. He was amazed at how grateful Adam had been. He ate it as if it had been a true meal, expressing sincere thanks. That's when Adam was on his meds. Now he was off them again and acting crazy.

Tim called me on the phone. "Dave, can you come over for a while?"

I was just about ten minutes away and arrived at his apartment soon after he called. The place had been our brother Doug's apartment before he moved his family to Kansas with Mom and Dad. Doug had a good relationship with the landlady, and kept it in his name so Tim could have a place.

"Man, I get it now," he commented. "It's weird to be on the other side of the medication thing. I'm getting a sense of how I acted and what it was like for everyone else."

"Well Tim, I'm glad you get the opportunity to see what it's like. And, at the same time, I'm sorry you have to experience it. It's alright to let Adam go until he's able to be consistent with his own medication."

"I was hoping to have another meal with Adam like we did last week. I liked being the one who has something to offer."

"I haven't eaten yet, what's on the menu?"

"Well, I just have a big pot of soup I was going to share."

"Sounds good."

"Dave, I'm grateful to all the people who have helped me, but someday I'd like to be the one who picks up the tab at restaurants."

We sat near the bay window overlooking Seventh Avenue near Irving Street.

"Dave, this is not…"

I could see tears welling in his eyes as he looked at the table.

"Not home?"

"Yeah, this isn't home. I'm glad to have it, but I never wanted to live in the city. Now here I am alone in this apartment. I miss Pleasant Hill."

"I know. Hang in there. This is not forever. In fact, it's probably not even for very long."

"Yeah, I think you're right. Working at the The Clayhouse every day is super helpful. At least I've got that."

"Yes, you have that. That job isn't going anywhere."

Tim chuckled. "Not going anywhere? Why am I working in a job that's not going anywhere?"

I caught the double meaning and we both laughed.

Little did I know those words would become prophetic.

BALLOONS AND BUFFOONS

"Uh… What's this?" I asked, walking into the shop. I had arrived earlier than usual and was met with a huge, caramel-colored, rubbery blob, spread out over the shop floor. Reminiscent of an air mattress, but much bigger, this thing was fully fifteen feet across. Tim was there with Alan, a friend and also one of my employees.

CHAPTER EIGHT: 1988 - 1998

"Oh," said Alan, looking startled and a bit sheepish. "We didn't expect you so early."

Tim and Alan were attempting to inflate a giant weather balloon Tim had recently acquired. They thought it would be funny to see everyone else arrive for work with a huge portion of the room taken up by a super giant balloon. They hadn't accounted for me showing up early, nor had they realized how much air it takes to inflate such a thing.

The previous day, my partner Ron and I had spent a while talking about the level of professionalism in the shop. "I love how our workers love their jobs," I had told Ron. "The morale in the place is usually quite high."

"That's great, Dave, as long as they don't have so much fun they forget to work."

I stood there over the slowly growing amorphous object. "Ron will be coming by sometime soon," I told them. "He won't enjoy this. And I'm not sure I do either. I get that this could be fun, but at the moment, it's way out of bounds."

"No problem," they both responded. "We'll get this out of here before the others arrive."

The following day, about mid-morning, sitting at my desk, I was startled by Charles, barging into the office, looking very frustrated.

"Dave, I can't get any work done. Your brother is driving me crazy. I try to mind my own business, but Tim is bouncing that big balloon around the room, laughing constantly. It's unprofessional and... just weird."

I was pretty occupied and hadn't noticed, but as Charles spoke, especially with the door now open, I could hear Tim's high-energy laughter.

"He's playing with a balloon?"

"It's that big weather balloon thing he bought."

As it turned out, Tim had purchased more than one old weather balloon the previous week. I had already encountered the biggest one.

On this particular morning, he had arrived at work with the smaller of the two giant tools-turned-toys. He made use of our shop's air compressor and inflated the balloon until it was an impressive six-foot diameter, mustard colored, rubber sphere.

Walking out into the shop, it was exactly as Charles described. Tim was moving around the shop, keeping the giant balloon aloft, bouncing it with a series of upward fist-bumps, and each time, laughing as if he'd never seen such a thing before.

Diego, one of our coworkers, was also distracted by Tim's balloon bouncing. Primarily a Spanish speaker, Diego had been learning English in our shop and was putting together a sentence, which he then said, slowly, word by word.

"Tim – did – you – have – your – medicine – today?"

"See?" said Charles. "I wasn't going to say anything, but dang, man, this is ridiculous."

"Dave, isn't this awesome?" shouted Tim. "I've always wanted one of these!"

I didn't want to ruin his fun, but I was also trying to run a business. "Tim, can you settle that thing down somewhere, and visit me in the office?"

Tim and I talked awhile about the nature of a workplace, and how, without realizing it, he'd been making it hard for the others. He was more than eager to please, and said he'd deflate the balloon and get to work.

A little while later, I was out in the shop preparing to light the main kiln. The platform under the firing chamber was about five feet wide and seven feet long, with sixteen gas burners that produced flames about two feet tall each. For some reason, it was being stubborn. I got down on the floor, extending one arm under the firing platform with a long lighter we sometimes used in such moments. Normally, we'd turn the gas down low, light one of the sixteen burners, and then turn it up as necessary. Today it wouldn't light. I raised the level of gas flow. Still no luck. I raised it more. And more. Finally, with far more gas flow than usual, all sixteen burners suddenly ignited. "Foom!" A deafening concussion of heat burst out across the room. I shot away from the kiln, still on the floor, feeling the heat slam against me. I turned to see Charles in midair, legs out in front of him, then falling, landing on his butt on the concrete floor. Simultaneously, Tim, Alan, and Diego yelled out random monosyllabic sounds of surprise.

The kiln sat there firing nicely as if nothing had happened.

"Whoa!" said Charles, getting up off the floor.

"Good going, Dave," said Tim

"No offense, Dave," said Charles, now more perturbed than before, "but you're a buffoon. What are you trying to do, kill us all? What kind of people do I work with?"

"Buffoon. Balloon," said Tim calmly from across the room.

Charles looked at Tim, incredulous—a quizzical expression forming on his face.

Tim's odd comment was like comedic medicine.

"Who needs schizophrenia," said Tim. "We're already a bunch of buffoons."

Diego burst into laughter.

Charles stood there shaking his head trying to keep it serious, but failed as his own stifled laughter betrayed him.

GRADUATING INTO COLLEGE

Tim and I worked quietly but steadily, sitting on opposite sides of the sculpture, our four hands in the clay. The work was nearly finished.

Tim frowned thoughtfully. "I think the whole thing needs to be about an inch longer."

"It's practically done," I said, a little annoyed. "How are we supposed to just make it an inch longer?"

"Just cut it in half, and add clay to the middle," answered Tim, matter-of-factly.

I stared at the shape, turning it around a few times on the table. I got up and stepped back a few feet. "Hmmm, maybe you're right."

I could always count on Tim when sculpting new designs. I would produce the basic idea in clay, and he would invariably see some way to improve it.

Our finished piece that day was a dinosaur—a triceratops about sixteen inches long from nose to tail. It was followed soon after by a brontosaurus and a T-Rex.

We made molds of the three sculptures and set up the shop to produce them, hopefully by the hundreds. During this process, the movie Jurassic Park came out in theaters, propelling dinosaurs into the consciousness of moviegoers everywhere.

That summer was a sweet success. We made the dinosaurs into coin banks which was apparently a good idea, as nearly six thousand of our ceramic beasts shipped out across the country. For Tim and me, the experience of conceiving of the project and seeing it through fulfilled a huge piece of what we always hoped for from our little factory. That summer came and went, but it left a nice echo of success.

As great as that summer had been, its echo was insufficient to sustain the business. Something was causing our sales to drop and the cash flow had become inconsistent. Even items that sold well for years no longer moved. We lost some people but trudged ahead with a crew of six.

Kate watched with concern as I leaned into creative ways to keep the business going. She became less interested and put more of her energy into other more independent activities.

Despite occasional minor setbacks, Tim had been doing extremely well over the previous months, with consistent commitment to his work and even showing leadership from time to time as I left him in charge of the shop.

"Dave, we need to talk," said Tim, late one afternoon as the others were finishing for the day.

We sat down in a comfortable area of the shop just outside the office—the closest thing we had to a lunchroom. Tim's face expressed both seriousness and excitement.

"I think it's time for me to leave. I've been looking into the surveying program at Fresno State. I'm gonna go for it."

My mind divided, heading in two directions at once. I felt resistance, wanting him to stay and continue running the shop with me. At the same time, some part of me knew he was right—that this job had run its course and he needed to pursue what would be next.

I let out a long slow sigh. "Well, maybe you're right."

"I think so," he responded.

"And maybe you're wrong," I added hastily. "This place needs you."

"I'm glad for that," said Tim, with real gratitude in his voice.

We sat awhile in silence, looking around the shop. The air compressor kicked on, filling the room with its pulsating rumble. When it stopped, the shop seemed extra quiet.

The conflicted, divided feeling increased within me. For years, I had committed myself to this very end—to help Tim make the leap to appropriate independence—to help him finish the growing up process that had been so severely truncated. I knew this was it, but I had grown accustomed to his work in the shop. Without realizing it, I had begun to assume I'd have his presence and his work as I made plans for the business. This moment represented a big loss, even though it was also a victory.

"Why would such a good thing hurt?" I asked.

"Dave, I gotta be straight with you. I'll miss this place, but I'm ready. I'm not hurting. I'm pretty excited."

"I know. I get it. I can see it."

"Remember when I was all excited about going to Mars?"

"Yes," I laughed.

"This isn't like that. It's Fresno State University, not Mars. I think I've set my sights at the right level. And it's land surveying; I could get a real career out of this."

"Yes, you could. And I believe you will."

"I love working here. Every day here has been fun for me. But I gotta say, the pay has been pretty inconsistent lately."

"That's true. I'm not sure how long we're gonna survive, business-wise. It's been awfully slow lately. Your timing might be smart."

"Dave, if I'm ever going to get married, I need a career that pays well. What are the chances this job will take me there?"

"I see your point. The way things are going, this job may take both of us backward."

We spent the next ten minutes shutting down the shop for the night.

A few weeks later, I was once again shutting everything

down for the night, this time alone. I sat down again in the same place where Tim and I had talked a few weeks earlier. I felt alone, but I also felt a familiar presence.

"Please don't let it fall apart for him in Fresno," I prayed. "He deserves to have this work out."

Those seven years at The Clayhouse proved to be a perfect context to allow Tim to heal and grow. Sometimes in the middle of a workday, he needed to drop what he was doing, go out to his little Honda Civic, and take a nap. He couldn't handle stress and he couldn't have done the job during that stage of his recovery if he'd had a demanding or harsh boss who didn't understand his needs at the time.

Tim's words echoed in my head: "Every day here has been fun for me." In a job with almost no stress, he got to see his creative work sell, which gave him huge encouragement.

It also meant a lot to Tim to have marketable abilities. Ceramic mold-makers may not be in high demand, but he had acquired a bona fide skill, which transformed the way he saw himself.

Tim said his experience of that job felt like a caterpillar in a chrysalis, transforming him from an unskilled laborer with awkward social skills into a competent shop foreman. This would be his fourth attempt at college. He had integrated well with others, and was ready to take the next step.

MY EMPTY MISTRESS

Despite Ron's investment and moving to the new shop, the expenses of my business climbed higher than its income, which frightened Kate. It frightened me too, but we each reacted differently. She wanted me to reconsider the business and maybe even call it quits. Instead, I dove deeper into my work. The resulting conflict cost us dearly. She seemed less invested in our marriage than she had been. I claimed to be invested, but my behavior sometimes said otherwise. The business took most of my attention.

"It feels like the The Clayhouse is your mistress," said Kate one morning as we prepared some breakfast.

I didn't understand her comment, but it got my attention. "My mistress?"

"Yeah. Your shop is my competition. I can never quite tell whether I have all of you, or if I have to share you with your mistress—your clay shop." She spoke matter-of-factly, but I sensed a lot of feeling under the surface.

Instead of receiving the opportunity to connect with her, I ran to my own rescue, proving her point as I did so.

I spoke emphatically. "The Clayhouse is not my mistress." I knew in my heart those were the wrong words and the wrong attitude, but I felt an inexplicable need to defend myself.

Looking back, it's easy to see she was right. The thought of losing Kate was terrible. I could hardly allow myself to think about it. But somewhere in my subconscious mind, the thought of losing the shop threatened me in ways I didn't understand.

Deep in my psyche, I felt the shop was the only thing that defined me as an actual grown-up. I carried a deep fear that if I lost it, I would no longer know who I was or what my life was about. These were not conscious thoughts, but like most fears, they guided my choices.

Over the next couple of months, the tension between us solidified. Kate seemed to want out, and she started living as if she was single again.

One morning she was getting ready to go to work. She

spoke in a casual tone mixed with sternness as she walked out the door. "I can't live with poverty and uncertainty."

When I realized she might actually leave, I threw all my efforts into saving our marriage, but it was too late. One Saturday morning, a moving truck backed up in front of our house and two men began loading up her stuff.

I drove to my shop, of course. My mistress. My comforter. The one who was always there no matter what. I pretended to work, but I was distracting myself with the familiarity the shop offered my five senses. She would never surprise me and never give herself to another. She would always open for me when she felt the touch of my key in the door.

Arriving back home, I was unprepared for the emptiness. It was almost its own sort of presence—dismal, flat, and dull. I had to keep telling myself to exhale.

Most of our stuff was gone. My favorite chair sat in the corner of the room surrounded by nothing.

Bobo stood looking at me with a questioning face.

"Well, you're still here," I said to the dog.

She made a throaty sound, looked out the window, then back at me.

"I don't know," I said. "I think you'll see her again, but I can't promise. I guess it's just you and me now, Bose."

The echoes hit me hard the first night: the constant expectation of Kate's voice, now replaced by this emptiness. I missed her terribly. I felt like something left in the back of the fridge too long—like I got so far past my "use by" date that I needed to be discarded.

I lived with Bobo and the emptiness for a month. Then I came home to a note from Kate. She had come by and taken Bobo with her.

The emptiness expanded.

She visited again, many months later, this time with divorce papers. After we talked, I watched as she walked away toward her new life. All I had now was my unprofitable shop, to which I devoted myself like a foolish lover.

CASCADE OF LOSS

"Hang on for a second, Drew, I need to answer the other line."

"No worries, Dave, we can hang up. I don't need anything this month anyway."

Drew hung up and I paused for a moment before answering the other line. The sales I was expecting were not coming through. My wholesale customers seemed to be satisfied that they had sufficient stock of my designs.

"Why aren't they selling anymore?" I asked myself as I picked up the other phone line.

Tim's voice sounded happy. "Hey Dave, how's it going?"

"Well, okay, I guess. Business is slow, and it feels like my life is falling apart. I'm just trying to keep going."

"I'm sorry, Dave. I know it's been hard lately. I hope it gets better. You should come visit me here sometime. It's great, and I'm meeting some very cool people. And wait until you hear this: I climbed Royal Arches in Yosemite with Rich."

"Dang, man, that's a big one. How much of a climb are we talking about?"

"It's a fifteen-hundred-foot cliff. We went all the way up. I didn't know if my hand could do it—you know, I don't have the fingers I used to. I can't spread them, but I can grip pretty well. Anyway, we did it."

I never expected Tim to climb with Rich again. After recovering from the reattachment, he regained about sixty percent usage of his hand. That was considered quite good, but the thought of him climbing a cliff in Yosemite surprised me. "Congratulations, man, that's amazing. I confess, I'm pretty surprised."

"It was so great. I'm glad my hand was up for it." He paused for a few moments. "Dave, can you come visit me here? A lot of things have changed and I wanna stay connected."

"Well, yeah. I'm not sure when, but let's make that happen."

It felt good to know he was taking care of himself, and that he was happy down in Fresno. Our call was interrupted by the other line ringing.

"I'm gonna take this call, Tim. I'll catch you later." It was after hours, but I picked it up anyway.

"Clayhouse – Dave here."

"Dave, this is Drew again."

"Oh, hey Drew. Did you change your mind? I'd love to pack up a shipment for you."

"No, but I wanted to ask you about something. I keep seeing your items in much larger stores. If you keep doing that, you'll push us little guys out. I like you, but this is bugging me, and I just wanted to say something."

"I've sold to a couple of large stores, but nothing in your area."

Drew proceeded to name the places where he'd seen my items for sale. None of them were my customers. Mystified, I told Drew I'd investigate and get back to him.

The next morning, I got the crew going for the day, then took myself on a field trip to one of the large companies Drew had mentioned. Sure enough, there on the shelves sat nearly all my designs, copied exactly, and made in China. For a few moments, I forgot to breathe. I just stood there in the aisle of the store—a store I used to like—its nefarious nature now revealed.

Letting out a slow sigh, I felt my body tighten and my skin flush, anger surfacing. The presence of these items on the shelf explained a lot about my recent drop in business.

After several long conversations with a couple of lawyers, it became obvious that I'd been wronged, but I couldn't afford to do much. Most of the damage was already done and the main problem was occurring in China. I was also nearly out of money.

Ron had already stepped away from the business, no longer seeing it as lucrative.

The fear of losing my shop became vividly conscious. I had to lay off all but two of my employees. I made sacrificial deals with some of my wholesale customers—deals that brought only short-term cash flow. Word got out that the shop was going under, causing other businesses to investigate what I had that they might want.

My obsession with keeping the business afloat blinded me. By the time it was over, the shop that had been my mistress was violated in a feeding frenzy over my equipment.

The emptiness expanded again.

I woke in the night to chest pain followed by abdominal pain; then again the next night; and the next. Swallowing was painful; I couldn't get some foods to go down at all, and acid reflux kept me awake at night.

I eventually dragged myself to the hospital.

"Have you been under any stress?" asked the doctor after he examined me.

"I guess. Yeah."

"We'll see if we can get you fixed up," he said calmly.

Among other things, the fix involved heart medication and a week in the hospital. My stomach was misbehaving, and the condition of my esophagus was alarming, requiring immediate surgery so I could eat normally again.

I recovered at a friend's house where I tried to discern what my life was about now. I had lost my Kate. I lost my shop, a place of hard work, but also a place of joy and camaraderie. I lost my equipment and my tools. I lost my home. I lost my work truck—my only vehicle at the time. I lost all my money; I couldn't even afford bankruptcy. And not only was I broke, but I also owed money to people who were still lined up to get it.

———————

Using a friend's phone, I called Tim to check in. "Hey Tim, how's it going?"

"Hey, Dave. It's just great. It's going great. I can't believe it. School's going well, and the people down here are my kind of people. I love it here."

"Man, I'm glad to hear that. I'm glad you're finding a community of people. That's awesome."

"How are things on your end?"

"Well, I don't know. At this point, all my goals are pretty short term, like where am I going to stay next."

"Hey, I know what—you could move down here."

"Uh… I'm not sure…"

"Never mind. Sorry, Dave, I don't know what I'm saying. I don't have anywhere for you down here."

"That's fine. Somehow, I'll be alright. You focus on your studies, and I'll come visit before too long."

"Sounds good. Just let me know when."

That phone call was very ordinary—no big news, no breakthrough—nothing all that memorable. But I hung up knowing he was alright. For the first time, I was in a position where I couldn't offer Tim much help. And for the first time, he was in a position where he didn't need it. This was not lost on me. I was extremely grateful that he was doing well and had caring people around him. Now I just had to find a path for myself.

"Thank you," I said to Maria as she passed a large paper cup of coffee across the counter. She had no idea what was happening with me in that moment. I felt like that cup was my last meal. I had exactly thirty-two cents in my pocket after paying for it. I mumbled to myself as I walked out onto the street. "No cash, no credit card, no bank account, and nothing left to sell."

Out in the Irving Street evening, I saw Sherry sitting in her usual spot next to the ATM machines. She brushed her black hair as she watched people walk by. For someone who lived on the street, Sherry surprised me. Every morning, she swept the entire block of the south side of Irving between Eighth and Ninth Avenues. She slept in the doorway of Progress Hardware across the street. They're the ones who gave her the broom.

I slowly walked over to a fire hydrant and sat down, using it as a stool. Scanning the area, I took a sip and looked into the darkness. It wasn't the darkness of the night, but the darkness of my own future. I recalled my mom's words from ten years earlier: "I'm not accustomed to hopelessness," she'd said through sobs.

I wasn't accustomed to it either, but I was getting there. I felt like the bare bones of my former self. The skeleton of my being was still there, but not much else. I didn't know what I looked like anymore. All the things that defined me—husband, artist, business owner—all of it was gone. I was like the smoke after a fire's been put out: empty, vacuous, and without purpose. I sat there until I took the final sip of now-cold coffee.

I sensed a subtle but strong presence in the darkness. With it came a strange mix of confrontation and comfort. I didn't hear any words, but I felt the message. "You can despair, or you can move forward."

"Into what? Darkness?"

"Yes, even into darkness."

The streets of that neighborhood became very familiar as I spent the next six months foraging for ways to move forward and clues as to what that might mean. A few generous friends offered their couches from time to time, so I often had a warm place to sleep, but not always.

HAIGHT-ASHBURY

Andrew smiled down at me from his six-foot, six-inch stature. I usually felt tall, but not when I was around him. His face was confident. "Dave, we want you to move in and join us in the house we're setting up in the Haight."

I looked at Debbie who stood with him. Her whole face smiled, framed by her full red hair. She knew what this meant to me. It had been a while since I had a place I could call home and the idea hooked me.

I hadn't known either of them very long, but they had become good friends who knew my circumstances and still believed in me. They were setting up a household in the Haight-Ashbury district that would involve community living with a focus on helping young people who lived on the street.

"That would be awesome, but I'm still scraping together money to pay off debts. I wouldn't be able to pay the rent." I figured my lack of finances would cause them to count me out.

"We know that," they both said at the same time. "We want to cover your rent."

"Um…" I thought about it for a second, making sure I'd heard them right. "Seriously?"

"Yes. We think you'll be a real asset. We want you with us."

"No rent?" I still couldn't believe what I was hearing. Part of me nearly burst into tears. I had acquired some serious doubts about myself, and the respect they showed me moved me deeply.

Andrew had given me a car a couple of months before that—an old AMC Rambler from the mid-sixties. I liked that car, not only because I had some transportation, but also because it gave me hope; Andrew thought I was worth investing in. I was homeless at the time and had filled the trunk of that car with items of value. That trunk became my treasure box. And now he was offering me a place to live as well.

I moved in and fully participated in the life of the house. I experienced being valued, not for what I possessed or for what I could do, but simply for who I was at the core. My outer life was broken, but the more I allowed people to see my inner life, the more I could feel my value. That experience was a game-changer for me, altering my perspective on life forever. It changed the way I saw others who were also in various states of brokenness.

After one fascinating year, Andrew and Debbie needed to move, and the rest of us went our separate ways. I moved to another house in the city with a few friends where I continued to explore how to live based on who I was, and how to let my life choices flow from that.

NOW LOOK WHO'S STABLE

Down in Fresno, Tim was taking in new experiences. We spoke on the phone often. After a brief stay in an apartment, he moved into what he called "the Guys' House." It was a home shared with four other students, not far from the campus. The guys were about ten years younger than Tim, but they happily welcomed him, even after hearing about his history.

Sometimes I took the four-hour train ride to his place and helped him with various projects. I built him some bookshelves, a desk, and other wood furnishings. He showed me Fresno and introduced me to his new circle of friends.

Tim was a decade behind in his personal and professional development, and the hospitality offered by his housemates encouraged him tremendously. He felt more of a sense of home at the Guys' House than he had felt in years. His housemate Trevor became a close friend and would remain so for life. He was welcomed and included in a network of friends who genuinely enjoyed him.

Tim drove an old Chevrolet Biscayne at the time, a fairly large car made to seat six people. One night after watching a movie at home with his housemates and other friends, they talked him into driving to Dave's Donuts. They called this "Club Midnight," telling Tim it was one of the house rules: "You can only go to Dave's Donuts after midnight." They arrived, and like a clown car at the circus, ten people got out of Tim's car. Such experiences may seem frivolous, but to Tim, it meant he was included in ways he never had been, which mattered a great deal.

He breathed easily when he realized he could rent a room in a house with friends and support himself, even on minimum wage if it came to that. Meanwhile, he knew if he could get a surveying job in the Central Valley, he might also be able to afford his own home.

He set up a potter's wheel and a small kiln at the house, continuing his creative work in clay. This activity fit right in. They hosted Art Nights at the house—something Tim very much enjoyed. Other students and friends would bring their creative expressions to share in a supportive atmosphere. He flourished around all the creativity and found himself socially integrating into a community for the first time since the onset of his illness.

Tim flourished in the surveying program, getting good grades and earning the respect of peers and professors alike. The program offered summer employment for all students who applied. In his interview with Pacific Gas and Electric, they asked Tim, "Why should we hire you?"

"Because I'm bright and chipper, and worth my wages," he answered.

I guess that was the right answer. They offered him the job, and he worked on a field crew throughout the summer. It felt great to get some actual surveying work. And for the first time in his life, he made decent money, which also felt great.

That summer, as they worked in a grassy field, the aroma of tarweed took Tim back to childhood memories of playing in the field in Spring Valley as a little boy. That wonderful smell filled his mind with old visions of golden wild oat grass, the buzz of a hundred cicadas, and lizards scurrying over dusty brown trails. Those feelings from a happy childhood brought joy to the work as he measured and surveyed the land.

The utility company rehired him the next summer as well. His work took him from Lassen County in the North to the Mojave Desert in the South. He learned to set up and operate a total station as well as an optical level, and he began to put into practice concepts he'd learned in school. He enjoyed the stable income, and for the first time, he was delighted to be the one who picked up the tab at restaurants.

CLEARING THE AIR AND THE TABLE

During the early years of Tim's healing, he sometimes experienced episodes of inner rage toward our parents. He described it as coming out of nowhere and the feelings terrified him. He feared that if he gave in to them, he might attack our parents. I wasn't sure what he meant by "give in to them," but I listened and helped him process his thoughts and feelings on more than one occasion. He never expressed them outwardly and he didn't know why he would feel such strong negative emotions.

In general, and despite all the difficulty, Tim usually felt close to Mom and Dad, but the angry emotions affected his interactions with them. After four or five strong episodes over a period of two years, he found himself at their kitchen table one evening while visiting them in Kansas and decided to open up about his anger. They were gracious and receptive, and they listened carefully.

As he talked, he made a discovery. "I've begun to realize how deeply I was wounded by our family's move to San Francisco all those years ago."

They both sat quietly, allowing him to gather his thoughts. "I was just about to get into high school where Doug and Dave went. Then suddenly we uproot, leave all that beautiful land, and move to the cold city."

He looked up and began to realize that Mom and Dad were both still listening without any sign of getting up, changing the subject, or rushing the conversation. That in itself was a huge gift and reflected the wisdom they'd learned from their journey. Mom's hair was white now, and Dad's was gray and thin. Time was doing its work.

"All the adults in my life seemed to think the move was the right thing to do, and Dad kept saying it was God's will, which scared me; I didn't want to go against God." Tim stopped and thought for a minute. "It was like Dad got all excited about an investment, but over time it turned out to be a bad investment and we lost everything."

"Investment?" asked Dad.

"It's a metaphor," snapped Tim, showing some anger. "When we moved, it's like you had blinders on. Nothing could have swayed you. I was feeling terrible about the exact thing you were so excited about. What was I supposed to do? I stuffed it all inside and went crazy."

Dad looked thoughtful. "Tim, are you saying the schizo-phrenia came because of our move?"

Tim looked exasperated. "Dad," he clenched his teeth, then stopped and let out a sigh. "No, of course not, but how was I supposed to handle that inner pain as a kid? The schizo-phrenia happened right after that, and no one knew what was happening to me. I'm not saying you were wrong; I'm saying I was hurt, and you were too busy to notice."

Real tears formed in Dad's eyes. "I'm sorry Tim." His voice was open and truthful. Mom looked surprisingly calm—even peaceful.

"I know," responded Tim. They all just stared at each other for a few moments, then Tim spoke up again. "I'm actually feeling pretty good suddenly."

They sat awhile in silence, which was helpful to Tim. He could see they were open to more listening.

"Dad, I get that you were in a lot of pain yourself when

we ended up moving back to Pleasant Hill."

"Yes," said Dad, "I felt like part of me had been cut off. It was awful."

When Dad said the words "cut off," they all glanced at Tim's right hand, kind of a symbol of how life can be broken and how our family was broken.

After sharing a few more comments, they got up and cleared the table together. At one point, Dad gave Tim a hug. "I love you son."

"I love you too Dad."

Since the conversation that evening, Tim's anger at our parents has never returned. I believe the reason has something to do with Tim feeling heard and having his perspective honored.

A lot of families experience tremendous loss. A lot of children feel anger they cannot adequately express. A lot of fathers and mothers make what they believe to be wise decisions and still disappoint their kids. A lot of people in the world experience emotional pain. A family such as ours, moving from the country to the city, is not abnormal; many families do that. These things have nothing to do with mental illness.

Or do they?

I have watched my brother's life from its beginning. The schizophrenia may have shown up regardless of the parenting he received or the life circumstances of our family. Nevertheless, I see a basic truth: the healthier the relationships, the better equipped to handle mental illness when it emerges. If a family, or any community of people, faces the hard work of keeping their communication open, honest, and frequent, then when a member experiences mental illness, the difficult communication required will come easier.

Tim's survival is not mere happenstance. It is the result of enormous commitment from a good number of people who decided they would listen to him and stay with him when it cost them something to do so.

CHAPTER NINE
1999 – 2009

The secret of life, though, is to fall seven times
and to get up eight times."

~ Paulo Coelho, The Alchemist

HAPPY GRADUATION

Tim's laugh got the whole crowd laughing as he opened our friend Corey's gift on the back patio at the Guys' House. "Wow! A potato canon! I've always wanted one of these!"

"That's an important instrument you'll need in your land surveying arsenal," commented Tim's housemate Trevor.

"Definitely!" responded Tim with that big smile.

Something about Tim suddenly caught my attention. There was a quality about him that sparked an old forgotten feeling, something I thought was lost long ago. Here was the happy kid I remembered from childhood. His childlike joy had returned. Everyone at the party was caught up in it. To varying degrees, they all knew something of his dark journey. That awareness added to the occasion, like the stories one hears about an injured person who wasn't supposed to walk again yet ends up running a marathon.

I moved to an open area behind everyone to take in the moment, because some reservoir of emotion would not let me join the laughter. I was happy, but I was also releasing a weight I had carried for years—a weight so attached to me that my own story had developed underneath it. And now it was coming off—or at least beginning to. I went into the house, trying to hold myself together as I found a bathroom and locked myself inside.

The tears flowed as I realized what was happening. "Tim just graduated from college with an engineering degree!" I exclaimed to no one. But it wasn't no one. The old presence was like a nurse that day, untying the knots that held this burden in place, gently pulling it off. I stayed there for a while breathing in a new layer of freedom.

I returned to the party and gave Tim a huge hug. He responded energetically and then hollered out, "Okay, let's fire up this potato canon!"

Trevor and Corey were ready with proper ammo, and the festivities went from happy to hilarious as potatoes left their messy marks on the back fence about twenty yards away.

Mom and Dad must also have felt some of their burdens lighten that day. Their affection was open and generous. Beth came with other family and friends. Beth and Tim had become very close and shared a relationship of trust that would have seemed impossible at one time. Ned and Jean made the journey from their ranch, along with their daughter Nancy and her husband Scott. Doug's family couldn't make it, but they sent their joy from afar. Tim's people gathered to celebrate his path of obvious healing, smacking down the darkness with their joy.

Late in the day, as the celebration became calm, Tim and I sat and talked.

"Dave, remember when I decided to move to Fresno and start this program?"

"Of course. Yes."

"I have to say, that one moment of decision—choosing to move and enroll here—I accomplished more in that moment than all the work following through with these four years of college. Deciding to go turned out to be harder than earning the degree itself."

We sat there in familiar silence.

"Are you going to accept the Belmont offer?" I asked.

"Yeah. I like those guys. They're down-to-earth. I've had four offers, and I've had a lot of doubts, but I'm going for that one. It's the closest to where we grew up. For some reason, I like that."

Tim would continue to experience doubts after starting the surveying work at his new job, but the doubts didn't disable him. He enjoyed reading John Bunyan's old book, *Grace Abounding*, written hundreds of years ago. Bunyan's decades-long struggle with doubts gave Tim hope as he struggled with his own doubts and frequent bouts of anxiety. The reasons for feeling anxious were real, but the feelings were out of proportion to the circumstances. Bunyan's story helped to strengthen Tim's faith.

One day, while working at his computer after several hours of fieldwork, a peace came over him. He stopped and spoke to himself.

"I decided to take this job. I'm following through on my decision. I respect my decision. I am on track."

SEMINARY? SERIOUSLY?

I was on a phone call with my friend Linda when she suddenly surprised me. "Dave, I think you should move up to Marin County and enroll in the seminary."

"Seminary? Seriously?"

"Yes. They've got pretty cheap housing, which you could use, and who knows, you might learn something."

I responded through laughter. "Yeah, I'm sure I would learn *something*. Oh my gosh—seminary?"

Linda was someone I deeply respected. I knew her to be wise and I knew she was employed for her abilities as a strategic thinker.

I had never been interested in returning to school in general, let alone seminary. But Linda had the ability to influence me.

"You're a natural, Dave. You might be prejudging the idea without realizing what the possibilities are."

It was a strange moment. Deep in my mind, I wondered

if she might be right, but I had developed a distaste for getting into ministry as a vocation. Given my family, it was certainly a familiar kind of life, and I had continued with church involvement throughout my adulthood. Nevertheless, I had repeatedly encountered painful disappointment when trusting church leaders—not always, but enough to leave me grimacing at the thought of seminary.

"Well, give it some thought," said Linda before we ended the call.

I did. And I confess, one of the main reasons was the cheap housing. Since losing the clay shop, I had taken several random jobs to try to regain some financial stability: serving in a coffee shop, installing window coverings, and some freelance mold-making. I still had a ways to go. I could move to the campus, and if I found decent work, I felt I could manage the tuition.

The first person I encountered at the school was a woman named Karen in the admissions office. She explained everything to me: the sort of school it was, its history, expectations for campus residents, and a lot more.

"If you need anything else," she said, pointing to herself, "just come back and ask this girl."

Those words echoed in my head as I walked away from her office. She was reasonable, positive, helpful, friendly, and knowledgeable—not to mention beautiful. It had been eight years since Kate's departure, and I couldn't help wondering if this girl from the admissions office was available.

I found work with a local coffee business and was able to pay the rent and tuition. I also found occasional work using my artistic skills. After some initial adjustment to the culture of the school, I got into a good rhythm.

✧ ✧ ✧

THAT GIRL IN THE ADMISSIONS OFFICE

I stopped by the admissions office one day and stuck my head in to see if Karen was in. She was. She stood up from her desk, wearing a dark blue dress. She smiled, brushing back her long dark hair.

"Ah, mints! I love these," I said, grabbing three mints out of a bowl on the reception desk.

"That's what they're there for."

"How's it going today?" I asked.

"Oh, fine. How are you?"

"Oh, fine," I responded, imitating her. "Well, I got my mints, I guess I'll see you later."

"Okay."

Walking down the hall outside her office I resolved to ask her to lunch the next day. Then I stopped. "Why wait?" I asked myself. I turned around and went back. This time I went in and closed the door behind me. She had been approaching the door when I came in, so now we stood facing each other, just a few feet between us.

"Are you free for lunch?"

She looked a little surprised. Her smile faded slightly, and she folded her arms in front of her. "I'm not spontaneous."

I suddenly realized it was already noon.

I spent the next three seconds rethinking my plan—or lack thereof. "How much time do you need? How 'bout tomorrow?"

A long four seconds passed.

"Um... yeah, I can do lunch tomorrow."

"Nice. Shall I meet you here?"

"Sure."

I walked from her office again. It was the same hall as a minute earlier, but everything felt different.

The next day we shared a patio table at a nice cafe about

a mile from campus. The food was good, but we had a hard time eating, as we were both caught up in our conversation.

Finally, there was a pause. Karen looked at me with an interesting expression. "You know, you come highly recommended."

"What do you mean?"

"Well, after you asked me to lunch, I took a closer look at your file."

"My file?" I said, laughing. "I have a file?"

"Yeah, remember the paperwork you filled out for my office? Remember the recommendations you had to provide? I went back and read all that. And you come highly recommended."

"Great. Does that mean you'll go out with me again?"

"We'll see. Probably."

"Probably?"

"Yes."

"Yes 'probably' or yes you will."

"Yes probably."

"I can work with that," I said with a chuckle.

I was surprised by how good it felt to be in a new setting, meeting new people. It also felt good to be out of the city.

A BEAUTIFUL MIND, BUT A LITTLE SCARY

Tim leaned over in the dark theater, still looking straight at the screen. "Dave, that's exactly what it's like."

We were watching the movie *A Beautiful Mind,* in which Russel Crowe played the Nobel Prize-winning mathematician, John Nash. Nash was a smart guy: a graduate of MIT, winner of several awards, and something of a fixture at Princeton University.

"Really?"

"Yeah." He paused, looking a little disturbed. "They nailed it."

In this scene, Nash was trying to teach a class when Enemy Russian Agents entered the back of the room attempting to corner him. He ran from the building, doing everything he could to escape capture. Or so he thought. John Nash struggled with schizophrenia and delusions brought about by the illness. In reality, there were no enemy agents after him; it was just another day on campus.

I discreetly kept an eye on Tim as the film continued. Many scenes followed depicting Nash's frightening struggle trying to discern fact from fantasy. In many cases, he failed to see reality for what it was. He got caught up in imaginary circumstances that wreaked havoc in his profession, his reputation, his marriage, and perhaps most of all, in his own soul.

Had the lights been on, any observant person could have seen that Tim was very uncomfortable. When it was over, the two of us walked out to the car where we sat awhile before hitting the road.

Feeling a little worried, I wondered if I'd made a mistake bringing him to this film. "Was this a bad idea?" I asked.

"I don't know."

"I thought it might be interesting to talk about with you in particular."

"Yeah, I can see that." He spoke quietly with a faraway look. "Maybe I'm not ready yet. I'm having a hard time right now."

"What did you mean when you said, 'That's exactly what it's like?'"

"Yeah." He let out a big sigh. "It's not the specifics, like Russian agents or whatever, but the way he couldn't tell what was real. That's what they got right. It's terrifying to try to relate to people when you're navigating this other reality where the people you're with may or may not be who they say they are. And you can't ask anyone. You're forced to figure everything out on your own. And the whole time, there's this constant "help"—voices inside trying to tell you what's really going on—and they're wrong. They're wrong all the time."

He suddenly sounded angry. "They're always wrong! But you can't stop listening to them. It's torture!"

We just sat awhile.

I started the car.

The ride home was quiet.

When we got back to my dorm at the seminary, Tim spoke up. "I feel like calling in sick tomorrow, but I don't want to lie."

"Lie? What do you mean?"

"I really don't feel up to going to work, but I'm not sick."

"Tim, if you need a little recovery time after that movie, I think that's fine. Maybe you're not "sick" in the usual sense, but this qualifies."

"You're right. Yes, it does. I'll call work in the morning and tell them I can't come in. Thanks, Dave, you're right. I'm still recovering from that sickness. This counts."

"Absolutely."

"Can I stay here tonight?"

"Sure, no one will mind."

We stayed up late talking and were joined by a fellow student, Eric, who had seen *A Beautiful Mind* the previous day. Tim had met Eric before and liked him.

"Wasn't that a good film?" asked Eric.

I looked at Tim.

Tim looked at the floor.

I spoke up. "Yeah, I liked it. Tim's having a little trouble though. It sort of triggered a few things. Tim struggled with the same sort of problems the character in the movie did."

"Tim, you have schizophrenia?"

"Well, yeah, I did. Or maybe I still do. I'm never sure how to look at it."

"Wow. I didn't know that."

We all three sat in a very long pause.

"If you don't mind my asking, what's that like? I'm curious."

Tim sat back, looking at Eric, who suddenly reacted. "Sorry man, you don't have to answer me. I was just curious."

"No, I don't mind you asking. I can understand being curious about what it's like to be schizophrenic. I can tell you this. I grew up with some arachnophobia too, but I would rather eat a pile of wolf spiders than go through what I went through before."

Eric gave a sudden loud laugh, then apologized. "Dude, I'm so sorry, you just surprised me with your 'pile of wolf spiders' thing."

Before he finished, Tim was laughing too.

Another pause.

"If you've ever had self-consciousness or social anxiety, schizophrenia is like putting the two together, amped up ten times. For me, it's been so awkward, I've sometimes lost people before my eyes; someone seems like a friend at first, then they can't handle the awkwardness and bail."

Tim thought for a moment, then continued.

"Imagine if instead of having a bad dream, and waking up realizing it's just a dream, you wake up from a sweet sleep to find out your reality is a bad dream—at least that's what it felt like to me. I can understand being curious, but man, it's awful. There's a lot of schizophrenic jokes out there, but I can tell you, the actual experience has no humor."

I was still sitting there, shaking my head, chuckling. "A pile of wolf spiders?"

Tim smiled. "Hey, I needed an appropriate metaphor."

Eric spoke up again. "Tim, I would have never guessed you had to go through that. You're one of the sanest people I know. I hope you'll be around for a long time."

He took a risk, got up, and gave Tim a big hug. "Thanks for hanging out, Tim, I like it when you're around."

That comment set Tim's mind at ease for the night, and the hug was good medicine.

EVERY SECOND SATURDAY

"Never underestimate the power of a small group of people sharing their creative expressions with each other over time." That sentence lodged in my mind as I sat with a hundred or so people at a breakfast gathering in the hotel banquet hall. The speaker was Os Guinness, who was the reason I was there. For years I had been thinking about that very thing—the results people get when they encourage creativity in each other, then go create something, then come back and share what they did. I found that pattern to deliver great results.

Over the next few weeks, Karen and I made a plan. We started an art group. By this time, we were engaged to be married, and very much enjoyed working together.

On a Saturday morning, we set up twelve chairs in a circle. We made coffee and put out some pastries. We wanted to host a forum for artists in a noncompetitive atmosphere designed to encourage more creative expression. We spent the previous few weeks getting the word out as best we could, inviting artists of any sort.

Eight people showed up. The pieces shared included a

small sculpture, an edible creation, some paintings, and an original song. It wasn't a big crowd, but we had a great time and wanted to do it again. I pulled out a box of random items with a lid on it so no one could see inside. A volunteer put his hand into the box and pulled out an item. It was a piece of torn paper with words written on it. The words read, "Beauty on the other side." I then asked everyone to spend the next month creating anything they wanted based on that phrase. Karen and I debriefed after everyone else had gone.

"That was really cool," I said.

She smiled. "I agree. I feel great about it. I'm so curious what people might bring next time."

The next time was even better. I was amazed at the variety of creative expressions that came from that shared stimulus pulled from the box. The group took root quickly. Within a year, it was about twenty artists each time, and not always the same people. If everyone came at once, it would have been fifty or sixty. The art forms were diverse: visual art, music, fashion, performing arts, film-making, and more. They gathered, gave, and received feedback and encouragement in a competition-free atmosphere. The group continued to grow, and we got permission to meet in a local auditorium.

One day Tim joined us. He sat quietly with a large spiral notebook, writing in it from time to time. We talked afterward.

"Dave, I love this. I feel inspired."

During many gatherings, he sat with his notebook, writing down ideas as they came to him.

After our first year, we planned an art show to share the group's works with the public. I asked Tim if he wanted to be included.

"Yes. I'd like to read some of my poetry. I've been writing

it during the gatherings, but I haven't shown anyone yet."

"That's awesome! Yes, please share it."

The show was more successful than we anticipated. A crowd came and didn't seem to want to leave. They enjoyed the visual art for a while, then our performers took to the stage to share their music, dance, dramatic monologues, and poetry.

Tim read his poetry. He was so nervous he couldn't hold the microphone without shaking it. I held it for him. When he finished, he heard wild applause—all for him.

Many months and many poems later, Tim told me that the Second Saturday group had become as important to him as the clay shop had been. The group had supported him in his creative growth, encouraging him as he found his voice and grew in confidence. Once again, I found myself in the mysterious and fortunate position of pursuing an idea that inadvertently provided a healing context for Tim—and it wouldn't be the last.

DAD LOSES HIS COMPOSURE – FINALLY

As the announcer called my name, I stepped out onto the stage in my cap and gown, scarlet master's hood positioned perfectly, and walked toward the school president's outstretched hand. He was about to present me with a Master of Divinity degree with studies focused in counseling.

The eruption of cheers caught me off guard. I almost stopped. I quickly scanned the crowd looking for familiar faces. About twelve rows back, near the middle, my father was on his feet waving his arms and bellowing out pure happy cheers. I hardly recognized him. Dad was the type to maintain a disciplined composure—applaud when appropriate, but nothing else. That persona was now gone and in its place was something I didn't know existed—my dad looking on me with so much love and pride that he forgot his dignity. Mom sat next to him, beaming.

After the ceremony, it was Tim's turn.

"Dave! Well done!" he exclaimed, planting a big kiss on my cheek. That familiar smile landed on his face: that same smile he'd flashed from his crib, the one he wore when Dad bought him a toy drum on that road trip through the desert, the one that watched me from the window as I rode past the house on my unicycle, the one he wore when he discovered five puppies one morning after Keesha gave birth—the same one that survived the outskirts of hell itself.

Those reactions made the academic work of the previous five years worth it.

Karen and I were married by the time I graduated. She had grown close to Tim as well as the rest of our family. She became a voice of encouragement, not only to me but also to Tim as he continued to recover and thrive.

MOM'S MYSTICAL VISIT

When I arrived home, I noticed the little blinking light indicating I had a voicemail message waiting. "Hi, son. I'm going into the hospital for a heart procedure. I expect to come out alright, but I just wanted to let you know and to tell you I love you."

Mom came out alright at first, but a stroke in the recovery room changed everything. She was left paralyzed and unable to speak.

Tim immediately took off for Kansas. I was glad he was able to go. I knew he would be a comfort to her, which amazed me as I thought about it. He had become safe and sane, and it didn't stop there. People now described him as loving and helpful. I thought about these things as I parked my car while running some errands.

I hurried across the parking lot toward the door to the bank. I needed to make a deposit before they closed. I passed a small enclosure that housed a dumpster surrounded by a chain-link fence.

Suddenly, out of the corner of my eye, I noticed a chair next to the dumpster with an old woman sitting in it. "What's she doing in there?" I thought to myself, as I trotted past. Looking back, I saw the dumpster and the chair, but no woman.

"Weird," I thought as I paused, not sure what I had just seen. The image stayed with me awhile, then faded from my mind as I finished my errands and got back to whatever I'd been doing at home.

Before dawn the following morning, I woke with the sounds and images of a dream occupying my mind like a riddle that needed answering. In the dream, I parked at the bank as I had the day before. As I crossed the parking lot, I noticed the woman in the chair next to the dumpster. It was Mom.

"David," she said, "I don't know where to go from here."

She looked uncomfortable and deeply concerned about whatever it was she didn't know. I grabbed hold of the chain-link fence and looked at her, trying to console her—to encourage her to trust that she would know what she needed to know in time. My effort to reach her seemed to help calm her. We just looked at each other. She was still uncomfortable, but she looked a little more at peace. That was the dream.

Tim called later that day. "Dave, how are you doing?"

"I'm alright, how's it going on your end? How's Mom?"

"Oh, you don't know?" He paused. "She's already passed."

"Uh... wait... she died?"

"Sorry, I thought you knew."

"No." I sat down, letting myself feel the moment. "That's alright." A long pause followed. I pictured Mom in my dream, sitting in that chair in the fenced enclosure with the dumpster—the place where things were discarded, never to return.

"I'm so glad you got to be there," I commented.

"Me too."

After the call I noticed my phone machine blinking, indicating another voicemail, This time it was my dad: "I was driving back from the store to the hospital with some items for your mom when I got the news that she'd already gone home."

At the words "already gone home," his voice broke, and I heard the first sob that I'm sure was followed by many. I felt his loss, perhaps even more than my own.

"Gone home." That's how he figured it.

She'd gone somewhere for sure. And while I can't account for it, it felt like she checked in with me on the way out.

MOTHER'S COLD HANDS

"Whatever your hand finds to do, do it with all your might," our mom would say, usually when we were demonstrating laziness. She was quoting the book of Ecclesiastes, in the Bible.

The author who originally penned those words may have been expressing resignation, meaning that if there's no higher purpose, one may as well just lean into their life's work, and perhaps find some satisfaction.

Mom meant something else. She didn't want us to be slackers. She respected the idea of working with one's hands, and always encouraged us to find ways to contribute rather than be carried by someone else. She consistently modeled this with her own hands.

I leaned over the coffin in front of me and placed my hands on hers. The unresponsiveness was startling. Even a rock or a piece of wood responds in some way, offering it's essence when touched. Her hands were, even now, doing what they found to do with all her might. They were dead and were delivering the deadness without compromise. I thought I might feel just a tiny bit of her presence. This was after all my mom. But it wasn't. These things looked like her hands, but even with her death so recent, they felt like empty papier mache. I touched her face. Nothing. This was just another skeleton.

I missed my mom and wanted to focus my sadness on something. I thought it would be her body, but to me, it seemed that she had already abandoned it fully, and if she had, then so would I. Turning my grief from the dead to the living, I focused on the others present, especially my brothers and my sister. Their presence was real, and it felt good to share the sorrow with each other.

Mom's journey from the trails and "hollers" of Breathitt County, Kentucky was a long one.

I spoke softly to Tim: "I'm glad you were there with her at the end."

"Yeah, me too."

"Do you think she was aware of you?"

"Oh, yeah. She couldn't speak, but I know she could hear me. She responded by moving one foot in an obvious way."

We walked out onto the Kansas grass and sat down. It was warm that day and the ground felt clean; mostly because it was November and there weren't bugs everywhere.

"Dave, what's the difference between a living body and a dead body?"

It seemed like an odd time for a joke. "Um… I give up."

"No, no, it's not a joke. Really, what's the difference? What is it that makes a body alive? I mean, a dead body can be in perfect condition, and still be dead, right? So, what's missing? Life, of course. But what is that? Are we the missing part—the life? I think yes."

I loved his question. It stimulated my inner philosopher but aside from that, I appreciated the fact that Tim would ask this.

"That's a wonderful question. I think yes, we're the missing part, for sure."

We sat in silence for a while as I looked for more words. "I think we're the story. The body is nothing if it's dead, but if it's living, then there's a story to see. Bearing witness to each other's stories—being present with each other while also remembering the past—learning from it, that's the thing. I think we're stories more than anything."

Tim nodded. "I'm so grateful to Mom. She could have easily decided I was too much to handle, but she never even thought about that. Or maybe she did and I didn't notice. My story is possible because of her and others too, like you."

"My brother, your story is a really good one."

"Well, it's real, that's for sure."

"Tim, if you were a book, you would be a great read. Your plot is unpredictable, the characters are interesting, there's an undercurrent of humor, the scary parts are really scary, the end is elusive, and the hope is believable."

He teared up a bit as I spoke, and I could see his shoulders beginning to shake as he spent a few minutes letting out some of his grief.

✦ ✦ ✦

TREASURES OLD AND NEW

"Oh my gosh," I quietly exclaimed to myself. "How did these things survive?" I couldn't believe what I was seeing.

Unpacking was underway at our new place. Karen and I had chosen four other people who shared our vision for a creativity-oriented community house. We envisioned hosting art shows, writer's workshops, and musical events. The vision required a good-sized place in a neighborhood where such things would be appreciated.

We found such a place, and the owner was highly supportive of our vision. The fully renovated 1909 Craftsman structure was perfect. It took time to get moved in, and in the process, many boxes were left unopened for a while. Tim was visiting, helping us as we unpacked.

Somehow, against all odds, this particular box had not been opened for many years. It must have been moved from storage to storage without much notice.

"Hey Tim, look at this!"

"Whatcha got?"

"Remember these?"

"Wow." He stared, incredulous. "Are those the same ones from that trip?"

"Yeah."

In my hand was the small wooden box with the secret lock, containing the three polished stones I had acquired on that road trip where we stopped at the Indian trading post... over forty years ago.

"Symbolic," said Tim. "They're like this house—an old treasure being rediscovered and brought back."

I picked up the three polished stones, one at a time, out of the small wooden box. A feeling I can't name came over me—the feeling of my own story. "After all I've lost, how is it possible I still have these?" I said out loud.

"Yup," said Tim with a chuckle, "definitely symbolic. Moving into this house is bringing out the treasure."

"I'm not sure what that means," I responded, "but I like it." I walked outside, carrying my old treasure. I sat on the porch for a while, lost in memories and giving thanks for this new home.

We proceeded to implement our ideas, quickly gaining support from locals who enjoyed what we were doing. So, we kept doing it: art shows, art workshops, writer's workshops, house concerts, and other such events. We focused on the artists more than the art. We wanted to support creativity—something Karen and I found to be psychologically and spiritually healthy. The house had a large porch, which became the preferred spot for great conversations with many people.

Somehow we acquired the name Cedar House, possibly because the house is covered with cedar shakes. And Tim's words became true. The house indeed became a treasure for residents and visitors alike.

During one of Tim's visits, we sat on the porch enjoying fresh scones that Karen made. She loved baking, much to everyone's delight.

"So, Tim."

"Yeah?"

"Several people have suggested that I take my education further—that I go for a doctorate, maybe something connected to spiritual formation and the arts."

I wanted to see what he thought of the idea. I expected a casual conversation, but that's not exactly what happened.

"Dave!" He repositioned himself, setting down his scone so he could gesture with both hands. "Man!" He was getting excited, practically standing up. "You have to do that!"

"Whoa. You sound pretty excited. That's not the reaction I expected."

"Dave, you don't get it. You have to do that! Everything you're doing now is too good not to take it further."

"Why would getting a doctorate take it further?"

"I don't know, but it would. You have to do this. How can I help you?"

I sat back, thinking. I didn't indicate any decision at that moment, but deep inside, I instinctively responded.

"Well, I'll keep thinking about it," I said.

"You do that, and then you go for it."

We both reached for another scone, very much enjoying the Cedar House porch.

CHAPTER TEN
2010 – 2024

*Most days include some tedium—
work that can be laborious.
In those moments, I try to remember
the lessons I've learned:
Keep going. Give thanks.
Contribute generously.*

~ Tim Robinson

The Master Suite

It was a gorgeous September evening at Cedar House. Tim was visiting for the weekend, talking with one of the residents about her plans to move out. He joked about taking over her room after she left.

She was preparing for her wedding, and in the process, was also preparing to vacate the master suite. It was a beautiful room with its own balcony, a cozy little reading nook, and a full bathroom with a lovely antique claw-foot tub.

The moving day arrived, and we all helped her load up her things. Once again, Tim was around, observing the changes. He spent Friday night and Saturday with us. "Hey Dave, since the master suite is vacant, can I camp in there?"

"Sure, go ahead. Hopefully, we'll find someone to move in, but until we do, feel free."

Tim spent several weekends in the room throughout October and November. On one of those weekends, he seemed more thoughtful than usual.

"Dave, do you remember a while back when I was talking about moving in here, but it didn't work out?"

"Yes."

"I'm glad things worked out the way they did. Living completely on my own has been important. I needed to be able to do that."

"Yes. I agree."

"Well, I think the time might be right."

"Really?"

"Yeah, I always look forward to coming up on weekends, and I love it here. I'd be willing to commute to work during the week and pay rent here. What do you think? Does the timing seem right? And the idea of me living here; how does that seem to you? Would I fit? Does it make sense?"

"The only empty room is the master suite."

"Well, that's what got me thinking." He paused, thoughtfully. "I've decided that's the room I want, and I don't think I'd settle for anything else. I've always been the guy in someone's spare room, or a room upstairs at work, or some such thing. I had that apartment for a while, but it was small and felt temporary. I want to experience my own home."

"Well, this is a community house with a lot of shared space. Would it feel like your own home?"

"I've been thinking about that, too. If I had one of the regular bedrooms, I don't think so. But if I had the master suite, that would be different."

We talked about the possibilities. The biggest hurdle was the expense. Even though we shared expenses among six or more adults, the house was not cheap.

After a couple more conversations over that weekend, Tim decided to pay one month's rent, and see how it felt. Since we had no one in mind for the room, we had no reason to object. He would still have his room near his work, about an hour's drive away, but this way he could begin to get a taste of what it might be like to live at Cedar House.

The month Tim paid for was December, and he was with us for Christmas. "I like this a lot," he said, one night after dinner. "I don't know if I can afford it, but I want to make it happen."

The next night, we had several friends over. Karen and I hosted a study group each week, and this meeting was a casual Christmas get-together.

"Tim, are you living here now?" Mary, one of our friends, asked him.

"Well, sort of."

Mary laughed. "You're sort of living here? Tell me about that."

Tim explained how he was trying out the master suite. "It's kind of a step of faith," he told her. "I want to move in, but I can only commit to one month. We'll see what happens in January."

Mary was enjoying a plate of delicious items made by Karen that day. She quietly took a few bites, then said, "I want to see what happens, too. I respect your step of faith. I'd like to pay January's rent for you."

Tim was dumbfounded, staring at her, not sure how to respond. She laughed again, enjoying his reaction. "I'm completely serious. I'd like to do that."

Mary paid January's rent for Tim, and toward the end of the month, he had worked through the financial questions and had February's rent ready. After a few months, he moved in fully.

One day he hung a sign above the door to his master suite. The sign was a bit of a riddle. "Vanbarnor" is what it said. For just a moment, I felt an old familiar nervousness, triggered by memories of the way he used to mess with language as part of schizophrenic thinking.

"What's it mean?" I asked.

"It's a word I put together based on the Elvish language in the book The Lord of the Rings. It means 'fair dwelling above.'"

Over the years, I had learned much about the difference between crazy and creative. This struck me as creative.

"Vanbarnor it is," I responded, happy to see him owning his space and making it his home.

USEFUL TOOLS

"Man, I love this group," commented Tim with a tone of delight. The two of us were locking up the building after one of our Second Saturday art gatherings. I was just about to leave when he stopped me.

"Hey Dave, hold on a minute. I think I'll go get an exposure."

"An exposure?" I laughed. "What do you mean? Exposure to what?"

Tim smiled confidently. "To the spooky room back behind the stage."

He disappeared through a door we seldom used, and about two minutes passed before he reemerged with a satisfied look on his face.

"That room gives me the creeps," he said, "so I thought I'd go in there for a nice exposure."

I was intrigued. "I think maybe I know what you mean."

"You know that group therapy I used to go to for social anxiety?"

"Yeah."

"Dr. Chang, the woman who facilitated the group, told us about "exposures," which just means deliberately exposing yourself to something that sparks anxiety. She said exposing yourself to the anxiety gets much better results than avoiding it. You can do it whenever you're ready for as long as you'd like. You're in control."

I thought about that for a moment. "Interesting. I can see how that would be a useful tool."

"It's very useful. In Dr. Chang's group, we used to role-play. She had me practice asking women out—women who were part of the group. It was helpful. But it works with other fears too. I go into that dark, creepy room, stay for a minute, and leave when I choose. Now it bothers me less."

"So, it's a way of getting over your fears?"

"Exactly. You get enough exposure to scary situations that aren't actually dangerous, and eventually, you lose your fear. Pretty cool."

"Yeah, very cool. I'm glad you got to be part of that group."

As I drove home, I felt inspired by Tim's confident use of the tools he'd learned. He was rechanneling his courage in brilliant ways. I thought about the time he climbed to the top of the huge pillars at the Palace of Fine Arts and the time he stood on the very top of the Golden Gate Bridge. I recalled other experiences, like his climb up the granite wall of Royal Arches, jumping from an airplane, the descent into the old coal mine, and digging his own cave above the beach. He experienced some fear at each of those events, but he also showed courage. There were other fears too, that he avoided rather than facing. Those fears brought about tremendous anxiety, causing him to withdraw into isolation.

Now, it was like he'd found a way to take his courage and redirect it to the things that scared him. Instead of succumbing, he was now handling his anxieties and fears like puzzles to be solved.

SCHIZOPHRENIC ROMANCE

Sandy had been diagnosed with schizophrenia when she was in college. It made her education much harder, but she coped with her illness, stayed in school, and eventually completed a program at the Rhode Island School of Design. She wore creative, colorful clothing, much of it designed by her. She had a bright face with an easy smile that shone from under a lively whirl of curly auburn hair.

She was a favorite at our monthly art gatherings. One

day, after sharing some of her colorful design work, she told everyone about her struggle with schizophrenia. The response was applause. She smiled with understanding, knowing she was being encouraged for having done well despite her illness. I was moved by the group's strong show of support.

She pulled me aside one day as we were finishing up.

"Can we talk for a minute in private?"

"Sure," I said, showing her to an adjacent room.

She seemed a little nervous. "Okay," she paused, letting me have one phrase at a time. "I'm attracted to your brother Tim. I think he's great. I love the way he brings so much creativity everywhere he goes. And I know he's had schizophrenia. I know what that's like." She looked relieved, but also a little scared. "Should I be saying this? Do I sound like I'm in middle school?"

"You're just sharing your thoughts," I laughed. "You can sound any way you need to."

"Maybe I should be talking to him. But I don't know, I thought it might help to mention it to you first. If you want to talk to him about it, that's okay too."

We talked a little more and agreed to check in with each other again soon.

I wondered to myself: Should a person with schizophrenia date another person with the same struggle? This was suddenly a relevant question since I was aware that Tim liked Sandy and the thought of a romance with her had occurred to him before. My inner reaction to the question, was "No, that would not be a good idea." But I began to argue within myself. My thoughts went back and forth inside:

"They aren't 'schizophrenics,' they're just people, both of whom have had to deal with the illness."

"But it's not that simple. That disease wreaks havoc

everywhere it goes. Don't expect it to behave itself in a romantic relationship."

"But I can picture something beautiful. They like each other. They're in a strong, supportive community. It could work."

"But I can't picture them fully on their own. They seem to bring out the kid in each other. They'll always need support and guidance."

"But who doesn't need that? We all do!"

And so went my inner dialog ricocheting through my brain. There was also the fact that if they ever had children together, it's highly likely their kids would also have the dreaded illness.

I finally looked a simple fact in the face. It wasn't up to me. I would always offer whatever feedback they asked for and would offer counsel if necessary, but in the end, this was about their choices, not mine. That would normally be obvious, but I had grown accustomed to helping Tim process his thoughts, and I knew this situation would need a lot of processing. And to top it off, not only would he certainly ask for my help, but she was also asking.

I got together with Tim later that day. "Tim, you might want to have a conversation with Sandy. She mentioned to me that she has feelings for you. You have an opportunity to explore that if you think you should."

He stood with his hands in his pockets, looking at the floor. "Do you think I should?"

"Actually, I have some doubts. But you might have a growth opportunity here. You've got a history of anxiety when you get close to a woman and you're already comfortable with Sandy. I'm not suggesting anything other than some open conversations if you feel it's right for you. And romance may not be where it goes. You may just form a deeper friendship which could be good."

Three weeks later, Tim invited Karen and me to meet him and Sandy for a double date at a local coffee shop—just a simple hour or so over drinks. We grabbed a table out on the patio, enjoyed our drinks for a while, and talked a little about what the two of them were experiencing. The conversation was subdued. I was used to Sandy's colorful personality, but she was quiet, as was Tim. Neither of them seemed to know how to converse with us as peers. There was a sense that they were waiting for us to lead.

They spent a lot of time together either at Cedar House or at her place. Months passed, and though I still had doubts, their relationship seemed to be lasting.

One day I came into the house and heard Tim and Sandy upstairs laughing. At first, it made me smile, but after a few minutes, I became uncomfortable. They were laughing almost non-stop. I tried to ignore them—it wasn't any of my business.

"Hey, Dave!" yelled Tim from his room.

I went up to the master suite. "Hey, Tim. Hi Sandy. How's it going up here?"

Tim explained excitedly: "Sandy's making banners for my front window."

"Banners?"

"Yeah, these are so cool! Instead of curtains, I'm gonna hang these!"

He seemed a little too excited, and a bit disconnected. Sometimes a manic state looks like happiness, and I had learned to watch for the differences.

"Sounds interesting. Can I see?"

"Of course!"

Sandy got up from her sewing machine and spread out three brightly colored banners about sixteen inches wide, three feet tall, pointed at the bottom, with a long tassel hanging from the point. They were beautiful, which wasn't surprising, given Sandy's ability. They reminded me of something you might see at a Renaissance fair. They looked kind of cool, but I also felt a little uncomfortable about them.

"What are they for?" I asked.

"Just pure beauty," said Tim, causing Sandy to start laughing again. "And of course for the window."

I found myself thinking hard. I'm all for making beautiful things, but something was off.

In the months they'd spent together, Tim had developed a silly sense of humor that had him making jokes out of just about everything. And Sandy laughed at everything he said. This new humor sometimes hampered communication with everyone but Sandy who seemed to thrive on it. They were gradually making a little world only the two of them understood.

Sandy started sewing again. I decided to share some of my thoughts openly. "I like these—they're beautiful, but I don't think they fit this old craftsman house. And to be honest, they look like theater props."

Sandy spoke up. "I was thinking that too, but Tim was very specific about what he wanted, so I made what he asked." She seemed perfectly comfortable with what I'd said.

"Wow," said Tim. "Do you think I'm being schizo here?" He wasn't defensive at all, just honestly asking.

"It feels a little that way to me."

I had learned a long time ago to be gentle but straightforward in such moments. Tim thanked me for the feedback. That gratitude seemed to ground him in the moment and the disconnected feeling disappeared. I hadn't noticed the tension inside me, until I suddenly felt a little relief.

After Sandy was gone, we talked further.

"Dave, I want to know more about what you observed."

"Well, the effect the two of you have on each other doesn't seem to lead anywhere. It's like you're both having fun, but that's it. It's hard to picture the two of you setting any real goals or growing much. You both seem completely satisfied to just be together doing fun things. It's not enough of a foundation on which to build a future. And, I hate to say it, but it does remind me a little of the way you interacted with other patients in the psych ward."

Tim exhaled slowly, looking at the floor. "She's great. I really enjoy her."

"Of course you do—that's fine. And at the same time I'm afraid you might be going backward. I don't know that for sure but I'm not willing to just go on and not say anything, either."

"Dave, thank you. Thank you. There's no one else to tell me these things."

"Of course. And it's also important that you govern your life, and not let me do it for you. I'm just sharing my thoughts."

"I know. I understand that. I really do."

A few weeks later, Tim asked if he could speak with me again.

"Dave, Sandy and I decided not to pursue romance any further. We want to remain friends, and I think we can do that, but I don't think it's a good match for a marriage."

"I'm glad to hear that. I have mixed feelings, mostly because I enjoy her too and I like having her around. But in the end, I agree with you."

"We've never been sexually involved at all, which is a good thing—when breaking up, there's not as much to break."

"That makes a ton of sense. I'm glad for that too."

Tim learned a lot from Sandy. He became a better communicator, gained confidence, and felt much more comfortable around women. And the two of them remained good friends.

MEASURING THE EARTH

"Okay Dave, I need you to man the rod while I run the instrument."

"Sounds good."

Tim walked about a hundred feet up the small hill next to the science building where he set up the total station.

Beyond his normal employment as a surveyor, he would also do occasional freelance projects, like today's job for a large private school. It was a two-man job which is why I was with him. The tables had turned; I was working for him now, albeit only for a day or two.

Soon my walkie-talkie began to broadcast Tim's voice. "You ready?"

"All ready."

It was a beautiful day on a beautiful campus. Tim was in his surveying element. He was competent. He was in charge. He was respected and appreciated by those who hired him. He had come far through puzzles and obstacles on a very long road.

I watched him from a distance. He was a long way from The Quiet Room at the McAuley Institute and the sleepless nights of fear he once lived through. The level of recovery was remarkable.

I thought about other things he'd accomplished. Aside from surveying, he'd also finished several creative projects.

He'd made at least twenty intriguing art pieces, finished a book of poetry, and a beautiful, illustrated children's book about bugs.

His surveying work required a huge amount of disciplined study for which many people were proud of him. He chose a good career and he's never been bored with it. To be a full-fledged Land Surveyor, he had to pass a rather daunting test. It's a test offered once a year, and each year most candidates fail. It might be compared with someone who graduates from law school, but then needs to pass the bar. After graduating, he worked as a tech for a few years, then decided he'd like to go further. The test proved to be a test in more than one way: he needed to pass it to earn the title Professional Land Surveyor, but aside from that, it also tested his determination and persistence. He failed his first attempt. When he tried a second time, the test had been divided into two parts: national and state. He passed the national part but failed the state section which was much more rigorous. He studied harder and took the state test a third time. Again, he failed, and again, and again. After six failures, he joined a study group of others also working on it. On the seventh attempt, he passed.

He says working as a surveyor is simultaneously "blue collar" and "white collar." He's enjoyed searching for survey monuments shown on old maps from decades past. He says it reminds him of hunting for treasure. Often, after unearthing a particular marker—an old iron pipe or wood hub—he feels a pleasing rush, like the joy of finding quartz crystals in the embankment above Taylor Boulevard when he was a kid.

Tim has surveyed more properties than he can remember, determining boundaries and taking hundreds of topographic measurements on each job, then staking out newly designed homes.

He has surveyed beautiful rural areas and wild open spaces. He's taken topography shots in the Mojave Desert in the summer heat and recorded measurements as night falls in the short days of winter. From hammering iron property markers deep into brown sand at the beach, to traversing redwood forests and country streams with a tripod on his shoulder, most days have been good. He's seen coyotes, bobcats, hawks and eagles while he's worked. He's heard the warning sounds of rattlesnakes and the gobbling of turkeys. He's paused many times to take in the fields of orange poppies next to yellow and purple blooming wildflowers. He particularly enjoyed it when one time, while surveying, a scrub jay landed on his head and plucked at his hair.

He's also measured the earth in the middle of the city, in crowds of people that often blocked the view of his equipment.

Yet even in this career he loves, most days include some tedium. Whether it's slow, careful repetitive fieldwork, or hours drafting in CAD at his computer, the work can be laborious. In those moments, he's mindful of the lessons he's learned: Keep going, give thanks, and contribute generously.

THE REAL THING

I met Annemarie when she attended a public reading event that Karen and I hosted featuring several local writers. Afterward, her dark hair, bright eyes, and notably lovely smile caught my attention as she approached me.

"I enjoyed myself tonight. Please keep me posted when you do other events. I want to come back!"

She came back to other events we hosted at Cedar House and after a while our household became familiar with her.

One Saturday afternoon, Tim walked into the kitchen with

a smirk on his face. He was holding his phone and seemed very pleased with himself.

"What's goin' on?" I inquired.

"Oh, I've been texting Annemarie off and on all day." He let out a huge, satisfied, smiling sigh, pulled out a stool from the kitchen island, and looked out the window at nothing. His voice was wistful and happy. "This is so great."

I found myself laughing at his exceptionally blithe demeanor. "And this is what, exactly?"

"She says I'm doing it right."

"Which means…"

"She says I'm taking it slow, which she appreciates. It gives her a chance to adjust to the possibilities at her own pace. So instead of feeling pushed, she feels free."

"Tim! Wow! Well done! And you seem totally confident. What happened to the worried, fearful guy complaining about not knowing how to do this?" I found myself laughing at the way he was sitting there in his own little bliss-cloud.

Annemarie already knew about Tim's schizophrenia because she had participated in one of our groups in which Tim and Sandy had both shared about their past with mental illness. That knowledge didn't keep her from warming up to Tim.

When Tim showed interest in her, something inside me cheered. He had worked through social anxiety and fear of rejection. He had gained enormous confidence. With the exception of Sandy, I had not yet seen that confidence in his interactions with a woman for whom he had feelings. So, this was new. Whatever the outcome, Annemarie seemed like a person who would only leave Tim better than she found him. And after all this time, I could finally say the same thing about him.

The next time Annemarie attended a reading event at Cedar House, it was at Tim's invitation, and he was one of the readers. They talked afterward, and the next day, he was blissfully texting her and getting responses, pretty much all day—the day he walked into the kitchen with that smirk on his face.

One day after attending the same church, Annemarie asked Tim if they could step aside and talk. "This is it," he thought. "She'll tell me what so many other women have told me before: 'I consider you a good friend, but I'm not open to dating right now.'" Trying to keep his head up, he followed her outside, bracing himself.

She looked serious, but her look was not one of rejection. "I have a serious health problem. It's a rare kidney disease, and it's life-threatening. I need a transplant, and my doctors and I are in the process of searching for a donor. I wanted to confide in you because you deserve to know, and because I know you're the kind of person who will pray."

"Yes, I absolutely will." He felt honored that she would tell him this. He walked back into the church with a slowly growing awareness that, not only had he not been rejected, but the opposite—he had been brought in closer. He was trusted.

They each shared their faith in common and even prayed together sometimes. Their main concern at this point was her health. She needed to start dialysis unless she could find a suitable kidney donor. Tim was not qualified to donate. Other friends offered, but none were compatible.

As it turned out, Annemarie's sister was a perfect DNA match and was willing to give her a kidney. The answer was there in her own family. The surgery went well, and Annemarie's health was restored.

After her recovery, they were out with Tim's telescope taking in the night sky. Annemarie told Tim she was having fun. The cover of night hid his big smile. This was one of his favorite pastimes—talking with friends under a starry sky and viewing planets, nebulae, and galaxies through his telescope. Many more dates followed until they were seeing each other regularly.

Tim and I talked a few days later. "Dave, what would you think if Annemarie moved into the house here with me?"

"Hmm… interesting idea. We've had people move out to get married, but we've never had anyone marry *into* the house."

"She's been part of our house in many ways already, and I think she'd like it. And she's open to it."

"Open to it?" I asked. "You've already talked with her about it?"

"Well, I've asked her what she would think about it. I know it's not what a new bride would usually go for—moving into a community living situation. But I think it would be great."

"Actually, Karen and I have mentioned it to each other before. We're already on board with the idea. I think the household will happily welcome her."

Tim designed an engagement ring with a ruby accompanied by small diamonds. He commissioned a jeweler to create the ring out of the gold from the ring our dad's father gave to our grandmother a century earlier.

When she happily received the ring and agreed to marry him, something deep in Tim's soul began to relax into a settled peace.

A WEDDING AND A ROAD TRIP

"Tim, no. That's too many." Annemarie put the brakes on when Tim wanted to invite everyone he'd ever known to their wedding. He had put together a list of hundreds.

"Tim, our wedding venue has a limit. And besides, I want to invite people too!"

"I know, I know. I'm just excited."

The two planned a wedding that worked well for both of them, and it happened just as they planned.

While most of Tim's excitement at the wedding was focused on Annemarie, he was also thrilled to see so many people from his past. There were even a few people from The Barn, back in Concord when he was just a kid running around causing mischief. His old friend Bryan was there, as was Rich, still a rock climber after all these years. Many people came, some from a great distance, to applaud Tim's life: his recovery, his happiness, and of course his marriage to Annemarie.

"I gave more hugs in a single day than ever in my life by a long shot," said Tim as the festivities wound down. "I wish I could stay in this space for a few days and talk with everyone." His joy was huge, and his gratitude palpable.

Instead of a homily or sermon, a tradition at Christian weddings, Tim and Annemarie had written a portion of their life stories which were read aloud by Annemarie's sister and by me. Life had not gone as planned for either of them, but the crossing and merging of their paths was a story worth telling, to the delight of everyone there.

Part of their honeymoon took them to the places of Tim's childhood. He revisited the Scripps Institute aquarium—changed, but still familiar. They explored the Star of India, the old sailing ship Tim enjoyed when he was five years old.

They stopped by our family's old house in Spring Valley, where Tim had sat in the grass next to our dog Inky when she was killed, and where he had turned three. Looking at the house, Tim silently gave thanks for his life and for all the stories he'd been part of.

Then they headed east to the Grand Canyon.

With his lovely bride beside him, he admired the desert vistas he'd seen from the backseat as a child, and he enjoyed being fully present with the land.

They savored the beautiful seashores, the green-forested mountains, and wide deserts. He showed Annemarie the Great Meteor Crater in Arizona, one of his memorable childhood stops. He felt the blessing of being able to touch the sights, sounds, and loves of his childhood—finally from a healthy, grown-up perspective.

Annemarie is an outstanding fit for Tim. She came with two grown kids whom he loves dearly and who love him back. He loves her family, and she loves ours. He's come far and done extremely well.

GRAVE INTERACTIONS

"Dave, I remember looking at that exact place when I was a little kid."

He pointed to a conspicuous notch in the mountains ahead where the road found its way through them.

Tim, Annemarie, Karen, and I had embarked on a road trip to Kansas, and we were now in Utah.

A few days earlier I had answered my door to find Tim and Annemarie standing there. Tim had a troubled look on his face. "Well Dave," he said slowly, "we're orphans."

The three of us just stood there for several moments.

"Dad passed?"

"Yes."

"I guess we're a little old to be orphans, but I take your meaning."

This was a harder moment for Tim, as he had grown closer to Dad than I had. Nevertheless, a feeling came over me—the feeling of becoming the older generation ourselves.

Tim's grief was palpable. He used the word "orphans" because it matched how he felt.

Karen walked up at that moment and heard the news.

That's how the four of us ended up on the road together, off to visit Dad, this time for his funeral.

Two days later we sat with a small crowd in the cemetery where Mom was buried. I found myself staring at the American flag beautifully draped over Dad's coffin. I listened to the military Honor Guard playing Taps, followed by the flag-folding ceremony. I kept thinking the same thing: "Dad would love this."

Tears came easily, which seemed strange because the grief was difficult. I had trouble thinking of any specific memory. I just felt a generalized, all-over sense of grief. I missed him, but mostly I missed what could have been. I had always wished for closeness with my father, but I never knew how to make it happen.

"Hey, can we pull over here?" I realized we were about to pass the cemetery.

Tim, Annemarie, Karen, and I were up early for our drive back to California.

Tim was driving. "Sure," he replied.

"I'd like to spend a while here. How would you guys feel about waiting for me?"

They all indicated they'd be happy to wait. The three of them sat in the car talking, while I walked out to Dad's grave where he lay next to Mom. I stood on the loose dirt piled slightly higher than the grass. The morning air was crisp as the light had just begun to return to the sky, but the stars were still visible and the sun would not be seen for a while yet.

I wanted to say something to Dad. I wasn't sure what, but I didn't want to miss this opportunity.

I wasn't quite ready, so I walked awhile in the predawn glow, taking in the early morning air and reading the headstones around me. A lifetime of memories ran through my mind as I walked—tales of our boyhood, memories of fumbling so unprepared into adulthood without much guidance. In the solitude of the graveyard, memories floated through my mind like little stories, each one part of a whole. I stood out there longer than I expected, just remembering.

Eventually, slowly, I approached Dad's grave.

He'd been in the ground for less than twenty-four hours, but it seemed very real. I've heard people say things like "it doesn't seem real" when they lose someone. For whatever reason, this wasn't like that. I was profoundly aware that Dad was gone, his body the newest occupant in the dirt beneath my feet.

Graves are strange. The presence of the deceased mixes with their absence, both in the same space. I thought about the skeleton we dug up when we were kids. "Well Dad, now you're the box of bones in the ground. Maybe some crazy kids will dig you up in a hundred years."

Standing over his grave felt like standing over him— like he was somehow forced to listen. One never expects a response from a grave. Perhaps that's why we talk to them. They can't respond, but they're not distracted, either. They don't walk away, and they don't interrupt.

"It would have been nice if you could have known me," I said matter-of-factly, but with a vague awareness of a longing I had carried forever.

"I tried," he said, in my imagination.

"You tried? Yeah, I don't think so. You never really tried. You were too occupied with your plans, with your projects, and your ministry. Couldn't you have checked in with your kids on occasion? Maybe ministered to us for a change?"

I didn't know why my thoughts were careening into such a negative space, but I figured I'd never be here again, so I just went with it.

"You were like the guy who sees kids as a free workforce. You never taught us how to be adults. All you cared about was getting us to help you with your work. Which reminds me, what made you think I knew how to counsel suicidal people when I was eighteen? Do you have any idea how much that terrified me? Of course you don't. And where were you when Tim was losing his mind? I think what upset you the most was that he messed up your plans. But he needed you to see him; to listen to him—a lot. Where were you? You cared about your kids in a generic sense as 'your kids', but you never tried to get to know us as individuals."

Anger and pain surfaced as one. "And what about—"

I suddenly saw Tim in my mind's eye, lying on the kitchen floor, bleeding out. For the first time, I was able to pull a dark and painful thought up from where it had snagged on my own fear long ago. "What about—" I got down with my hands pressed into the loose dirt, angry tears pressuring me to let them out. My throat locked up, but I forced out the words. "When you found Tim bleeding, why didn't you touch him? You didn't even check to see if he was alive. Mom saw him, left him there, and called me. Tim was still conscious. He was lying in absolute hell, and neither of you tried to reach him. He watched you freak out. Caleb had to tell you that Tim was still alive."

My throat was killing me. I held in my grief, not yet sure what I was grieving.

"When I was in my own hell, I don't recall you trying to reach out to me."

"I tried," he said, in my imagination.

"Damn it Dad, shut the— you're dead, now stop talking! You never tried! The only time you were attentive to me was when I was in trouble at school, or when I'd done something wrong. You were there for me then, ready to punish. Do you have any idea how badly I wanted to just spend time with you? Why is that so hard to understand?"

"I tried, but you wouldn't open up to me. Your mind always seemed to be somewhere else."

"I think you have us confused—that's you you're describing."

Then, somehow, underneath all my own pain, I heard him. There on his grave, I heard him. He had tried.

I was always independent—wandering off to fulfill some desire of my own—rarely choosing to open up to him.

Still kneeling in the dirt, shaking my head in defiance, I felt something give way inside me. I tried to push it back, but I couldn't. I had to own it. The pain in my throat was like a lock being picked from the other side. An internal pressure insisted on coming out. I couldn't speak. I tried but my throat wouldn't let me. I couldn't speak, but I could scream, which I did. I screamed into the earth. I filled that corner of the Kansas prairie with the sound of a rage that had never been released—the cries of a boy who didn't know if his dad could see him—and cries for a little brother who felt he had to court death to protect his parents. It all came out like vomit on that hallowed ground. I wailed like an angry baby, pouring my grief into my father's grave until it soaked into his bones. The last few sobs came out like drops of water from a pitcher now emptied.

I felt the old familiar presence, and with it, the feeling of being a child. The last drop was a word I can only say to one person.

"Daddy."

"I'm sorry," he said in my imagination. And then I realized that the words were familiar. He said them in life many times. He was well aware of his shortcomings and frequently expressed that he wanted to do better. Here on his grave, I heard him.

My viewpoint shifted, seeing everything in a new light. All was not okay, and my issues were not suddenly healed. But my dad had a perspective I had missed before.

"Dad, I'm sorry—I'm judging you harshly. I wish I had responded more when you tried. I never told you when I was afraid. I didn't trust you to listen, so I kept secrets from you. I didn't know for sure if you cared."

I looked deeper into my memories, past my judgments into a place under a different light. I think it was the light of grace. From there my dad looked different. Somehow he looked more like a father. He had blind spots and shortcomings, but my choice to love him did not require his perfection. Other memories surfaced, wanting to be voiced. "Dad, you came out and worked for me at the The Clayhouse for over a week. That was the time I understood that you actually loved me. And I remember the times you cheered so wildly when I graduated. And you drove two thousand miles across the country just to pick up Tim and drive him two thousand miles back so he could be with you when you were working in Kansas. Once you realized he was sick, you were patient with him. You sat for hours with your arm around him, doing nothing but sitting there loving him, hoping for him, wanting him with you. You did that, Dad. No one else."

I listened for a while to the silence. The pain in my throat had begun to fade.

I looked up. The sun rose directly in front of me. The golden light warmed the quiet graveyard. A vivid blue dragonfly flew from behind me, right past my head into the morning light.

"Thank you, Dad. Thank you for the many ways you tried to love us. I suppose it wasn't easy—we were more than a handful. Thank you for protecting us from many dangers when we were small. Thank you for the packages delivered by the Navy from the other side of the world. Thank you for giving us a ton of freedom—we loved it. Thank you for never leaving us. Thank you for living boldly, even when it was embarrassing. Thank you for holding onto faith. Thank you for loving Mom; we always knew you were crazy about her. Thank you for your unconventional style. Thank you for all of it."

Walking back to the car, I felt the presence of the other graves: the parents, the uncles and aunts, the children. "So many stories," I thought.

I got into the backseat with Karen. "Thank you, guys."

"Of course," said Annemarie.

Karen fondly took hold of my arm and smiled.

Tim gave me a knowing look, pulled the car back onto the road, and headed for home.

SITTING IN THE FUTURE

Tim got his coffee and waited for me on the sidewalk outside the cafe on Irving Street. "Thank you," I said to the young woman as she passed my cup across the counter. Like Maria twenty-five years earlier, she had no idea what was happening with me in that moment. I recalled that cup of coffee that felt like my last meal—the time I got down to thirty-two cents in my pocket and what I thought was no future.

"Hey Tim, would you mind hanging out here for a bit?" I asked as I walked out into the Irving Street afternoon.

"Sure, no problem."

Tim and I commandeered a bench on the sidewalk. "This is where I often sat in my homeless days," I commented, recalling those days. The memories were clear, but they also seemed like a long time ago.

"On this very bench?"

"Well, actually no. I would sit on that fire hydrant." I pointed to the hydrant, still there—a silent witness to another time.

I walked over and sat down on my old hydrant-stool. I took a sip, looking into the memories of the previous twenty-five years. "The last time I sat here, the future was nothing but darkness."

"Darkness," said Tim, laughing. "Some darkness. After everything you've done since then, that seems pretty funny."

"Hmm. Yeah, I suppose so," I said, glancing up and down the street recalling old images and the accompanying memories of fear and loss.

"You suppose so? Are you kidding? Your life took off after that. You've got Karen. You've got Cedar House." Then he gave his best Dad imitation. "You're Doctor Dave for crying out loud!"

We both laughed. "Yeah, who would have seen that coming? Life has been amazing."

Tim nodded his head emphatically, flashing his big smile.

I thought about the goodness that had poured itself over our lives, and how unlikely it all seemed. If I could have seen what was coming, sitting on the fire hydrant that night long ago, I don't know what I would have thought—probably that I was losing it—that the schizophrenia monster was after me now. I simply could not have comprehended what was possible.

"Bonus years," I said. "These are the unexpected bonus years."

"Exactly!"

There's a quote from Jesus I've pondered a lot: "A good tree cannot bear bad fruit, and a bad tree cannot bear good fruit." [5]

These good years, these blessings, are not the result of my strategic planning or good management. They're simply the fruit that came from clinging to that mysterious God-Presence like a dog tracking the scent of joy.

A TASTE OF RELAPSE

As I walked into the kitchen, I noticed Tim sitting on a stool at our island counter. I was glad to see him up and around as he was recovering from a gnarly bout with Covid and was finally beginning to feel normal again—or so I thought.

"Hey Tim, how's it going? Ooh, you don't look so good."

"Dave, I'm not sure what's happening. I haven't slept the last two nights."

"Due to the sickness or something else?"

"I don't know. It's not just more symptoms, it's mental or

---

[5] MATTHEW 7:18 (NIV)

spiritual or something."

I got my coffee and sat down across from him. "Tell me more. What's goin' on?"

"Last night I couldn't sleep because I kept seeing a hideous viper staring me down with furious venomous hatred. It felt like there was lava or molten metal in the middle of my head."

"Oh man—yuck. That sounds horrible."

"It's a little better now, but I'm already feeling anxious about what tonight might be like."

I spent part of that day looking up information about how Covid might affect someone with schizophrenia. I didn't learn anything conclusive but there did seem to be cases in which Covid may have contributed to psychotic experiences.

The next morning, Tim and Annemarie were both worried.

He seemed a little distant and very sober. "Dave, last night I just laid there in fear. It was like social anxiety lying next to Annemarie as she slept. I was afraid she would feel my anxiety and wake up, ruining her rest, too."

"Which didn't happen," commented Annemarie. "I slept fine, but I'm concerned."

The next night, the fourth night of the struggle, Tim found himself in a panic attack, But for the first time there was an upside: he expressed that during the episode, despite the anguish, he was able to maintain a deep inner peace, trusting that the episode would eventually pass.

This was huge news. It showed that the many years of recovery had resulted in a maturity that enabled him to navigate very difficult moments by employing the mental tools he'd learned. By this time, I didn't even know such things were still issues, but here we were.

Later that day, he was on the phone with his boss, checking in about his absence from work, and conversing about his yearly evaluation.

"Well Tim, how do you feel you're doing at this job?"

An awkward silence lasted several moments.

"Tim, are you okay?"

Tim froze up. "Um…" He barely got out one word—quietly, tentative, and nervous. "Yeah."

"You don't sound so good. I'll call again tomorrow, and we'll talk then."

Later, I found Tim in the kitchen looking dismal.

"Dave, what's happening? I feel like I'm losing it again."

His emotions were right on the surface. He was trying to keep a good attitude but still felt like he was slipping backward.

"Have you spoken with Dr. Kwun?"

"I already called her. We're getting together this Friday."

"Good. We'll focus on walking through this week and then see what she has to offer."

His voice sounded somewhat depressed but still hopeful. "Okay."

That Friday Tim's psychiatrist prescribed a slight increase to the dosage of his medication.

The symptoms stopped.

Within a week, Tim was back to normal. He had a healthy, productive conversation with his boss. His doctor adjusted the medication back down, almost to where it had been, without incident. Apparently, Covid had triggered something and the simple change in medication dosage put a stop to it.

Soon after that, we sat again at the island in the kitchen enjoying some morning coffee.

"Dave, I'm actually kinda glad that stuff happened."

"Seriously? Why?"

"I learned that I can remain at peace deep inside; those

episodes may happen in my brain, but they're not in my soul."

"Wow. I like the sound of that."

"And thank God for medication. I love that stuff!"

"Me too," I laughed.

"It's also sobering. It brings up a question: Did I used to have schizophrenia, or do I still have it?"

I let out a long slow sigh. "Yeah, I've been asking that one too."

Tim still has occasional feelings of social anxiety and even thoughts or feelings one might call schizophrenic. Usually, that means an hour or two of feeling mentally off balance. When this happens, he'll ask Annemarie about it. In most cases, she couldn't tell he was struggling at all.

When he talks with me about these times, I remind him that many people, including myself, have experiences like that occasionally. I also remind him of where he's come from, and how well he's doing.

✧ ✧ ✧

AMONG THE STARS

"Is The Pleiades up tonight?" I asked as Tim and I drove to a hilltop known for good telescope viewing.

"I think so, yeah, it should be."

"I haven't seen it through the scope in a long time. It's one of my favorites."

"Me too, That's a good one for sure," he responded.

"People have been looking at that thing for thousands of years," I noted. "It's mentioned more than once in ancient writings, including the Book of Job. It's amazing how the constellations and other things in the sky are written about throughout history. It makes me feel like we're connected to other people over time; we're looking at the same things they were looking at." I paused for a bit, then continued. "And the beauty—there's something about it—like it wants to be seen. The sight of profound beauty seems like more than just something in my eyes and my brain. It feels like something wants to reach us, to touch us. Does that make sense?"

Tim's big smile showed his understanding. "Totally. Yes."

We parked and opened the back doors of the van. After carrying some equipment to a choice location, we returned. Tim picked up one end of the large telescope while I took hold of the other. We carried it to where we had already set up its base, waiting to cradle the wonderful instrument. Seeing through one of Tim's telescopes was always rewarding, but even seeing one in use was itself an impressive sight. The light-gathering mirrors in his three scopes measured thirteen inches, seventeen inches, and twenty inches respectively. Since the time he was barely over two feet tall, he would look into the heavens transfixed. With the telescopes, he had taken that experience further—reaching deeper into the wonder.

Before we looked through it, we simply looked up, taking in the starry canopy above us.

"It's good to look up," commented Tim. "It's like Ned used to say back on the ranch: 'Look in, get depressed. Look out, get distressed. Look up, get blessed.'"

"Yeah, that sounds like Ned."

He clicked on a small red light, opened a box of eyepieces, and finished setting up, pointing the scope toward our first deep-space subject.

"Okay Dave, take a look."

I got on the step stool next to the large telescope and put my eye to the eyepiece.

"What am I looking at?"

"If you're asking that, you're not seeing it."

"Hmm… okay."

"Let me adjust the scope." Tim looked through the Telrad pointer attached to the side and moved the whole assembly slightly.

I looked into the eyepiece again. "Oh, wow!" I was staring into a tight cluster of stars. "That's a globular cluster, right?"

"Yes, that's M3, a fine globular indeed."

I stared at the glistening cluster of innumerable points of light hanging silently, shining out from the dark backdrop around them. "I can't believe they call this 'globular.' That word seems so inappropriate. A cluster of stars hardly seems like a glob."

"Yeah," Tim responded. "I can see why they call it that, given what it looks like, but of course in reality it's a huge field of stars." He paused for a moment. "Sometimes I think about how seeing it from this distance is looking into the past. The light we see left those stars long ago. When it reaches us here on Earth, we're seeing it as it was when the light left it, so we're seeing the past."

"Yeah, I love that."

Scanning the sky, Tim suddenly turned the scope in a different direction. "Let's check out Orion before it goes behind the hill."

Soon, from the starry expanse, the Orion Nebula brought its greenish drape-like image into our field of view.

"So beautiful," I said quietly, as the huge interstellar cloud appeared to sit there in our little eyepiece. "I love that emerald color."

"Emerald color? You see color in it?" asked Tim.

"Yeah, it always looks green to me," I responded. "What does it look like to you?"

"I just see it in black and white."

"Huh. Interesting."

"Astronomers say it's over thirteen hundred light years from here," commented Tim. "They also say it's about twenty-four light-years across."

"Wait. The nebula itself is twenty-four light-years across?"

"Yup."

I let out a sigh. "I can't even process that—it's way too…"

"Too cool!" interrupted Tim, smiling with his eyes wide.

I sat down in a folding camping chair we'd brought along. Tim repositioned the scope and peered again into the eyepiece.

The starlight was generous. After its incomprehensibly long voyage across the vast field of space, it flew into Tim's telescope, reflected off his mirror, through his eyepiece and into his eyes, sharing the beauty it had carried the whole way. This was Tim's way of touching the wonder of the heavens, the mysteries beyond our world.

As I watched, I reflected on the journey that had brought us to this point. Like a telescope, our memory looks into the past. We see what was, but not all of it. What we see back there depends on how we aim the scope of memory. Sometimes not much is visible. Other times we find a globular cluster of memories.

The light of memory was generous that night as well, bringing visions from long ago that still shape my sense of things—of everything.

I pictured Tim in his crib when he was too small to participate in life. He could only see and watch the wonder around him. Now here he was with his telescope on this hilltop in the night, still seeing and watching what was out of his reach.

"Dave, do you have regrets?"

I looked into the sky, considering his question. "Yeah, maybe. I feel like I'm supposed to say 'no,' but actually, yeah, I do."

Tim thought for a moment, then continued slowly, his words uncertain. "I wish there was a way… Hmm… I hope I can help other people find some meaning. If my story can be helpful, then I don't have regrets. If I can help, then my soul is comfortable—which is not what it was."

"Are you saying that if your story can help someone else find healing and meaning, then it was all worth it?"

He took a step back, fully present now on the earth, well aware of the gravity of my question. He stared down at the dark ground around him, his body tightening. I could see his shoulders shaking as the emotions surfaced and he struggled with the memories. Then, after a long pause, he looked up again, starlight reflecting in moist eyes.

"Yes."

We were silent for a while, and then Tim spoke up again. "When I used to tell Mom what I wanted, she would always say, 'All in good time.' That used to frustrate me, but she was right. The wait was worth it."

Tim put his eye to the telescope and a few minutes passed before he spoke again. "I'm banking on the next life, beyond the grave, to really cash in. I'm looking forward to seeing Mom and Dad again—and Keesha—and a hundred other people."

I felt the chill of the night through the canvas of my collapsible chair. It was a familiar chill, a part of being out with Tim and his telescopes. I thought about what he said about the next life. Such thoughts came naturally to Tim. His religious perspective had changed from time to time over the years, but his core spirituality—that very personal connection to God—always seemed the same. Even after all the crazy schizophrenic thinking, a simple childlike faith had survived.

I continued watching as Tim moved the scope to different parts of the night sky, each time looking into the eyepiece to see what the universe might show him. I could almost feel the earth beneath us rolling through space among the stars. I pictured what it might be like to view the Earth from far away—one object among many, one place among many places.

This place, this earth, is where it all happens. This is my place, and it's our place. All our stories are lived on earth; we ride on its grand back as it carries its precious cargo through the universe to God-knows-where. We seem to orbit a stationary sun, yet the sun is on its own journey through this galaxy of its fellows—ever circling but never in quite the same place. The galaxy moves onward, joined by the other galaxies, each carrying its own suns and stars. And while many stories may be written on those distant worlds circling distant suns, we know only our own. Our shared story is our shared humanity. Our shared humanity is a shared family: one huge group of aunts, uncles, nephews, nieces, cousins, grandparents, mothers, fathers, sisters, and, of course, brothers. This amazing bubble of life stretched over the earth like a skin across its continents, oceans, and islands—this is where we have everything we've ever had. It's where we've known everyone we've ever known. This is where we love each other and lie to each other. It's where we hold each other at bay, all the while longing for closeness. It's where we're afraid and where we hope for rescue. This is the place we're afraid of leaving, even though, one way or another, we know we will.

Tim's voice suddenly interrupted my reverie. "Dave, you wanna see something cool?"

"Sure."

He adjusted the scope slightly. "Okay, look now."

The light that met me in the eyepiece was the light of the Pleiades.

"One of the great treasures of the night sky," commented Tim.

"Yes. Although viewed from out there, Earth is also in the night sky. I'd like to think that we, too, are one of the great treasures."

"Yeah!" he exclaimed, that familiar smile lighting up his face.

He paused awhile, continuing to look up into the starlight.

"Dave, it's good to be alive."

I let out one of my long slow sighs. "Yes. Yes, it is."

PHOTOS

Mom and Dad on an outing together while Dad was stationed in Germany with the Army

Mom and Dad during his early days in the Navy

Tim and Dad enjoying a happy moment

Tim's kindergarten school photo

The lower jaw of the skeleton, she recalled, was intact (Continued on Page 8A, Col. 7)

The boys' picture in the paper after they happened upon an old grave while digging. (L-R) Doug, Tim, our friend Skipper, and Dave

Tim wearing one of his hand braces after reattachment surgery. The desert landscape in this shot seems symbolic of how he felt at that time

Tim tried hard to remain positive, although his face often showed an inner struggle

Tim during his time living on Ned and Jean's ranch

Tim on a rock climbing trip in Yosemite National Park

Tim and his beloved mentor Ned

*Tim and Dave celebrating Tim's graduation from
Fresno State University*

*Dave and Tim enjoying time with sister Beth and
her son Jason*

Dave and Karen early in their marriage

Tim with his sister Beth after much healing

Tim on the porch at Cedar House

Annemarie out with Tim and one of his large telescopes

Tim and Annemarie celebrating their wedding to the applause of friends and family

AFTERWORD

AUTHOR'S COMMENTS

I have deeply enjoyed telling my brother Tim's story. He and I went over every part of it throughout the process. I wanted his full approval and endorsement, which he gave wholeheartedly. It was fun to compare memories as we discovered that our recollections of events matched up well. The process was also difficult, as we delved directly into memories that triggered feelings of pain, sorrow, embarrassment, and loss.

It's impossible to fully account for Tim's return to normal life after stumbling into the kind of darkness he had to live with during his illness. The level to which Tim has been restored is far from normal.

From his place of exceptional recovery, I've asked Tim if he would share some thoughts about how he maintains a healthy course in life. He was more than happy to do so, and offers his comments in the following pages.

After Tim's comments, Marty Schwebel, a mental health professional who has been a helpful influence in Tim's life, will share his thoughts about Tim's story. Marty's comments come from a clinical perspective after years of experience as a therapist. I am delighted at the opportunity to include his thoughtful words.

After Marty's comments, he's included a number of resources for those in need of assistance with issues surrounding mental health.

TIM'S COMMENTS

I'm still mystified by many aspects of my illness, but I've also learned a lot during my long recovery.

If I have chest pains, I may ask my friend who had heart surgery for advice. His advice might help, but not as much as a doctor's. I knew Sam, an engineer who had a heart transplant. He lived long into old age, many years after his successful transplant. He was a civil engineer, not a medical doctor. While his experience with his heart issues gave him special insight, it didn't make him a doctor.

I say this as a recovering schizophrenic. I am not a psychiatrist, a psychologist, or a therapist. I am a surveyor. I don't have all the answers, but many other people are qualified. I have met some of them.

Having said that, I would like to share some things I have been learning over my continuing healing process.

First, attitude is everything. My mentor, Ned, mastered attitude better than anyone I've ever met. I learned these two gems from him: "The main thing is to keep the main thing the main thing," and "Life is 10% what happens to you, and 90% how you respond to it."

To put Ned's wisdom into practice, I offer you seven tools I'm learning how to use:

Seven Tools from My Mental Toolbox

TOOL #1 – Gratitude

I can't overstate this. A billionaire who feels no gratitude is, in many ways, worse off than a poor man who appreciates what he has. I have met people who are truly happy, even when struggling, because they practice an attitude of gratitude.

Gratitude is the key to enjoying life as it is right now.

It also greases the skids to bring more and more good things. Expressing gratitude can reprogram your brain to be happier. If you struggle to think of what to be grateful for, think smaller; your brain does not know the difference between your good attitude about big things and your good attitude about small things. Gratitude, whether over something large or something small, produces the same healthy outlook. Meanwhile, no one likes spending time with resentful, ungrateful people; they're draining to be around.

TOOL #2 – Faith

I use the word in a general way—it doesn't have to be religious faith. It can be a confidence that carries you through horrible circumstances because you have hope in something bigger, deeper, and more lasting. I believe there is always something larger and more lasting than my current circumstances—something to put my faith in.

I see faith as part of receiving help, just as success in twelve-step programs depends on admitting we have a problem and need help from a higher power. I believe I survived my schizophrenia due to the prayers of people around me.

My faith, and the faith of others, has so far carried me through. If you don't believe in God, perhaps you can recognize the transcendent possibility of a love that cares for others and offers love generously, even sacrificially. Faith is a comfort and an inner strength drawn from a life greater than one's own.

TOOL #3 – Action

When circumstances are hard, I try to stay present and work through the problem rather than escape with substances, fantasies, self-pity, complaints, or bitterness. Though we sometimes think the universe is out to get us, we must begin again, and again, as many times as it takes.

According to King Solomon, "All hard work brings a profit." This is true even if you build a business that fails, because the experience and knowledge you gain can be worth even more than money. There will be a payoff. Work is hard but doable, and a harvest will come if you keep going.

Dr. Chang, who facilitated a social anxiety group I attended, taught me a very helpful kind of work—to deliberately face my fears. If I cower from my fears, they grow, but if I face them through intentional exposures, they fade. Of course, I'm talking of mental anxieties (like fear of the dark) not fear involving actual danger (like swimming with crocodiles).

Another work is learning not to feed thoughts that produce anxiety. An anxious thought can appear in my mind, but I choose whether to fuel it or to let the feelings dissipate by turning my mind to other things. Even a panic attack can be diminished, at least somewhat, by thinking, "This is a physiological biochemical sequence that only lasts a few minutes."

TOOL #4 – Communication

When I was finally open about my problems (with safe people, like Jean at the ranch) that opened the door for help. Openness with safe people is huge. If you can find a safe person, share your thoughts and concerns. Some of my heaviest fears dissolved completely when I revealed them to wise, mature and trustworthy friends. My guess is that most fears are similar—that they would not stand up to the light of open, truthful communication.

TOOL #5 – Initiative

Often, we don't even know about the help that is already waiting for us. Initiative starts the search for that help. Initiative is like a spark plug in an engine. We may have plenty of fuel, but we can't start the motor without a spark. Initiative creates something out of nothing, by means of our deciding and then acting. We all have this power.

TOOL #6 – Hope

As Dr. Abraham Lowe said, "Helplessness is not hopelessness."

"This too shall pass" is a helpful phrase. We can still have hope under any circumstances—perhaps not for a specific outcome, but hope that good itself will ultimately win the day, even if we must endure a difficult time of darkness.

TOOL #7 – Medication

Most countries, as I write this, offer many helpful medications. Despite side effects, the benefits of the right medication can far outweigh the drawbacks.

In my younger years, there was much more stigma, so I resisted taking medication. I needed to accept my medication before I could start recovering. For those who suffer where medication is not available or affordable, the other tools I've listed can still help.

To repeat what my brother Dave quoted earlier: medication stabilized me and gave me an opportunity for growth, but it didn't make me wise, improve my abilities, or alter my life circumstances. That's why the other tools are just as important.

In addition to those seven tools, I continue to benefit from professional help from time to time. I recently received significant help from EMDR Therapy (Eye Movement Desensitization and Reprocessing) with a certified therapist. I have found it helps a lot in defusing the triggers of my traumatic memories.

THERAPIST'S COMMENTS

I had the privilege of meeting Tim a few years ago, long after he had endured the darkest chapters of his mental health journey. The man I encountered exuded kindness and possessed a remarkable sense of inner peace. I felt an immediate sense of safety in his presence, completely unaware of the horrors he had endured in his younger years.

As time went on, Tim graciously allowed me to delve into the depths of his extraordinary story. He is someone who has traversed the depths of severe mental illness, yet his life is brimming with inspiration and wisdom for all of us, regardless of where we find ourselves in our own stories. I firmly believe that healing mental illness goes beyond the realm of psychology and its invaluable contributions. It involves connecting with the struggles of others and witnessing their triumphs. Unfortunately, stories of mental health battles often remain untold due to the pain and shame associated with them. However, Tim's story is now out in the open for all of us to hear. My hope is that we can imbue this narrative with even greater significance on our own mental health journeys and use it to aid others in their healing process.

Chances are, most of us have encountered individuals grappling with severe mental health challenges, whether it be a chance encounter on the street, within our social circles, at work, or even within our own homes. As a therapist, I am grateful that this story is being shared, as it has the potential to dismantle the stigma often attached to diagnoses such as Bipolar Disorder and Schizophrenia. When we hear these diagnoses, our minds tend to gravitate towards worst-case scenarios, causing us to overlook the person behind the label.

You may have encountered someone who is in a psychotic or delusional state, and it's natural for your initial thoughts and feelings to be filled with fear or even disgust. However, if you take the time to read Tim's story, you'll discover more about him as a person rather than just focusing on his mental health condition. Meeting Tim and delving into his full story allows us to see the real individual behind the mask of a diagnosis. It's important to remember that a diagnosis should never define who we are as individuals.

Is there a particular person in this story that you can relate to more than others? Perhaps you're going through your own mental health crisis and can empathize with Tim, or maybe you're a family member or friend of someone who is experiencing their own mental pain.

We often hear about the mental health crisis our world is facing, and I believe it to be true. So, what can we do about it? Hopefully, this book has helped you look beyond the label of a mental health diagnosis and the associated difficulties, allowing you to see a beautiful man who possesses kindness, intelligence, humor, and gentleness. I feel grateful to have come to know Tim and his story because it has enabled me to connect with many others, including my own family and clients, no matter where they may be on their mental health journey.

The book's title is absolutely fitting because it captures the contrasting symbolism of "skeletons" representing death and despair, while "stars" symbolize life and hope. It's a story brimming with hope, and I wholeheartedly urge you to share it with anyone you know who may have a loved one grappling with mental health challenges. As humans, we are intricate beings capable of growth, transformation, and evolution. Just as Tim and Dave molded raw clay into something beautiful and meaningful, our relationships with faith, family, friends, and communities can shape us into something extraordinary.

I truly hope that this book becomes a catalyst for positive change in your mental well-being. It would be amazing if you could generously share it with others as well. My wish is that this story inspires you to prioritize your own mental health and also encourages you to reach out to those in your family or friend circles who may be struggling. Whether it's going for a walk, enjoying a cup of tea, watching a movie, or simply sharing a meal, connecting with others can truly make a difference. Tim's journey towards improvement was largely due to his connections with others, and it's a reminder that staying connected is crucial for our mental well-being. It would be wonderful if each of us had a brother or friend like Dave in our lives, but unfortunately, that is not always the reality. Furthermore, it is my sincere wish that we can collectively glean valuable insights from Tim's narrative, emphasizing the significance of seeking professional assistance when we find ourselves unable to support or navigate someone else's mental well-being.

In my therapy practice, I have an expanding collection of mental health resources and tools. I'll provide a few options on the following page for you to contemplate for yourself or to share with a friend or family member. If you or someone you know is experiencing a mental health crisis, here is something worth considering. Firstly, prioritize taking care of yourself. Aim to reach a stable state, just like the instructions given on an airplane to put your own air mask on first before assisting others. Then, extend support to the other person by offering some of these resources. However, at the very least, be present in their life and genuinely listen to and validate the pain they are going through. Most of us simply desire someone who will hear us out and acknowledge the challenges that life can bring.

Fortunately, there is a wider range of mental health service options accessible now than in the past.

~ Marty Schwebel
LMFT IN CALIFORNIA (#103247) AND TEXAS (#203784)
www.newroadscounseling.com

RESOURCES

+ NAMI (National Alliance on Mental Illness) – www.nami.org

+ AFSP (American Foundation for Suicide Prevention) – https://afsp.org/get-help/

+ Recovery International – https://www.recoveryinternational.org/

+ Al Anon (for codependency and support for those with addicted friends and family) – https://al-anon.org/

+ Alcoholics Anonymous (for those whose mental health struggles include addictions) – https://www.aa.org/

+ Find a therapist through online search engines on the internet such as:
    www.psychologytoday.com
    www.zencare.co

+ Health Insurance – be sure to check with your health insurance plan for in network and out of network behavioral health options. Many healthcare plans are now covering talk therapy but are not being utilized.

+ Consider finding a therapist through the growing online services like Better Help (https://www.betterhelp.com) and Talkspace (https://www.talkspace.com).

+ Seek help and connection in a local faith community or club.

+ Volunteer in your local community through faith communities, food banks, shelters, etc.

+ National Institute of Mental Health (NIMH) – nimh.nih.gov

+ World Health Organization (WHO) – www.who.int

ABOUT THE AUTHOR

David Robinson, MDiv, DMin

Dave has been many things, including business owner, painter, sculptor, creative writer, mentor, counselor, and professor. He is the Director of Creative Interfaces, a nonprofit focused on fostering creativity, personal growth, and spiritual development. The website is creativeinterfaces.org.

He lives with his wife, Karen, in Marin County, California, where they have hosted creative events and managed a community house for over twenty years.

**THREE UNCLES
PUBLISHING**

Quality Written Works
Beautifully Produced

We respect writers, we love good books,
and we want to publish and promote
works by new authors.

Our current titles include both
fiction and non-fiction,
as well as poetry and children's books.

For other books by Three Uncles Publishing

Visit Amazon.com or

www.threeunclespublishing.com